THE POWER OF
PERSONALITY

*Unlock the Secrets to Understanding Everyone
in Your Life—Including Yourself!*

ERIC GEE

Prometheus Books

Guilford, Connecticut

Prometheus Books

An imprint of Globe Pequot, the trade division of The Rowman & Littlefield
Publishing Group, Inc.
4501 Forbes Blvd., Ste. 200
Lanham, MD 20706
www.rowman.com

Distributed by NATIONAL BOOK NETWORK

British Library Cataloguing in Publication Information Available

Library of Congress Cataloging-in-Publication Data Available

ISBN 978-1-63388-956-9 (cloth : alk. paper) | ISBN 978-1-63388-957-6
(ebook)

♾™ The paper used in this publication meets the minimum requirements of
American National Standard for Information Sciences—Permanence of Paper
for Printed Library Materials, ANSI/NISO Z39.48-1992

CONTENTS

PREFACE

~~THEORY~~

Everyone's an expert these days. Politics, sports, midcentury interior design—no subject is immune to being discussed on the internet by some random dude with a computer, wireless access, and an opinion. And personality theory is no different. There are books that tell you what color you are or what direction is your orientation—no, not that kind of orientation. There are tests that promise to find your strengths while conveniently ignoring your weaknesses. I know, I know, everyone has a right to their own thoughts on personality typing. What makes mine any different from the thousands of others amplified on the internet?

For starters, I've taught and coached personality typing for more than twenty years. In person. With real, live people. I didn't just read *Gifts Differing*—Isabel Myers's seminal work on personality theory—and call it a day. For ten years, I founded and operated an educational company that personality-typed more than twenty thousand students, parents, and teachers. I'd estimate that, over the course of my life, I've typed more than fifty thousand people. Is that more than anyone else on this planet? No. Is that more than 99.99999 percent of the population? Probably. So, forgive me if I recommend that you follow my advice on personality theory or that of the approximately 780 other people with requisite experience and expertise instead of that of some "master" on Reddit who makes personality memes about cats (no offense to memes about cats).

First off, let's stop using that word *theory*. *Theory* implies that something can be scientifically proven to the point of being widely accepted as fact. I don't care how effective a personality-typing system is, there is no way to prove it using the scientific method. Maybe, in the future, there will be research that proves that negative ions or brain waves—I believe there's an actual study pursuing this line of thought—or the size of one's pituitary gland at thirty-five dictates an individual's personality type, but we're not at that point yet. And even if we were, does it really matter? Certainly, the nature of something is far less important than how that something can help us live a happier, more fulfilling life.

And that's more or less how I view the mission of personality typing: to achieve a better understanding of ourselves and others. To do this requires a good eye for details and the ability to see how those details contribute to the totality of who we are as human beings. With each new observation, new paths of discovery and experience are revealed.

For that reason, *The Power of Personality*, or *PoP*, is not based around a theory. It is founded on a method—a method of understanding yourself and others in the hopes that it might build a better society or, at the very least, prevent societal conflict from getting so far gone that there's no turning back (which, in that case, I hope you've boned up on your zombie-apocalypse survival skills). Personality typing is *not* a science. It's a craft, like cooking or telling a good story. And just like those crafts are built on a foundation of recipes, three-act structures, knife skills, and narrative elements, the *PoP* method of personality typing possesses a solid base of structure and technique.

Structure

The varying personalities of the world population can be separated into four major groups. Within those groups, four subgroups can be found, making a total of sixteen distinct personality types, represented by animals. Here they are, along with their grade-school stereotypes (more in-depth, less flippant descriptions later, I promise):

1. **The Stag:** The bossy group leader
2. **The Beaver:** The rule follower/snitch
3. **The Elephant:** The friendly ignorer of personal space
4. **The Bear:** The quiet one who always volunteers to help the teacher
5. **The Fox:** The cool but sometimes two-faced kid
6. **The Shark:** The scary athlete
7. **The Peacock:** The loud diva/dancer
8. **The Butterfly:** The gentle sketchbook artist
9. **The Dolphin:** The popular do-gooder
10. **The Panda:** The reserved bookworm and closet shit talker
11. **The Baboon:** The class clown and closet *Magic: The Gathering* player
12. **The Humpback Whale:** The daydreamer

13. **The Killer Whale:** The valedictorian out for world domination
14. **The Spider:** The "adult" in the room
15. **The Chimpanzee:** The cool nerd
16. **The Owl:** The nerd

Technique

The distinguishing features of each type are numerous, and how they manifest themselves can be either easily observable or borderline indecipherable without a little added stimulus from the observer. This book goes over many techniques I've discovered over the years to draw out the kind of information you'll need to type someone, including yourself.

So who is this book for exactly? Someone open to learning about people in new and different ways and, most importantly, someone who wants to look deeper into themselves. Maybe you're dissatisfied with your current life situation. Maybe there are conflicts within your relationships that you'd like to resolve in a way that doesn't involve going to DEFCON 1. Maybe you're happy as a clam and just want to read commentary on your life performance as you take your victory lap. Whatever the reason, you're someone who's willing to look in the mirror for what is not always a pain-free self-examination. But mainly, this book is a reminder that, though we're all special in our own way, there's always room to grow.

Of course, any description of who *The Power of Personality* is for would be remiss without a description of who it is not for. A cynic might call the following portrayals a preemptive strike on any potential dissenters. I prefer to look at them as merely a brief attempt to understand those who might be offended, provoked, and put into a general state of discomfort by the contents of this book. Arguably, these are the people this book is *really* for. And in a book focused on personality typing, it seems only appropriate that these skeptics be divided into three categories.

HATERS, FASCISTS IN SHEEP'S CLOTHING, AND MASTERS OF THE PERSONALITY UNIVERSE

Haters

Haters pride themselves on being the smartest person in the room. Message board rebels without a cause, they are purveyors of the hot take for its own sake. Keyboard gangsters and overlords of whatever comments section they find the most troll worthy, they're the few people to whom I could say, without any equivocation, "*Stop* reading." The books they read only help to fuel their contrived arguments. If they went to college, then they probably majored in a hard science, like engineering or computer science, or something with purse strings, like business or accounting. If they didn't go to college, then they probably work in a practical field, think construction or home repair—though practically working in an actual field might be beneath them.

Haters often view personality typing as a sham or a con, preferring to stick to the "science," which is really just their method of adhering to the orthodoxies of the past while dressing them up as progress. Haters love to point to theories comparing human behavior to animals or ancient versions of ourselves. You know what I'm talking about. Books that recommend reverting to caveman habits or seem to justify patriarchal gender norms by connecting them to animal behavior. I've never seen the logic in this comparison. Sure, technically, we're animals too, but Darwin didn't write about evolutionary theory just for giggles. Humans are a far more complex species than any on the planet—come talk to me when you see an orangutan establish an HR department for fellow orangutans depressed on the job—and for us to look backward seems exactly that: backward. And don't tell me, "Animals use tools too!" Saying an otter uses tools just like a human is like saying my nine-year-old nephew uses a baseball bat just like Juan Soto. *Like* being a relative—the first of many puns—term.

As for the caveman nostalgia, should we really be basing our current values and behavior on the basest instincts of our evolutionary growth arc? How did that work out for our ancestors? There is such a thing as progress. I mean, when's the last time you heard someone say, "I love the new *Madden*, but I can't wait for them to bring back *Pong*!" Then again, Haters love to be contrarians. Not only is it their attempt at feeling special, but it's also a form of distrust that often masks a deep-seated insecurity. They feel like, if they were to ever really open up and leave themselves vulnerable, a person would perceive them in the same way they perceive themselves: ugly and stupid. It's a shame because Haters have much to contribute to the world and are quite bright—just not as bright as they think they are.

Fascists in Sheep's Clothing

These are the well-intentioned types who rail against personality typing because they feel like it puts people into immutable boxes. Of course, they are generally unaware of the fact that they do it, too:

- "Oh, you know the type. She's messy."
- "He's got that type A personality."
- "She likes the strong, silent type."

They can't help it. Their perspective of the world is also based on observation and categorization. So really, for them, it's not that the *PoP* method discourages free will and individuality; it's just that it does it in a way they don't understand.

I call them Fascists in Sheep's Clothing because they're the first people to castigate others for being different, and they do so under the guise of openness and potential. I used to coach youth basketball, and I remember discussing one of my players with his dad. His father thought he wasn't being aggressive on the court, which was true, and pleaded with me to try to bring that out of him. I told the dad, "Look, that's just the way he is. He's a gentle kid. He's unselfish, loves setting his teammates up for shots, and always makes the right decision. And no player is more coachable."

"Yeah, but I'm tired of seeing him get his ass pushed around."

He accused my coaching style of limiting his son and insisted that, with the right training, his son could be a great player. He was never able to break away from his narrow idea of what made a player great. It's also unfortunate that he never said anything about wanting his son to be a great person, but I guess that's beside the point. That's why the next time someone declares to you, "Anyone can be anything they want to be," just know that it's basically their way of saying, "Anyone can be what I want them to be."

Masters of the Personality Universe

There's a scene in the movie *Good Will Hunting* when a condescending Harvard student tries to embarrass working-class Chuckie (played by a pre-*Gigli* Ben Affleck), who is masquerading as a fellow Harvard kid to impress some coeds at a bar. The student patronizes Chuckie's "elementary" education, spouting off lines of what can generously be called intellectually masturbatory bullshit. He's basically regurgitating the last history lecture he attended, a fact that doesn't go unnoticed by Will (played by a pre–*The Great Wall* Matt Damon), a janitor by day and genius by night, who accuses him of "plagiarizing the whole thing" and coming into bars to "read some obscure passage, then pawn it off as [his] own idea to impress some girls" (Van Sant, 1997).

Unfortunately, this scene bears more than a strong resemblance to elements of the personality-typing community: "masters" on the internet preaching hundred-year-old theories as if they were their own. It's like the movie *Yesterday*, where everyone forgets the Beatles existed except for one struggling musician, who swoops in and takes credit for the songs the Beatles wrote (Boyle, 2019). And just like with the Beatles, everyone readily accepts the original material as being infallible. Look, I love me some "While My Guitar Gently Weeps," and the Beatles' songwriting is pretty damn brilliant, but let's face it, a lot of the production on the songs is like eating a mayonnaise sandwich. There's a reason their songs are covered so much. (Bobby Womack's version of "And I Love Her" is otherworldly, by the way.)

Masters of the Personality Universe are all reading the same books, memorizing the same information, and repeating the same jargon. No one bothers to make their own observations or create their own insights because, at that point, they're already slaves to confirmation bias, too busy seeing the world through the prism of the few seminal works on personality theory. They become so attached to the ideas that they become detached from the actual meaning, like an acolyte who believes the repetition of a mantra is enough to comprehend it. What they lack in depth of understanding, they make up for in certainty. They are *always* right, and if you don't agree with them, they'll be more than willing to prove your insights are false and fraudulent—by substituting another person's ideas for their own.

THE POWER OF PERSONALITY'S SEVEN-POINT CREED

It might seem unnecessary to finish this preface with a list of reasons on how this book is different from (i.e., better than) other books on personality. I mean, you've already purchased it at this point; Jeff Bezos is already diving into a pool of your money. I blame it on my almost obsessive habit of drawing distinctions, which is useful when personality typing but can also come off as overly critical. So in the spirit of Jalen Rose, a professional basketball player who, when asked why he didn't knock Kobe Bryant to the ground while Kobe was en route to scoring eighty-one points against Rose's Toronto Raptors, once said, "I didn't want to be a hater" (Rose, 2006). Therefore, the following is not a list of everything *The Power of Personality* stands against but rather a declaration of everything it stands for, a seven-point creed, if you will:

1. **Personality typing is not a science.** Don't forget this, no matter how many times someone tries to convince you that cognitive functions are a thing. They are merely the club that the "personality theory is a science" crowd uses to beat people over the head while name-dropping Carl Jung. Sure, it was a groundbreaking theory a hundred years ago, but so was the idea that electrotherapy could cure polio.

2. **Intuition: Train yours, then trust it.** Reliance on the "science" tricks us into neglecting our own natural gifts. Every single person has years of people-watching experience tucked away in their subconscious. Let's turn off the computer, tap into that wellspring of knowledge, blow up the Death Star, and go home. Of course, no number of books read—even this one—can beat good, old-fashioned practice. Type your parents. Type your friends. Type the creepy guy at the party whose number you've just grudgingly accepted while knowing full well you're deleting it later. And most importantly, type yourself.

3. **Tests are fallible.** Every personality assessment is a blunt tool. They're simple, easy to score, and therefore lack much of the complexity and human touch needed to properly type a person. Adherence to an algorithm might work on Spotify, but understanding the reason for the life choices you or others have made takes a little more prying than asking whether you're more talkative or more shy.

4. **Put in the work.** Everyone wants to know who they are, what it means, and whether it justifies their very existence. That's fine, but let's not forget about the hours of introspection and observation it takes to get to that point. A treatment is only as good as the diagnosis. As Einstein supposedly said (disputed, but I love the quote so I'm using it anyway), "If I had an hour to solve a problem, I'd spend fifty-five minutes thinking about the problem and five minutes thinking about solutions." The knowledge that,

as a certain personality type, you're more likely to do A, B, and C because of X, Y, and Z is only meaningful if that's your actual personality type. Anything else is just personality cosplay.

5. **Do not be afraid to reassess.** I'm frequently asked whether it's possible for someone's type to change. My frequent answer? No. But it *is* highly likely that your understanding of said person has deepened, and thus, from your perspective, their type has changed. New information can bring a new diagnosis. If we can be lifelong learners about physics or fantasy football, then we can be lifelong learners about the people we surround ourselves with every day. And that even includes the randos we meet on the street, if for no better reason than the fact that we're stuck on this planet with them anyway.

6. **Have fun!** I've already spent more than a few pages harping on the importance of personality typing. It behooves me to spend more than a few lines reminding you not to take the typing process too seriously. Those two truths are not mutually exclusive, which is why, in this book, you might find more than a fair share of pop culture references, personal anecdotes, and semiveiled references to topics ranging from Nietzschean relativism and Depeche Mode to scatology and the mating habits of the banana slug. Examining how our personality connects to others works best through a prism of familiarity. Personality *should* be personal. And just like looser muscles can increase flexibility and strength, a looser approach to typing others prevents rigidity and sharpens the senses.

7. **I am the test.** I've said this more than a few times in my life, always in response to a person arguing that their test results were different from how I had typed them in person. Now, in fairness, it's worth mentioning that I'm not always right. On the contrary, I continually find myself reassessing (see point 5), and for a moment in my early twenties, I was convinced that I was a different type than the one I am now. That being said, we must learn to trust the totality of our observations and insights over the results of a commonly self-administered checklist of multiple-choice questions. Remember, I am the test. And you can be, too.

CHAPTER ONE

PEOPLE'S HISTORY (OF TYPING)

FOUR

In the very loosely paraphrased words of George Santayana ([1905] 2013), if you don't know your history, you're bound to fuck up again. Likewise, any understanding of the present and future of personality typing would not be replete without knowledge of the past. Now, I know we didn't travel all this way down the highway of ideas to hear me regurgitate someone else's theories—especially after *Good Will Hunting* showed how asinine that is—but a crash course on the history of personality theory is vital to comprehending how *The Power of Personality* is influenced by and, most importantly, how it has evolved from the work that came before. It'll also be a way of paying our respects to all the personality typing forefathers, kind of like those "In Memoriam" segments during the Oscars: still filled with notable omissions and random sound editors but not as depressing. And you don't have to feel pressured to clap if you've never heard of any of these people.

The idea of a world constituted by four distinct elements has been around as early as sixth century BCE. In the beginning, these elements were earth, fire, water, and air. The belief was that each of these four substances carries their own unique qualities and characteristics, the combination of which gives our world balance and synergy. Yes, I know, this is sounding eerily similar to *Avatar: The Last Airbender*, but I promise you, these old farts came up with the idea first.

Ancient Persia

Old fart #1 was a Persian philosopher by the name of Zarathustra, also known by his rapper name Zoroaster. Zoroaster described the four mentioned elements as "essential for the survival of all living beings" (Habashi, 2000).

Ancient Greece

Ancient Greek discussions of the importance of the elements date back to seventh century BCE, with such philosophers as Thales and Anaximenes determining that individual elements like water (Thales) and air (Anaximenes) were the source of our existence. It wasn't until Empedocles came around in the fourth century BCE that a cosmogonic theory [a fancy way of saying "An idea that explains where the hell all of this (i.e., the universe) came from"] that included all four elements would be introduced to the Greek thinking palate (Russell, 1991).

India

Pancha Maha-Bhuta lists five great elements: earth, fire, water, air, and the aether (space), which I guess adds that extra special element, kind of like the ayurvedic version of *Captain Planet*, though I'm pretty sure it's argued in the Vedas that *Captain Planet* is the Saturday-morning-cartoon version of Hinduism (Venkatesan, 2013). A version of this 4 + 1 element theory can also be found in Bön, an ancient Tibetan philosophy that predates the arrival of Buddhism. Buddhism itself lists four great properties among its tenets: solidity (earth), energy (fire), cohesion (water), and expansion (air; Bodhi, 1995).

Over time, the four elements began to be replaced by symbolic incarnations, each one representing the characteristics long associated with earth (steady and grounded), fire (excitable and kinetic), water (emotional and empathetic), and air (detached and abstract).

The Bible

This symbolism is found in both the Old and New Testaments. Take, for instance, Ezekiel 1:10, where Ezekiel describes his vision of a cherubim with four faces as the "face of a man, and the face of a lion, on the right side: and they four had the face of an ox on the left side; they four also had the face of an eagle." These same four animals can be found in the apocalyptic vision described in Revelations 4:7: "And the first beast was like a lion, and the second beast like a calf, and the third beast had a face as a man, and the fourth beast was like a flying eagle." The representations seem clear: the fiery lion; the industrious, salt-of-the-earth ox; the emotional human; and the haughty, lighter-than-air eagle.

These archetypes can even be seen in the writing styles of the four gospels themselves. The quick pace and now-ness of Mark's action-driven gospel is as kinetically powered by fire as the stoic, serious, and detailed gospel of Matthew is grounded by earth. Luke's gospel is written in the style of a well-researched historian, almost ambivalent in its academic nature, a headiness often associated with air. And anyone who knows the New Testament is familiar with the words of John, practically overflowing with emotion, like a spiritual cup runneth over.

Hippocrates

This four-group classification found its way into the "sciences" courtesy of Hippocrates (a.k.a. the father of medicine, a.k.a. that guy with an oath named after him—to be honest, "do no harm" sounds great on a bumper sticker, but let's be real: getting your blood slowly sucked out of your body by leeches sure sounds like a whole lot of harm). Aside from the aforementioned CV material, Hippocrates was known for his theory of humorism, the belief that our health and behavior is regulated by chemical systems within our body connected to one of four fluids, or humors. Any disease or affliction we might contract is due to an imbalance of one, two, or maybe all four humors (black bile, blood, phlegm—not the spitting kind—and yellow bile; Kalachanis and Michailidis, 2015).

I know what you're thinking: What the hell is black bile? I mean, with the exception of blood, who knows what any of these fluids are? French physiologist and Nobel laureate Charles Richet (1910) once sarcastically tried to describe phlegm as "this strange liquid, which is the cause of tumours, of chlorosis, of rheumatism, and cacochymia—where is it? Who will ever see it? Who has ever seen it? What can we say of this fanciful classification of humours into four groups, of which two are absolutely imaginary?" That being said, for the purpose of our discussion here, humorism doesn't have to be medically accurate to be historical. Just like the systems before it, it's built on a group of four, with each humor representing a distinct personality trait:

1. **Blood:** hyperactive
2. **Black Bile:** sadness
3. **Yellow Bile:** moody
4. **Phlegm:** passive

Plato

Quite possibly the most pivotal figure in Western philosophy and a hay-maker name-drop in any intellectually pretentious, tuition-justifying discussion about ideas. It's like talking to old heads about anything; inevitably they bring up some old cat and throw the name down like a trump card. I see your Tupac and Biggie and raise you a Grandmaster Caz. LeBron is great. Jordan was better. But you know who could really hoop? Bill "Eleven Rings" Russell.

Plato believed in four kinds of knowledge, which he laid out in his divided-line analogy. (I won't explain it here, but feel free to wiki it. You'll be very unimpressed with the pictures.) The four kinds of knowledge are *pistis* (certainty), *eikasia* (instinct), *noesis* (intuition), and *dianoia* (intellect). The first two derive information on a concrete level and together are known as Doxa, or the visceral. The latter two combined are known as Episteme, or the intelligible, and pertain to information on an abstract level. This distinction between the concrete and abstract is incredibly relevant for reading about Keirsey later in this chapter (Plato, [360 BCE] 2009).

Galen

Greek physician, surgeon, and philosopher—an old-school version of a triple threat and another reminder that, back in the day, doctors used to think about things other than tee times. Of course, I guess there's more time to contemplate the meaning of life when you don't have to worry about malpractice suits every time you maim or kill one of your patients, which I'm surmising happened quite a lot back in Galen's time. The beauty of low expectations.

Galen came up with the idea of four distinct personality temperaments directly based on the four humors: melancholic (conscientious and reserved), sanguine (active and excitable), choleric (independent and irritable), and phlegmatic (unemotional and calm). This was one of the first, well-known instances where people were explicitly divided by a set of four personality traits (Jouanna, 2012).

Paracelsus

Another triple threat, Paracelsus was an influential member of the Renaissance's medical revolution and a noted alchemist. He took the idea of the four elements and paired it with an elemental, a mythic being described in occult literature around the time of the European Renaissance. Gnomes were his gatherers of the earth; salamanders, his denizens of the fire. Undines (water nymphs) and sylphs (fairies of the air) drew on the mystical nature of their element counterparts (Silver, 1999).

Carl Jung

If psychology had its version of the Recording Industry Association of America (RIAA), Jung would be a multi-diamond-certified artist. He pumped out top-forty psych concepts like archetypal phenomena, dream analysis, synchronicity, the psychological complex, the collective unconscious, and extraversion versus introversion. The latter led to him introducing a dichotomy of three preferences: extraversion versus introversion, sensing versus intuition, and thinking versus feeling (Jung, [1921] 1971). He called them function types. Myers-Briggs Type Indicator (MBTI) fanatics call them gospel. I call them a bit outdated.

Isabel Briggs Myers

Otherwise known as the mother of all MBTI-based personality theory, co-creator—along with her mother, Katherine Cook Briggs—of the MBTI, and a person I name-drop in the preface. Myers authored *Gifts Differing* (Myers and Myers, 1980), a seminal work that many people consider to be the personality bible. And much like the Bible, no one's actually read it, and yet it still manages to inspire bad take after bad take, each one expressed with more certainty than the last. Myers took Jung's work and added a fourth function type: judging versus perceiving, which translates to something akin to organized versus flexible.

The MBTI assesses our preferences based on the four function types (E vs. I, S vs. N, T vs. F, J vs. P), with the final result giving us a four-letter designation (e.g., ESTJ), sixteen different possible combinations, and thus personality types. This is personality theory in probably its most familiar form. Just ask anyone, and they'll vaguely recall taking it in high school or college, followed by a halfhearted stab at remembering the letters—basically, the same reaction if you ask them to recall anything they learned in high school or college.

David Keirsey

For me, Keirsey's *Please Understand Me II* (1998) is the real personality bible. Granted, the title is terrible—it sounds like the battle cry of the millennial, simultaneously pleading and entitled. Self-esteem-generation book titles aside, what Keirsey did was ingenious. He took the four-group classification model, as seen by many pre-Jung philosophers, and blended it with the work of Jung and Myers. Instead of sixteen individual types, Keirsey restructured it to feature four groups (Guardians, Artisans, Idealists, and Rationals), or temperaments, and four subgroups within each temperament.

This system has the benefit of maintaining sixteen distinct personalities while acknowledging that strong similarities exist between different types. It even addresses the division that Plato had previously observed between concrete knowledge (the visceral) and abstract knowledge (the intelligible). Out of the four temperaments, Keirsey believed that Guardians and Artisans prefer to understand the world concretely, collecting information mainly from their senses. Idealists and Rationals, however, naturally perceive the world abstractly, choosing to trust their intuition as they navigate the invisible world of feelings and ideas (Keirsey, 1998). And yes, it's true that all people can do a little bit of everything—let's just keep figure 1.1 pinned so I don't have to write it for the millionth time. But like in all things dealing with personality type, it's about what comes naturally. For all you visual learners out there, see figure 1.2.

Figure 1.1 Big Ass Reminder

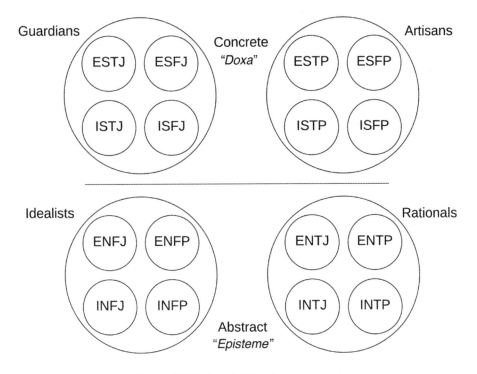

Figure 1.2 Keirsey's Four Temperaments

I am not exaggerating when I say I *love* Keirsey's system. I love it more than Robert Horry hitting a game winner against the Sacramento Kings. I love it more than the first time I heard Horace Andy singing on Massive Attack's "Angel" and said, "Damn this girl can sing!" There is a certain elegance to its construction, a clarity of concept, where information and distillation flow seamlessly as if it were always meant to be. Keirsey's four-temperament structure makes so much sense that it causes a visceral, doxa-powered anger to build up inside of me knowing that most MBTI "experts" have absolutely no familiarity with his work, like a professed music lover who's never heard Eva Cassidy sing. But as nature has proven, evolution is a powerful force. And as much as I respect and admire Keirsey's obscure yet groundbreaking work, the natural selection of ideas inevitably takes place, and just like the theories of the ancient Persians and Greeks before him, Keirsey's concepts can give way to better, modified forms of viewing personality.

"THE TIMES THEY ARE A-CHANGIN'" (DYLAN, 1964)

Before accusations of presumption come raining down on me like hellfire, let me remind all the readers that Keirsey's concepts are almost fifty years old. Myers started formulating the ideas that would become the MBTI assessment in the early to midtwentieth century. Jung was alive when most people still got around by riding something with a mind of its own. These are *old* theories. Even still, MBTI purists tend to cling to them religiously, as if it's perfectly believable that, in 150 years, we can go from performing surgery with just a bottle of moonshine and a bite rag to having access to centuries of human knowledge in the palm of our hands, and yet advancements in the way we understand people are impossible.

Now, I didn't rappel down the tree of our personality ancestors branch by branch just so I could trash their theories once I got to the bottom. It's unfair and, quite frankly, kind of an asshole move to criticize ideas for being antiquated just to prop up your own, especially those that have benefited from the luxury of time and hindsight. The advent of the iPhone doesn't make the wheel any less ingenious. Instead, I do my best to politely list the main ways that the *PoP* method deviates from the theories before it, with the tacit understanding that the former would not exist without the latter.

First Deviation

The Power of Personality uses animals to represent the sixteen different personality types.

Why: As symbolic representations, animals are far easier to remember than a four-letter combination. Plus, it's more fun telling people you're a Fox.

Second Deviation

The Power of Personality places its animal personality types into four major groups (packs), represented by roles rooted in ancient civilizations: Gatherers, Hunters, Shamans, and Smiths.

Why: These roles remind us of both the historical and practical nature of personality typing. Whether you grew up in the Mongolian Empire at its height or in a tiny Proto-Indo-European fishing village on the shores of the Black Sea, chances are you relied on similar things to survive (food, shelter, community). While these needs have evolved over the centuries, much of their essence remains the same. How the coexistence of these four groups has enabled our species to survive is examined in the next chapter.

Third Deviation

The Power of Personality eschews the letter dichotomy first introduced by Jung.

Why: Differences in types don't always manifest themselves according to letter designation. For example, the difference, theoretically, between an ENTP and INTP (MBTI designation; in the *PoP* system, they would be a Chimpanzee and Owl, respectively) is that one is extroverted and the other is introverted. However, the types often don't present themselves in that way. Chimpanzees, like Elon Musk, are much more likely to hole up in their workshop smoking weed and dreaming up new ways to revolutionize the energy sector or screw over cryptophiles with a single tweet (still going to use that word) than hit the social scene. They prefer trolling Twitter (okay, X) to trolling clubs. And the seemingly quiet Owls can be quite loquacious and energetic when discussing a topic they find fascinating. Trust me, I have an Owl friend who's a theoretical chemistry professor. I once asked him about string theory, and he still hasn't shut up.

Thankfully, having knowledge of both MBTI and Keirsey helps to elucidate the reasons for the blind spot. Keirsey reintroduced us to the idea of four distinct groups of people, and among those groups, Gatherers (related to Keirsey's Guardians) make up close to half of the population. They are also much more willing than the other temperaments to volunteer as subjects for observation, testing, and other forms of personality-based research, as they feel contributing to public knowledge is part of their civic duty.

So if we accept that Gatherers make up the largest sample size of test subjects, then it would also be reasonable to accept that their traits and behavior are probably overrepresented in personality theory. When you compare Gatherers, such as an ESTJ and an ISTJ, the extroverted and introverted traits are much more pronounced and consistent, confirming the E-versus-I dichotomy as accurate, especially after repeated observation. That's how the letters became gospel. Of course, it's a revelation that only ministers to half the population. For Hunters, Shamans, and Smiths, the letter distinctions don't just lead to mistyping and confusion, but they also give ammunition to skeptics. A Smith friend (a Killer Whale, to be specific) complained to me once about personality typing being inaccurate because he was techni-cally extroverted, but his outgoingness depended on the context. I could only agree. Nuance was sorely needed.

Fourth Deviation

The Power of Personality defines people by their core desires and needs (secu-rity, excitement, identity, and information), thus replacing the binary choices found in most MBTI-based personality assessments.

Why: The way an individual prioritizes those foundational values is the best determinant of their decision making. That doesn't mean that someone who prioritizes security over excitement is going to make that choice 100 percent of the time. A cautious person can take risks to have fun, just like a thrill seeker can decide to settle down and have a family. It's just harder. Kind of like a lefty using their right hand. It may be unfamiliar and most likely un-comfortable but not impossible—I know, I know, ambidextrous people screw up my whole metaphor. Perhaps my editor can think of a better one (if you're reading this, you'll know how that went).

WHAT DID WE LEARN?

So, a quick recap:

- Humans from various cultures have been dividing the world into four entities for a long, long time (see figure 1.3).
- In the last 150 years, it's become vogue to categorize humans into sixteen different types. Personality theory also became quite science-y, with actual tests and things that can be assessed by *experts* with *authority*.
- Keirsey was awesome and underappreciated.
- *The Power of Personality* uses animal types because they're fun and easy to remember, and it veers away from the letter dichotomy of function types and MBTI because they're inaccurate and not as precise as the "science" would have us believe.
- Individuals can be defined by what they value most, as best observed through the priorities they choose naturally.
- I use a lot of metaphors, some of which don't always work perfectly.

THE WORLD IN FOURS

Zoroaster (Ancient Persia)	Earth	Fire	Water	Air
Empedocles (Ancient Greece)	Earth	Fire	Water	Air
Pancha Maha-bhoot (India)	Earth	Fire	Water	Air
Bön (Tibet)	Earth	Fire	Water	Air
Buddhism (Four Tenets)	Solidity	Energy	Cohesion	Expansion
The Bible	Ox	Lion	Human	Eagle
The Gospels	Matthew	Mark	John	Luke
Hippocrates	Black Bile	Blood	Yellow Bile	Phlegm
Plato	Pistis ("certainty")	Eikasia ("instinct")	Noesis ("intuition")	Dianoia ("intellect")
Galen	Melancholic	Sanguine	Choleric	Phlegmatic
Paracelsus	Gnomes	Salamanders	Nymphs	Sylphs
Keirsey	Guardians	Artisans	Idealists	Rationals

Figure 1.3 The World in Fours

CHAPTER TWO

THE FOUR PACKS

WE'RE ALL PLAY-DOH (NOT THAT PLATO)

Now comes the CYA (as in cover your ass) portion of the book. At its surface, this chapter might seem like one long disclaimer, an elaborate expounding on the imperfect nature of personality typing as a means of excusing all the times I screw the pooch when typing people—all of which is true. But upon closer inspection, I hope you'll come to understand that, when trying to understand people, it's the nuances and imperfections, the mistakes and recalculations (especially when assessing ourselves), that make it such a worthwhile process in the first place.

Individual = Personality Type + Life Experience

Remember this equation. Always. Every time you think you know a person's type, then they go and do something completely unexpected, and you immediately want to retype them. *Remember.* Personality type and life experience are two separate things. The first is, for the most part, consistent. Whether you're a Fox, a Spider, or a Humpback Whale, you are going to share a great number of similarities to other Foxes, Spiders, or Humpback Whales. What separates us as individuals is always the life experience we have accrued.

Let's imagine our personality type as a brightly colored ball of Play-doh and life experience as the sometimes gentle, sometimes brutal hands that mold and shape it. The resulting sculpture is who we are: a manifestation of our individual self. Occasionally, life takes that initial clay and turns it into Michelangelo's *David*. Other times, it becomes so twisted and distorted it ends up looking like that Bob's Big Boy statue of Donald Trump they displayed at CPAC in 2021. But regardless of the result, the initial matter remains the same.

A question I get asked all the time is, Can a person change? It's a fair question. On its own, it sounds well meaning enough. Growing up, we're always taught that the best thing about making mistakes is that they're the impetus for growth. But growth and change are not the same thing. We can grow and mature, and as we do, our behavior changes and evolves, but that first ball of Play-doh, our personality type, cannot change, even if we want it to, at least not in any genuine and true way. Can an individual's behavior deviate from the expectations of their personality type? Of course. But it's not healthy. Things come naturally to us for a reason, and to force ourselves to do the opposite, aside from not making a whole lot of intuitive sense, will invariably tie our psyche into knots. What's worse is that the likely cause for any deviation is usually an outside influence that, while well meaning, is often self-serving.

Case in point: The question of whether a person can change usually comes up in one specific scenario. Someone wants to know if their romantic partner can change to better fit their needs. It's only natural for someone to want their significant other to be their perfect match—as if such a thing even existed. It's not uncommon for someone to project their own traits onto their partner to confirm the solidarity of their love. But of course, these are illusions, as fantastical as a lucid dream where all desires are met and relationships are animosity-free. There most certainly is conflict between all personalities, and that conflict is generally consistent according to the types involved. The question I always ask is, Can you accept that about your partner? Because if you can't, then wishfully thinking that he or she is going to change or that they're actually something they're not is detrimental to the maturation of both you and your partner.

Nietzsche ([1886] 1998) once wrote that true maturity "consists in having found again the seriousness one had as a child, at play." It means reconnecting with who we truly are, that initial Play-doh, and letting it guide us toward who we're meant to be. So to answer the initial question, Can a person change? No. But they can grow. And in the best of scenarios, they grow into better versions of themselves. After all, puppies mature into dogs, not cats.

Which brings me to the reason I bring all this up in the first place: When typing a person, don't forget to consider their life experiences and how those might affect their behavior. For example, we might expect a Peacock (one of the Hunters) to be naturally gregarious and spontaneous—I know I haven't gone over the specific types yet, but trust me, they are. But what if the Peacock's parents were extremely rigid Gatherers, so much so that the stringent restrictions they placed on their Peacock child sapped away any natural charisma? Or let's say a Beaver (one of the Gatherers) appears nothing like the organized, responsible, stickler for details they're destined to be because they were raised by immature Hunter parents who, while searching for self-gratification, left the Beaver bereft of good role models. In cases like these, appearances can be deceiving.

That's why it's important to remember, a Peacock without charisma is still a Peacock. An irresponsible Beaver is still a Beaver. Even though a person has lacked the requisite life experience to reach the full potential of their personality type, the situation can be easily rectified once they've been typed accurately. Put that same Peacock in a scenario away from their strict parents where they're encouraged to perform, and watch them become a star. Give that same Beaver just a taste of structure, and see the life that they can build—which might include literally building structures. The affinity was always there.

A HIERARCHY OF DESIRES

The first step to typing anyone is to ascertain which of four major groups they belong to—I call them packs, as it seems apropos with animal types. As briefly alluded to in chapter 1, these four roles (Gatherers, Hunters, Shamans, and Smiths) have been prevalent for centuries of human existence. Civilization has always needed people who can

1. grow, gather, and store the harvest;
2. scout unexplored terrain and hunt for food;
3. coalesce individuals around a single, communal identity; and
4. create new tools and improve old ones.

Each role has been essential to the evolution of our society, and like evolution, it can be theorized that a particular pack's percentage in the population is dictated by survival, or, more specifically, how many from each pack society needs to evolve. It makes sense that a larger number of Gatherers and Hunters would be needed. And while Hunters appear in smaller numbers than Gatherers (I don't know this from personal experience, but I'm assuming that hunting wildebeests with wooden spears comes with a less-than-stellar survival rate), they're still far more plentiful than Shamans and Smiths. In a rural hamlet, it takes several villagers to sow the fields but only one to sense when it's about to rain and many to join the hunt but only one to create the weapons.

As societies have evolved, so have the four packs. Whereas Gatherers in the past might have concentrated solely on agrarian needs, their present-day requirements, though similarly logistics focused, have expanded to such tasks as coordinating supply chains and supervising complex organizations. Hunters may have given up their spears but for no less risky occupations like firefighting, deep-sea fishing, and financial speculation. Shamans still heal the sick and tend to their flock, generally in counseling or advocacy roles, and Smiths still look to the future to innovate the tools at our disposal like they always have (though I highly doubt any Iron Age blacksmith foresaw the advent of the cloud). So, the present shows itself to be very much like the past and, in all likelihood, the future, but the question remains: How do we know which pack someone belongs to?

In the film *The Silence of the Lambs*, the incarcerated serial killer Dr. Hannibal "The Cannibal" Lecter counsels an ambitious FBI agent in training, Clarice Starling, as she attempts to apprehend a mysterious killer who has been murdering and skinning young women:

> HANNIBAL: First principles, Clarice, simplicity. Read Marcus Aurelius, "of each particular thing ask, 'What is it in itself? What is its nature?'" What does he do, this man you seek?
> CLARICE: He kills women.
> HANNIBAL: No! That is incidental. What is the first and principal thing he does? What needs does he serve by killing? (Demme, 1991)

Determining an individual's pack follows the exact same principle: simplicity. We must strip away a person's actions and delve deep into their core intent. We must ask ourselves, "What desire does this person seek to satisfy?"

There are four core desires: security, excitement, self-identity, and information. Now, regarding matters of desire and instinct, we can go back into the annals of psychology and find disagreements between the likes of Freud, Maslow, Skinner, and so on, and from a purely observational perspective, it's easy to see that human wants are varied and plentiful (fast cars, a house with a pool, a yoga studio in walking distance of a Trader Joe's). However, their essence can be boiled down to these four principal desires, as they dictate to all the others. As cinema's most famous, liver- and fava-bean-eating, chianti-drinking serial killer would attest, *that* is our nature.

Four Packs

1. **Gatherers = Security:** The need for safety benefits all who fall under the blanket of their protection and care.
2. **Hunters = Excitement:** The need for speed fuels their ability to engage in risky but often necessary behavior.
3. **Shamans = Self-Identity:** The need to connect with themselves extends to the rest of humanity's global village.
4. **Smiths = Information:** The need for data enables them to further stretch the boundaries of innovation.

This is the point in the conversation when everyone and their mother barges in to tell me, "All these things are important!" Yes, this is true. Desiring one does not preclude us from desiring any of the others. What it comes down to is, when push comes to shove, which one does a person choose first? Of course, the process is not infallible. Many Gatherers, if you ask them, will tell you they value information above all else. In fact, years ago, I used to use the term *knowledge* instead of *information*, and people from every pack would find the word too irresistible to pass up. Even *information* can be tempting for non-Smiths to claim atop their hierarchy. That is why, when typing, the choice needs to be presented as clearly as possible, with no wiggle room for rationalization.

When a Gatherer tells me that they prize information above all else, this is how the conversation usually goes:

ME: Would you risk your life for information?

GATHERER: Risk? What do you mean?

ME: Like, if you were researching the cure for cancer, would you be willing to experiment on yourself to get your answers?

GATHERER: Of course not! That's insane!

And like that, I have my answer. Notice how the thought of risking their life or *security* for knowledge had never even occurred to the Gatherer. The idea is so foreign, so unnatural, that it doesn't even register as a possibility. And I don't mean to make fun of Gatherers (well, at least not exclusively) because we're all susceptible to this insularity of values. Our core desires are powerful things, so much so that they can leave us with the subconscious assumption that everyone else prioritizes them just as much as we do. And it's not to say that a Smith, because they treasure information, would automatically risk their life in pursuit of it—but they would consider it.

I am aware that I've been throwing around these terms like you know them intimately, as if I'm already on chapter 2 of this book, and I have yet to describe them in any sort of detail. This is a fact I now rectify. Gatherer, Smith, a menagerie of animals—what do they all mean? We can't begin to start typing people into distinct personalities until we actually understand the complexities of those personalities first. Figures 2.1 and 2.2 are visual guides.

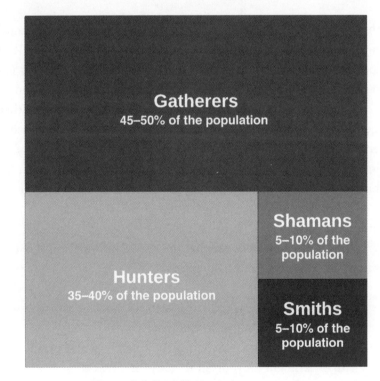

Figure 2.1 Pack Percentage

16

A
N
I
M
A
L

T
Y
P
E
S

Figure 2.2 Animal Type Percentage

Pay careful attention to those approximate population percentages, as they're extremely vital to comprehending the dynamics between the packs. Conflict between differing types is inevitable, but that conflict takes on a new dimension when one pack (Gatherers) makes up almost half the population, not to mention that the two concrete packs make up around 85 percent of people in the world.

Gatherers

It's not that Gatherers are the self-ordained sentinels of society as much as they *are* society. Civilization as we know it would not exist without the consistent, practical, organized strength of Stags, Beavers, Elephants, and Bears.

Past descriptions of the quadrant have not been particularly glamorous (news flash: this one isn't either), as being told that you have a natural talent for managing goods and services isn't exactly going to light up anyone's amygdala on an fMRI. And when told of their prevalence in society (approximately

45–50 percent of the population), some Gatherers choose to identify with other, rarer types, as if scarcity were somehow synonymous with quality. This need to feel special is unfortunate, for it distracts from the very thing that makes Gatherers legitimately special to begin with: the ability to provide order and comfort in a world that seems to be increasingly bent on chaos.

Gatherers are generally unselfish, responsible individuals who hold themselves to high standards of right and wrong. Their desire for security manifests itself in two powerful ways: their dedication to fulfilling proper societal obligations and their wish to provide comfort and support to their loved ones. Just think of the last time you needed help with anything. Which friend or family member did you call? Chances are, you called a Stag, Beaver, Elephant, or Bear.

Another thing that Gatherers have in common is a genuine faith in the idea of the traditional community. This is not a blind faith; Gatherers are quick to point out possible improvements that can be made to their respective organizations. It is more a belief that, as flawed as the current system might be, there is no better way to ensure the continued providence of human-kind than trusting what has already been established, proven, and accepted. Traditions are to be revered, if only out of respect for the fact that they have endured for so long—endurance being a trait that every Gatherer values.

Categorization is a skill that Gatherers are predisposed to, as it gives them a greater sense of certainty, which in turn makes them feel more secure. This, along with their keen understanding of societal norms, helps them do ex-tremely well in school as the stereotypical perfect student and citizen of the month. Gatherers generally love being around people, though they can be choosy about the company they keep and the context in which they interact; they have work buddies, friends in the inner circle, and friends they'd have sex with if asked—remember, they love categories.

There is a trust that Gatherers have with their fellow humans that is fueled by fear and practicality. They view the world as a dangerous place rife with serious peril (war, natural disasters, unemployment, rising temperatures, etc.), so it only makes sense to tackle these problems as a group. There is safety in numbers but only if you trust your teammates. That's why Gatherers work to create spaces where individuals can feel safe and comfortable around all manner of people, trusting in the knowledge that the culture and traditions of the past will sustain them in the present. And whether it's a kindergarten class, a hospital, a church, or an entire government, Gatherers usually succeed.

Hunters

Whether you're watching them from afar (some Hunters would refer to it as admiring) or interacting with them up close and personal, there is no doubt of a Hunter's purpose: to do something worthy of attention or, at the very least, to have fun trying. Spontaneous, action oriented, free flowing, and audacious, Foxes, Sharks, Peacocks, and Butterflies always seem to bring a needed bit of excitement and pizzazz wherever they go.

When it comes to their philosophy on life, Hunters are epicureans at heart, masters of maximizing pleasure and minimizing pain in all aspects of their lives. They are the free spirits, the rule benders, the gamblers, and the entertainers; they are the people most likely to skip dinner and go straight to dessert. For Hunters, life is all about living in the visceral intensity of the moment, and there is no better counselor to them than their own five senses. With their optimism and zest for the present, Hunters usually don't let their shortcomings or failures bring them down; in fact, falling on their face is the best—sometimes only—way for Hunters to learn. And the recklessness and overconsumption of their earlier days frequently evolves into the shrewdness and nuance that guide them for the rest of their lives.

All Hunters take pride in their respective talents and do not hesitate to showcase them at a moment's notice. Foxes and Peacocks are overt in their showmanship, while Sharks and Butterflies tend to be a bit more restrained, letting the brilliance of their craft do the talking. No matter the type, Hunters live by the motto "If you got it, flaunt it!" Perhaps this is a result of growing up in the tightly structured world of the Gatherers, a world whose categories and restrictions often chafe the hyperactive, "anything is possible" Hunters, who hate to be told what they can and cannot do.

School can be torturous. Its "learn first, apply later" paradigm is not exactly simpatico with the Hunter's need for instant gratification; it's not difficult to figure out how Hunter children performed on the marshmallow test. Risk takers who learn by doing, Hunters prefer practicing proven techniques over memorizing abstract theory. For them, technical mastery is the goal. Though that process might be arduous, Foxes, Sharks, Peacocks, and Butterflies don't mind getting their asses kicked, figuratively *and* literally, if they're learning to master something that is practical in action. And it is in that pursuit of greatness within their respective craft that a Hunter fights like a junkyard dog, regardless of whether they'll receive a grade for it or not.

In the mind of a Hunter, you're either good at something or you're not, no matter the method, means, or manner in which you achieved your results. It's almost more fun to do it the harder, more unconventional way, like a slap in the face to all those people who ever doubted them. Conceivably, Hunters' desire to exhibit their skills might be a form of vindication for years spent having to dodge the wrath of Gatherer orthodoxy. Despite that, it's also safe to say that Hunters strive to display their artistry no matter what kind of animosity they may or may not feel—just don't be surprised if they perform a touchdown dance or slip in a lighthearted wink on their way to victory.

Shamans

Shamans are the unicorns of temperament theory. I'm not trying to be flippant. Yes, it's true that such Shaman traits as empathy and optimism frequently cause Dolphins, Pandas, Baboons, and Humpback Whales to be caricatured as hypersensitive, hippie-dippie dreamers who fantasize all day about misty rainbows, magic, and a perfect world filled only with purity and grace. Of course, like the unicorn itself, this perception is fantasy, and the real Shaman, the one of flesh and blood, is no closer to virtue than the next person. Perhaps it's this myth that casts doubt on their existence at all. Identity seeking, with an imaginative streak that can veer on otherworldly, Shamans commonly feel marginalized by a society that values the concrete over the abstract, material success over spiritual wholeness, and fitting in rather than fitting out.

Unlike the equally rare Smiths, Shamans choose to assimilate with greater society, becoming quite adept at repressing some of their more esoteric proclivities. While hiding in plain sight gives them a sense of belonging, what a Shaman really needs is self-acceptance, and anything or any person who impedes is detrimental to their personal growth. Fortunately, many Shamans eventually find the confidence to be that one black horse in a stable of white horses or, better yet, a unicorn drifting in a sea of thoroughbreds.

Shamans not only seek their own identities but also help others do the same. In their heart of hearts, they believe that, if everyone were to discover and be appreciated for their true selves, the world would be a better place. Unfortunately, this often puts them at odds with a social structure that discourages individuality in favor of conforming to familiar traditions and standards. Enter identity crisis. Sorry, Shamans. No way to avoid this. But take comfort in the fact that you'll come out the other side stronger, more confident, and possessing the ability to change society in ways that will benefit all its people. *Or* you'll just lie on your couch, roll into a ball, and waste away in the fetal position. But let's be optimistic!

Though Dolphins, Pandas, Baboons, and Humpback Whales all have differing priorities and approaches, the singular thing that galvanizes them is the belief that true happiness lies solely in the province of the individual. Most of the time, this is a faith hard-earned, as each Shaman at some point in their life must fight their own battle with social conformity. For some, it's a brief skirmish. For others, it's like trying to establish order in Afghanistan, a never-ending war waged for the right to be themselves. In the end, however, Shamans always seem to emerge stronger, the bearers of emotional scars that serve not only as a display of the pain that they've suffered but also as evidence of their resolve.

It's a special kind of fortitude. It involves being so anchored to your moral center that even the wildest emotional storms can't move you. A Shaman might look at it as an epiphany: "I'm weird, and I'm okay with that." And like a secret treasure, they guard it with their life, only teaching it to those they deem worthy. After all, self-confidence and an appreciation of one's own individuality is far more valuable than any material wealth one could accumulate. Or as Nietzsche ([1886] 1998), a dyed-in-the-wool Shaman, once wrote, "No price is too high to pay for the privilege of owning yourself." And who needs a day job when you can have rainbows, purity, and grace?

Smiths

Long stereotyped as social outcasts, brilliant eccentrics, and unapologetic sociopaths, Smiths frequently find themselves as both beneficiary and victim to prejudice: It's not enough that they're powerful; they must be misanthropic, too. What is it about Killer Whales, Spiders, Chimpanzees, and Owls that makes society want to brand them as the mustache-twirling, cat-stroking archvillain that longs to rule—or destroy—the world? Conceivably, it's because a majority of Smiths rather like the idea of being a supergenius, albeit an evil one, and find pieces of truth in the caricature. Of course, those bits of verity are like that old Buddhist parable about a bunch of blind guys touching an elephant: Each one grasps only a portion of information and mistakes it for the whole truth. Smiths are more than a stereotype. They're not cold-blooded, graceful vampires with absolutely no feelings. That's impossible; Smiths are way too clumsy.

Smiths seek information, yet this accumulation of facts is not about achieving a level of certainty. After all, what can be confirmed can also be unconfirmed. Knowledge is fluid, expertise is fickle, and the assumption that possession of the former automatically bestows the latter is fallacious in the eyes of the skeptical Smiths. The mere mention of being an authority, especially in the intellectual arena, is bound to elicit eyerolls or disdain from people like Einstein (1973), as clear an example of a Smith that ever existed, who once said, "To punish me for my contempt for authority, fate made me an authority myself." Doubt isn't frowned upon. It's not perceived as a sign of weakness. It's viewed more as a guide, a yoga trainer, if you will, keeping a Smith's mind balanced and flexible.

Smiths worship ideas, new and old, and do not think twice about spending hours and hours in solitude trying to develop a better understanding of any novel concept brought to their attention. Of course, ideas in and of themselves are a contradiction. They hold tremendous power—the capability to drive the world—yet when it comes to their physical constitution, they are composed of nothing, save for the electrical charges bouncing from neuron to neuron within the human nervous system. This state of abstractness and detachment often mirrors Smiths' struggle to understand the intangible while remaining anchored to the physical world (family, friends, etc.).

Maybe that's why Smiths, whether it's as parents, lovers, or working professionals, find themselves so easily misunderstood as cold, dispassionate, and even lazy. It's not that they don't love; it's just that their love manifests itself in an atypical manner. When a Smith loves someone, their first instinct is not to protect but to understand and inform. When a Smith works, it's not for the sake of productivity as much as efficiency. Love. Work. For Killer Whales, Spiders, Chimpanzees, and Owls, the lines frequently blur, and the marriage of the two (of all the types, Smiths are the most likely to be workaholics) serves to express the passion that simmers just beneath their veneer of objectivity.

FOUR PACKS, FOUR ANIMALS, FOUR ARCS, FOUR ROLES

The *PoP* method is a typology method built on the number 4. This was not intentional. Chalk it up to a whole lot of history (see chapter 1) and a bit of tidy formatting. Put simply, there are four packs with four animals each and four arcs for every pack and four roles for every animal.

For every pack, there is a natural growth arc that its members generally follow. Keep in mind, this is not a map etched in stone. There's no Boy Scout handbook given to each new Gatherer, Hunter, Shaman, or Smith telling them what do, where to go, or how to build a fire with a ball of lint and a magnifying glass. Determined by the individual characteristics of each type, the development patterns manifest themselves so naturally that most people are unaware that they exist. Think of it like the hero's journey times four, with each path being remarkably unique to the pack. As the Greek philosopher Heraclitus (2001) once remarked, "A man's character is his fate."

And what is this character that we (obviously Heraclitus and I are close personal friends) speak of? Well, would it be terribly evasive of me to answer a question with a question? How about four questions? I know, I know, usually this is a stall tactic, kind of like when your girlfriend asks you if you're interested in having kids, and you ask her, "What do you want to eat tonight, sushi or tacos?" (which is, I swear to God, not autobiographical). However, in the spirit of stalling, let's put a pin in all that (detailed portraits of the sixteen animal types, growth arcs, those all-important four questions), and I promise to expound in greater detail in the next—you guessed it—four chapters.

CHAPTER THREE

THE GATHERERS

"THEY GOT THE GOLDEN ARCHES;
MINE IS THE GOLDEN ARCS" (LANDIS, 1988)

The popularity of personality typing always seems to surprise me. Let's face it. It's a pretty nerdy thing to be into, which is why every instinct I have for social preservation tells me that it should never be the first, second, or third thing to bring up in a conversation with a stranger. Is it prejudicial to assume that the average person wouldn't be interested in self-reflection? Possibly. Perhaps my writing this book is a form of absolution. Still, it fascinates me how one inadvertent mention of animal personality types seems to catch like wildfire in a social setting. It's like accidentally slipping a D&D reference into the middle of a conversation, and as you wait in fearful anticipation for the guillotine to drop, a person from somewhere else in the room yells, "There's no way your rogue succubus is leveled up higher than my halfling elf!"

Of course, not everyone is a fan. There's always the skeptics. I was at this party (more specifically, a movie night devoted to the narratively incoherent but strikingly beautiful *Upstream Color*) explaining personality typing to someone I had just met. She had heard about it from a friend of a friend and felt that was a good enough reason to pelt me with what felt like a thousand questions and eye rolls:

HER: So, how long did you study this in college?
ME: Oh, I studied screenwriting and English lit, but I'm not sure that counts since I only went to class about 15 percent of the time.
HER (with disdain): If you didn't study psychology, how can you prove these things are true?

At this point, I explained to her in a polite and, most importantly, concise manner (if that conversation was a plane, I was ready to jump, parachute or no parachute) that I had owned an education company where we had suc-cessfully applied the personality typing methods of *The Power of Personality* to address the individual needs of our students. I received a perfunctory "Interesting" in response, and that was the end of it. I bring up that story for two reasons.

The first reason is to explain the origin of *The Power of Personality* growth arcs. I didn't read them in some book so I could then regurgitate them here and pass them off as my own. They came from years of experience learning from students of all ages and personality types. Observing individuals for that long, patterns emerge. Sure, different personalities deal with failure and success in different ways; that's nothing new. But what I did find interesting was that different personalities seemed to have different emotional require-ments as they traveled on their path to maturation. Where one student might need to be assured, another might need to be humbled. Where one individual might need to be pushed to the limits of their imagination, another might need to be taught how to ground their ideas with a measure of practical application.

The second reason is that the woman in the story fits the epitome of a young Gatherer in the early stages of their growth arc. The fact that she pos-sesses a college degree (she made sure to announce her academic bona fides to me in a not-so-subtle way) is even further evidence that education does not necessarily equal maturation.

EXPAND THE BUBBLE

The best way to understand the Gatherer growth arc is to accept that all Gatherers live in a bubble: not 50 percent, not 99 percent. All. Of. Them. And I know that might sound equal parts patronizing and asshole-ish, but aside from it being true, it also has the benefit of being a form of low-key flattery, sort of a reverse backhanded compliment. I mean, what's wrong with bubbles? They're hermetically secure and squeaky clean, and their transparent nature represents a sort of honesty in its lack of deception—all traits that Gatherers cherish. Living in a bubble means that you're safer than most people. Of course, it can also imply that you inhabit an insular realm of ignorance and closed-mindedness, so I guess that's bad.

The problem is not the bubble itself but its size and willingness to ex-pand (insert tired dick joke here). Some Gatherers live in extremely small bubbles, made worse by their unwillingness to let anything else in. That which is found in the bubble is known and, thus, acceptable. Anything else represents the unknown (i.e., dangerous). Other Gatherers, much further along on their growth arc, exist in expansive bubbles, possessing extensive knowledge and experience in a vast range of areas. They are as global as the less mature Gatherers are provincial, and because they live in a bubble, the wisdom they've accrued feels safer and more stable and, in time, eventually is accepted as normal.

Back when I owned my education company, we'd hold annual professional development workshops for our teachers, lunch provided. One time, as everyone was standing in line to get food, one of my teachers, a Bear (a type of Gatherer), didn't recognize one of the dishes, so she turned to her friend, a Butterfly (a type of Hunter):

> BEAR: What's that?
> BUTTERFLY: I don't know.
> ME: It's falafel.
> BEAR AND BUTTERFLY (blank stare): . . .
> ME: It's like ground-up beans rolled up into a ball and deep-fried.
> BUTTERFLY: Ooooh! (Puts two on her plate)
> BEAR: Hmmmm . . .
> BUTTERFLY: Sounds awesome.
> BEAR: Okay . . . (takes one)

Fast-forward to two years later: same Bear, same lunch line, same falafel. But this time, it was the teacher in front of her with the blank stare.

> TEACHER: What is that?
> BEAR: Oh, that's falafel. It's ground-up beans rolled in a ball and fried. It's really good.

And like that, her bubble had expanded. Not because she was shamed for her lack of worldliness or mocked for her caution but rather with gentle prodding by someone she trusted. Trust. That's the cardinal word. Any attempt to manipulate or cajole a Gatherer without first establishing trust is futile. These are individuals who value safety and security at the utmost. And they're tough. Don't forget that their patron element is earth. You're not going to be able to move them unless they want to move themselves.

Once you accept that Gatherers live in a bubble, you'll realize that, like a bubble, their world can only be expanded from the inside. To grasp the unfamiliar, they must be able to do it while anchored to something or someone they know. Push too hard, and the bubble bursts. But if done correctly, there's no limit to how vast a Gatherer's bubble can expand and how wide their influence can extend. It's no surprise that Gatherers run a large percentage of the organizations in the world, whether we're talking as heads of state or heads of the PTA. They are the true "gatherers" of the global community. Planet earth is a sort of bubble, after all.

Four Questions for Gatherers

1. How do I see myself?
2. How do I see the world?
3. How do I interact with the world?
4. What is my flaw?

Remember these questions because the way a Gatherer answers them establishes one of the four roles that constitute their character. At the end of the chapter is figure 3.1, a handy little chart that tells you how each role answers each question, though perceptive readers are probably able to figure that out on their own. And that's pretty much how each of these chapters goes.

Somewhere out there, a Gatherer is reading this and thinking, "That's right. Our chapter is establishing the norms of how the other packs are explained. We rock." Aside from the faux-clever pun—you know, Gatherers, earth, rock (crickets . . .)—I really do hope that, for the sake of my book sales, there's more than one Gatherer reading this thing. And yes, the chapters on Hunters, Shamans, and Smiths pretty much follow the same formula as this chapter, which is awesome because I really hate explaining the same thing over and over. Let's be honest, I digress enough as it is; add redundancy to the mix, and this book's page count will rival *War and Peace*.

Special note: As you go through the profiles of the animal types, don't assume that the four roles follow the order of the questions above. A reasonable person might say, "Wouldn't that make a lot of sense from an organization-of-ideas perspective?" And they're right. It's a bit bass ackward. But trust me, it flows better this way.

THE STAG

Forceful yet disciplined; aggressive yet deferential to established authority. Stags are so influential and vital to the establishment of our society that they are often looked upon as the quintessential Gatherer. More than any of their Gatherer siblings, Stags embody the idea of community, teamwork, and order. More supervising than the auditing Beavers, Stags are natural leaders who believe they have a responsibility to ensure that every individual is on the same page when it comes to reaching a common objective, one that will benefit society in a practical way.

The Authority Figure

I don't gripe to you, Reiben. I'm a Captain. We have a chain of command. Gripes go up, not down. Always up. You gripe to me, I gripe to my superior officer, and so on and so on. I don't gripe to you. I don't gripe in front of you. You should know that, as a Ranger.

–Captain James Miller (Spielberg, 1998)

Much like Beavers, Stags prioritize dutiful obligations over family ties. It's not that they don't care about family. It's that their role as a parent, for example, and the subsequent responsibility to ingrain in their child a reasonable respect for authority supersede their feelings as a parent. This ability to remain objective enables Stags to make reasoned, impartial decisions. However, as opposed to Beavers, whose objectivity is best utilized in positions of judgment and inspection, Stags are frequently found in supervisory roles, where their impersonal decision making and leadership skills, when combined, prove vital to guaranteeing the success of the group. Individual whims are often disregarded by Stags—even their own.

Whereas rules are paramount for the Beavers, Stags adhere to the chain of command. A clear line of authority, predicated on qualifications and experience, is important to them. There is a comfort in knowing that the person you're following has reached the mountaintop before via hard work and experience and that the men and women following your lead feel the same way about you. This can be misconstrued by other types as blind obedience, and Stags are commonly accused of not thinking for themselves. While this might be true when it comes to immature Stags, the same can't be said for mature Stags, whose ability to reason and ponder the ramifications of their decisions rival any type. Stags who have effectively expanded their bubble (see, you didn't read that section in vain) appreciate the value of critical examination, but they also know that there is a time and place for everything (arguing with your superior in the heat of battle rarely works out for either of you), and consistently questioning authority, even on a Smith basis, can only lead to the eventual upheaval of the structure that authority is based on; if the choice is between conformity and chaos—well, for the Stag, that's no choice at all.

The Compartmentalizer

By enforcing the Clauses, we have kept religion a matter for the individual conscience, not for the prosecutor or bureaucrat. At a time when we see around the world the violent consequences of the assumption of religious authority by government, Americans may count themselves fortunate: Our regard for constitutional boundaries has protected us from similar travails, while allowing private religious exercise to flourish. . . . Those who would renegotiate the boundaries between church and state must therefore answer a difficult question: Why would we trade a system that has served us so well for one that has served others so poorly?

—Sandra Day O'Connor (2005)

Order is paramount for Stags. Like Beavers, who ensure that everything is in its proper place, Stags strive for a world with clearly delineated niches and designations, and they make sure that these categorizations are accepted by all. If the Beaver is the anvil, the support on which the laws of society lean on, then the Stag is the mighty hammer that drops when those laws are not followed. Stags do not fear confrontation. In fact, they take pride in the straightforward, confident style with which they dictate their opinions on what is right and wrong, though this is not to be confused with the dominating Killer Whales, who can sometimes be rather oblivious to the needs of others. Stags, beacons of the community, are always aware of the needs of their group members, so any critique they dole out is, in their minds, beneficial to the team in the long run. They are the hard-driving drill sergeant, the screaming football coach, or the taskmaster boss.

Regarding their role in an organization, Stags do not view themselves as specialists but rather as great judges of character. Unlike their fellow administrators, the Killer Whales, Stags, when recruiting, place a higher premium on such traits as loyalty, practicality, and trustworthiness over knowledge or skill. To a Stag, practicality is intelligence, and while they acknowledge the virtues of speculation and experimentation—albeit through gritted teeth— Stags find it hard to trust that which has not already been proven and established as truth.

The Inflexible Bureaucrat

You're going to keep your mouth shut until I come to you and ask you a question, then you're going to speak; otherwise, Byrd will take you outside until you understand the rules, 'cause here, I'm in charge.

—Judith Sheindlin (1996–2021)

A Stag's purpose in life is to determine the most practical method of reaching a certain echelon of success and then to hold themselves, their family, and the other members of their organization accountable to this standard of achievement. Unfortunately, this can lead to a tremendous amount of conflict when they fail to realize that there are different strokes for different folks; Stags too often follow a virtual manual on how a person should properly behave themselves, with specific rules for specific contexts. At their worst, Stags aggressively engage with those who would challenge their authority or the authority of the system they adhere to. In such cases, it is not uncommon for them to be perceived as overbearing, obtuse, and virulently closed-minded, unwilling to view a situation from any other perspective but their "correct" one.

Their devotion to the chain of command and their penchant for delegating, when combined, can cause them to form committee after committee of "authorities," creating a weighty bureaucracy that is as unwieldy as it is progress stagnating. Lucky for us, the same knee-jerk reaction toward established virtue that leads Stags into the aforementioned problems can also lead them out of it, as it usually only takes an intervention from an individual they respect (in words that every Stag has said at least twice in their life) to get their shit together.

The Natural-Born Leader

There is nothing that gives a man consequence and renders him fit for command, like a support that renders him independent of everybody but the State he serves.

−George Washington (1776)

As opposed to Elephants, the other herding, team-building type among the Gatherers, Stags are less about turning their organization into one big, happy family and more about directing it toward attainable goals—think SMART goals (specific, measurable, achievable, relevant, and time-based), which Stags love to preach as gospel. To achieve this, Stags take it upon themselves to make sure that every member of the team is fulfilling their prescribed duties. They are practical individuals who prefer when plans are laid out in an applicable fashion and address concrete questions: What is the benefit from a specific course of action? Is the goal feasible? What are the steps needed to accomplish said goal?

The reality-based Stags focus on immediate, tangible results rather than distant, projected outcomes. They're the general manager of a sports franchise that exchanges young prospects for grizzled veterans at the trade deadline. They are always in win-now mode. In no way does this mean that Stags avoid establishing long-term objectives. It's just that they need to see continual progress, or else they begin to doubt the efficacy of the plan. Due to their hard work, social awareness, and loyalty, Stags are often high-ranking individuals who climbed their respective organizational ladders with relative ease. And yet, it is their team-first mentality, not their industriousness, that is at the core of their followers' respect and admiration. Individuals under their leadership can always feel safe in the knowledge that the ship is being steered by a solid, straight-shooting captain who has their best interests at heart.

THE BEAVER

Low maintenance and industrious, Beavers are the quiet backbone of most, if not all, institutions. Like their Gatherer siblings, the supervising Stags, Beavers prioritize duty above all things, whether it is in their role as parent, boss, employee, student body treasurer, or any position with even a modicum of responsibility. However, unlike the Stags, who take it upon themselves to command the group toward a common objective, Beavers assume the role of inspector general, gatekeeper to the rules and regulations that society is built on.

The Impartial Critic

I confront the European elite's self-image as tolerant while under their noses women are living like slaves.

–Ayaan Hirsi Ali (quoted in Caldwell, 2005)

When it comes to practical details, no type is more on top of things than the fastidious Beavers. Differing from the strategic Spiders, whose mastery of details usually pertains to the abstract concepts that buttress their long-term plans, Beavers prefer to focus on the concrete particulars of the present. No manner of minutiae is too trivial for their inspection. For a Beaver, it's those precise specifics, the ones that other types—particularly Shamans and Smiths—frequently disregard, that are necessary to keeping society intact. For example, when it comes to troubleshooting, a Chimpanzee, with their Smith curiosity, is prone to examining every interesting aspect of a machine. A Beaver, however, is the one who discovers in seconds that the machine is merely unplugged. This method may not be exciting, but Beavers don't really care. They just want things to work.

This no-nonsense approach, along with their humble skepticism (a Beaver usually labels grand ideas for the future as unrealistic hubris), is the major reason they make great judges and umpires. No one is above the rules, not even themselves, and their insistence on sticking to the facts of the case, contest, or competition without adding any superfluous context ensures that the results are as fair as humanly possible; Beavers check their personal convictions at the door.

As critics, they're insightful and unbiased, pointing out specific objections, and unwilling to pull punches when critiquing those with whom they share a close personal or social connection. Because of this, other types sometimes perceive Beavers as being rigid or uncaring, especially when compared to their more compassionate Gatherer siblings, the Elephants and Bears. However, this is far from the truth. A Beaver's adherence to the rules is actually just a reflection of their concern for the welfare of society as whole; and what's more compassionate than that?

The Workhorse

In 1966, Andy Dufresne escaped from Shawshank prison. All they found of him was a muddy set of prison clothes, a bar of soap, and an old rock hammer, damn near worn down to the nub. I remember thinking it would take a man six hundred years to tunnel through the wall with it. Old Andy did it in less than twenty.

—Ellis Redding (Darabont, 1994)

Industriousness is easy enough to define. Merriam-Webster describes it as being "constantly, regularly, or habitually active or occupied." But what if there was a competition between animal types as to which was the most industrious? Who would win? The career-minded Killer Whales and Spiders are relentless students, just as the Sharks and Butterflies practice endlessly to perfect their craft. And we cannot forget the Stags, Elephants, and Bears, all of whom possess the Gatherer traits of consistency and diligence. Nonetheless, it's the Beavers who can claim the title of hardest-working type. Whether they're fixing things around the house, taking part in menial and tedious tasks, or inspecting the structural integrity of a proposed freeway project, Beavers are unparalleled in their determination to see that the task is completed.

Their willpower is second to none; to shirk responsibility, no matter how daunting or unglamorous, is absolute failure. Beavers feel an almost nagging proclivity to be productive at all times. Dirty work is like catnip—pardon the mixed animal metaphors (though I know it's technically a simile). Don't be surprised to see a Beaver taking out the trash or washing the dishes. Bears might do the same, though they're motivated more by loyalty to their friends than to any obligation to serve. Beavers are usually the first to offer help and the last to ask for it; they hate being a hassle, and the idea of not being able to carry their own weight horrifies them. Because much of their work is done outside the spotlight, Beavers are commonly taken for granted. Recognition is not a necessity, but appreciation goes a long way toward making a Beaver supremely happy. Just don't try doing the work for them. That would be an insult.

The Worrywart

The Freedom Bell in Berlin is, like the Liberty Bell in Philadelphia, a symbol which reminds us that freedom does not come about of itself. It must be struggled for and then defended anew every day of our lives.

—Angela Merkel (2009)

Naturally cautious, Beavers are like the Boy Scout motto incarnate: "Be prepared" is basically every day of their lives. They have a defensive mindset, always at the ready for whatever life might throw at them. Because of this, it's not unusual for them to worry about possible outcomes that have very little chance of happening. If there's a 99 percent chance for a positive outcome, leave it to a Beaver to stress out about the 1 percent. And unfortunately, no matter the outcome, it's the perfect set-up for confirmation bias. If, by chance, the negative, one-in-a-hundred scenario occurs, the Beaver will declare that they told you so. If the probability-blessed positive outcome occurs, the Beaver will attribute the good fortune to their stressing out about the negative possibility. Either way, it reinforces the idea that their unnecessary stress is, in fact, necessary.

In many contexts, this reflexive caution serves Beavers well. They make terrific accountants and civil engineers; when it comes to building bridges, I'll take the person who's constantly stressing about ways to make sure it doesn't collapse. That being said, a Beaver's hesitance to take risks can be frustratingly closed-minded and stifling to progress in any field and, at worst, leads to the continuation of a status quo that could be detrimental to society in the long—and short—term.

The Patient Builder

I call investing the greatest business in the world . . . because you never have to swing. . . . All day you wait for the pitch you like; then when the fielders are asleep, you step up and hit it.

—Warren Buffett (1974)

Mature Beavers learn to channel their carefulness and risk aversion into a disciplined patience. They never rush. They never give in to the temptation of easy rewards. On the surface, this makes them appear similar to Bears, their Gatherer siblings. But unlike Bears, whose protective qualities make them skittish when it comes to investing money or developing projects, Beavers can become extremely proficient at taking calculated risks. There's no doubt that they'll put in the time and effort to read all the instructions, take all the necessary precautions, and research all the relevant information. Engineering is regularly assumed to be the sole province of the Smiths. While this may be true when it comes to computer science, where abstract design is key, structural engineering is another thing entirely. Let's not forget, actual beavers are known for constructing dams.

Precision, cost analysis, and risk assessment—skills that translate to the financial sector, as well—are all necessary if one plans on building the massive structures that serve as foundations to cities both large and small. Though like much of what Beavers do, these logistical afterthoughts get outshined by flashier achievements. I mean, when's the last time anyone got excited about a new sewer system? Or fixed potholes? Which is a shame. The next time you marvel at the wonder of the Golden Gate Bridge, think about that stretch of California highway you took to get there, and remember that it was probably a Beaver who built it.

THE ELEPHANT

Rivaling the Peacock for the title of most outgoing type, Elephants are well known for their warmth, chattiness, and generosity. Unlike the Peacocks, who are socially aggressive to the point of brazenness, Elephants exude an easygoing friendliness, an air of social comfort that enables those around them to feel comfortable. On a grander scale, the collective work of Elephants helps create and maintain the social structure that our civilizations are centered around.

The Head of the Family

Everything I think and everything I do is wrong. I was wrong about Elton, I was wrong about Christian, and now Josh hated me. It all boiled down to one inevitable conclusion: I was just totally clueless. Oh, and this Josh and Tai thing was wigging me more than anything. I mean, what was my problem? Tai is my pal. I don't begrudge her a boyfriend. I really—Oooh, I wonder if they have that in my size.

—Cher (Heckerling, 1995)

Herders by nature, Elephants share many traits with the other herding types, the Stags and Dolphins. However, unlike their fellow Gatherers, the authoritative, bossy Stags, Elephants tend to herd their companions using a lighter touch, so much so that it's easy to confuse them with the sensitive, Shaman Dolphins. Still, whereas Dolphins stress self-empowerment and individuality, Elephants emphasize compassion and togetherness and, above all else, seek to create a family environment for every person they come in contact with. It cannot be stressed enough how crucial the idea of family is to Elephants, whether it refers to their spouse and children, their extended family, their tightly knit group of friends, or the menagerie of pets they are likely to have roaming around the house. Just as society relies on them for social stability, Elephants rely on a strong, familial support system that they can turn to in times of need.

Let's not forget that Elephants are Gatherers; safety is paramount, and the greatest benefit of being safe is living a life of comfort. For this reason, abstract musing tends to disinterest them. It's not that they're incapable of introspection; it's just that time is precious, and they'd rather spend their life kicking back on their front porch playing with their grandchildren than combing the back alleys of their subconscious. Being in an ivory tower is like detention for an Elephant; they suffer in solitude while all their friends get to go out and play. In an Elephant's mind, what's the point of gaining a better understanding of the world—or yourself, for that matter—if you don't have time to share it with anyone?

The Optimist

Humans are by nature, too complicated to be understood fully. So, we can choose either to approach our fellow human beings with suspicion, or to approach them with an open mind, a dash of optimism, and a great deal of candor.

—Tom Hanks (quoted in Daum, 2016)

Elephants see the very best in people. Staying true to their Gatherer roots, this optimism is grounded in their belief in the sanctity of the community. They are not ignorant to the fact that negativity exists. They just choose to live their lives in a positive manner, believing that positivity breeds positivity and that any goodwill they throw into the world will come back tenfold. Insults and slights slide off them like water off a duck's back (when the hell did I start using folksy idioms?). Anyway, Elephants are usually the first person to initiate social interaction, and in contrast to the freewheeling Peacocks and Foxes and the businesslike Killer Whales, they do it with a polite, unpretentious style, turning strangers into acquaintances and acquaintances into friends, all in a matter of minutes.

Once they have established friendships, those connections tend to last, strengthened by the Elephant's silly musings, good-natured ribbings, and habit for laughing. Rejection does not deter them—they're social juggernauts, bitch (a childish X-Men animated series reference I was too tempted to not drop *and* rewatch on YouTube)—as they are relentless when it comes to bringing new people into the group. Whether it's the kid sitting by himself during lunch or the coworker hiding away in the corner cubicle, Elephants make it their mission to ensure that every single individual feels like part of the team. Their archnemesis is loneliness, a villain they would love to eradicate from the Earth.

The Gossip

Show me someone who never gossips, and I will show you someone who is not interested in people.

—Barbara Walters (quoted in Sarkis, 2012)

The downside to an Elephant's social maneuvering is that they can often be viewed as busybodies. They routinely involve themselves in other people's affairs, applying a tremendous amount of pressure on individuals who aren't on the right social track. Elephants are popular, and they want you to be popular, too. It never occurs to them that what makes them happy, their dream of idyllic social bliss, is not particularly high on the list of priorities for other types (the reclusive Owls and calculating Spiders are particularly annoyed by Elephants). What if John from HR really does just want to be left alone? Perhaps cousin Margaret doesn't want to be reminded of her "unsuccessful" marital status every Thanksgiving or set up with some random guy you met in the wine aisle at your local Whole Foods.

The type most likely to know everything about everybody, Elephants can usually be found heading various societal institutions, like church groups, PTAs, social clubs, reunion committees, and so on. Even though they're extremely outgoing and avid party throwers, Elephants are not really party animals per se. For them, parties are an extension of the community, and you're more likely to see them organizing a baby shower or planning a game night than doing body shots in Cabo—though it's worth noting that, of all the Gatherers, Elephants are far and away the most adventurous. They love trying new things and traveling to new places, as long as the novelty of the experience is grounded by the companionship of familiar, trusted faces.

The Host

Honestly, it's the greatest show on television. It's live. It's topical. It makes you laugh. It's just a great vibe.

—Jimmy Fallon (*USA Today*, 2004)

Generally speaking, the humor of an Elephant is based on their vast collection of silly expressions, coupled with a playful, bubbly, nice-guy/-gal demeanor. This engaging behavior serves them well in the workplace, where they tend to work best in fields that provide ample opportunities for bonding between themselves and their coworkers. Thus, Elephants frequently hold management roles in the health-care, education, and nonprofit sectors. Because they're so conscious of the welfare of others, Elephants make the best hosts; they always seem to know what their guests need at any given moment.

That same busybody approach that might annoy others in a different context is almost necessary as a host. How else can Elephants pull shy guests from out of their shells and ensure that modest visitors take full advantage of their Elephant generosity? Unfortunately, Elephants occasionally go overboard with the affable host routine. When this occurs, they may be accused of being, at best, smothering or, at worst, overly pleasant and uncritical to the point of being weak. Mature Elephants, however, realize that not everybody can—or should—be their friend and that sometimes understanding a loved one's need for privacy and personal space is the best way to love them.

THE BEAR

On the outside, the quiet, shy Bears bear a strong resemblance (is it possible to overdose on puns?) to the gentle Butterflies. However, whereas the Butterflies' never-say-no mentality derives from their easygoing nature, the Bear's penchant for going with the flow is driven by loyalty to those closest to them. They exude kindness, but make no mistake, Bears have a strong backbone, one they readily display if you threaten their loved ones.

The Bodyguard

Whose life would be on my hands as the commander-in-chief because I, unilaterally, went beyond the international law, went beyond the stated mission, and said we're going to show we're macho? We're going into Baghdad. We're going to be an occupying power—America in an Arab land—with no allies at our side. It would have been disastrous. We don't measure the size of our victory by how many innocent kids are running away.

                                        —George H. W. Bush (quoted in Kelly, 1999)

Like their Gatherer siblings the Elephants, Bears hold family and friends as their top priority. Unlike the Elephants, though, who focus on creating a pleasant space where all can live in comfort, Bears seek to safeguard the protection and security of those fortunate few who have been allowed into their inner circle. Bears are stalwart defenders; once their trust has been gained, their loyalty to whomever they love and serve is as solid as the Rock of Gibraltar.

They are commonly described as being kind, and while this is incredibly accurate, it would be wise to not let that description lull you into thinking that Bears are complete pushovers. They can exhibit tremendous force on behalf of others. And on those occasions where Bears veer to unnecessary extremes in their protective zeal, their behavior can be borderline vicious. Fortunately, moments like that are not only rare but also fleeting, as Bears quickly revert to their customary gentle persona, often riddling themselves with guilt over crossing the line.

The Humble Servant

What makes Superman a hero is not that he has power, but that he has the wisdom and the maturity to use the power wisely. From an acting point of view, that's how I approached the part.

                                        —Christopher Reeve (quoted in Smith, 2002)

In social situations, the humble Bears are always conscious about not throwing their weight around. Quiet by nature but sharing the community-minded traits of their fellow Gatherers, Bears are moderately social; they enjoy being around others as long as the interaction is harmonious and peaceful. In environments like these, where Bears feel safe and loved, it's not unusual to see the normally reserved Bears become quite talkative, with their opinions being expressed in the nicest and least-threatening manner—unless, of course, they're standing up for someone else.

This is a consistent trait for Bears: steadfast resolve when in defense of others, utmost humility in matters dealing with themselves. In times of conflict, they would much rather turn the other cheek than engage their opponents. The least aggressive of all the types, Bears view aggression with an almost palpable disdain. They know full well the destruction it can cause, and they attempt to repress even the slightest hint of hostility within themselves. To a Bear, power is not something one should strive to attain; it is something one should fear, especially considering its potential for misuse.

The POW

Rich gifts wax poor when givers prove unkind.

–Ophelia (Shakespeare, [c. 1600] 2016)

Bears can withstand a substantial amount of physical pain and voluntarily bear (I know, again) the burden of suffering for others if need be. This willingness to suffer extends to emotional pain, as well, which often causes a problem when it coincides with a Bear being in an unhealthy relationship. Whether it's a romantic pairing, a platonic friendship, or a professional partnership, Bears give of themselves completely. Akin to their Gatherer siblings, Bears entrust their faith in established value systems. Unlike the duty-bound Stags and Beavers, however, Bears will forgo their belief system if it means helping those closest to them.

As lovers, a Bear might find themselves constantly deferring to their partner, relinquishing much of their power in the relationship. Their partner's choices become their choices. Their partner's likes and dislikes become their likes and dislikes. Inevitably, Bears begin to lose aspects of their identity entirely. The same resolve that is so essential when defending loved ones serves them poorly when in conflict with those same loved ones. And the vigilance that makes Bears such staunch protectors can twist and contort itself into paranoia and insecurity, the need for companionship being so strong that they refuse to entertain the thought of being left alone, even when the relationship is deleterious to their physical and emotional well-being. On a positive note, mature Bears find the courage and strength to disentangle themselves, drawing on the powerful support of family and friends—a fitting reciprocation of a Bear's loyalty and dedication.

The Caregiver

Don't look for big things, just do small things with great love.

—Mother Teresa (2007)

Because of their need for comfort, Bears can be quite predictable, following set routines they know and trust. This is not to say they don't like to experience new things. It's just that Bears don't need to try new things, especially if they come with a certain degree of risk. This steadiness is unwavering, even during the toughest times; when Hollywood used to put out a casting call for the "strong, silent type" (pretty sure that's a relic of the past), it's Bears whom they had in mind.

They are compassionate, devoted, and lack pretense. The mere notion of self-promotion disgusts them. Due to these traits, Bears are perfect when it comes to looking after the welfare of others—think doctors, nurses, and other health-care professionals. Having a soft spot for the weak, the helpless, and the bullied, it is not uncommon for Bears to volunteer their time to relief efforts and charities or to work as addiction counselors and special education teachers. Bears like to feel safe, and they'll devote 100 percent of their energy to making sure that others can feel that way, too.

	How do I see myself?	How do I see the world?	How do I interact with the world?	What is my flaw?
Stags	The Authority Figure	The Compartmentalizer	The Natural Born Leader	The Inflexible Bureaucrat
Beavers	The Workhorse	The Impartial Critic	The Patient Builder	The Worrywart
Elephants	The Head of the Family	The Optimist	The Host	The Gossip
Bears	The Bodyguard	The Humble Servant	The Caregiver	The POW

Figure 3.1 Gatherer Roles

CHAPTER FOUR

THE HUNTERS

"WE TALKING ABOUT PRACTICE, MAN"

Long before I owned an education company and started working with kids, I was a sixteen-year-old Boy Scout, responsible for leading a group of new recruits, all a few years younger than I was. For those unfamiliar with the Boy Scouts of America, it's a haven for nature-loving Gatherers. Patriotic, rules based (twelve laws, to be exact), and built on a foundation of comity and responsibility, it's equal parts military school and finishing school, with a touch of John Muir for good measure. And while the organization technically has a rule against hazing (a.k.a. physical punishment), my troop chose to ignore it. If discipline was a currency, then our rate of exchange was five push-ups for every one demerit, and boy, business was booming. Missing a part of your uniform? One demerit. Neckerchief folded incorrectly? Two demerits. Late for a meeting? Four demerits. And don't ask me what happened if you missed a meeting, excuse or not. Despite this somewhat draconian atmosphere, this was a space where I saw boys of all personality types grow and thrive. But it was not without struggle.

Aside from being popular with Gatherers, my troop was also extremely popular with Hunters, who leapt at the opportunity to run around in the woods, light fires, shoot guns, and basically cause havoc away from the meddling of their parents. They enjoyed it so much that most Hunters tolerated the rules. Some accepted them as a necessary evil, a small price to pay for freedom from parental supervision. Others saw the benefits. They didn't want to follow the rules; they wanted to bend them, and they knew that mastering discipline and self-control was the best way to learn how to do just that. Of course, I did say most tolerated the rules. There were exceptions, one of whom I was tasked to train.

The boy was charismatic but spiteful toward his parents. It wasn't that they had given up on him. They tried. But at this point, they had already exhausted all their parental energy on his two older brothers, both of whom I knew. They were older than me by a few years, and I had grown up in the Scouts with them. All three brothers were Hunters, and I'm guessing both parents were, too. Five Hunters under one roof; that's a lot of chaos. Perhaps too much to expect two teens to assimilate to a rigid disciplinary structure. The two older boys bristled at the rules and left without learning much of anything; not surprisingly, they found ways to cause serious trouble outside the shelter of the troop that had failed them. The youngest of the brothers would be my troop's last chance with this family to get it right.

That's when I learned the power of one word. One. We were going over how to chop wood, and the boy (I'll call him Dan for the sake of anonymity) was taking instruction—ignoring would be more accurate—from one of the older boys. The older boy kept telling Dan that he needed to "be careful" with the ax. He said "be careful" so many times that I started to get annoyed. I thought to myself, "Damn, if I was this kid, and I had to hear this nagging all the time, I'd be spiteful, too." That's when an epiphany hit me. Dan was clearly a confident kid, and the last thing he needed was someone trying to make him worry. I told him, "Dude, just concentrate, and it'll be easy." And that was it. He took the ax and put on his best Paul Bunyan impression, chopping wood faster than any of the other kids. I couldn't believe it. It was as if I had cast a spell. In my mind, I was like, "What crazy dark magic is this?" With just one word, his attitude had changed completely. Well, more like seven words, but I'm pretty sure the only one that mattered was concentrate.

I didn't realize this at the time, as my personality-reading skills were still nascent, but his reaction made a lot of sense for his type. Hunters seek excitement and pride themselves on their ability to take risks. The greater the risk, the greater the uncertainty of its success, and that feeling of not knowing, that suspense, is what fuels the Hunter fire. It's only natural for a Gatherer, like the older boy, to harp on safety first, as that's their number-one priority. But by constantly warning him to "be careful," the Gatherer was unknowingly taking away Dan's greatest strength: courage. He was unconsciously telling Dan that who he was, a risk-taking Hunter, was wrong. Conversely, telling Dan to "concentrate" was like saying, "Hey, there's nothing wrong with you taking risks. Just make sure you're concentrating when you do." The funny thing is, "be careful" and "concentrate" are trying to reach the same objective.

We both wanted Dan to focus on what he was doing. But as you'll find when interacting with people of all different types, it's not the intent that matters; it's what the listener hears.

EXPAND TECHNIQUE

As a sixteen-year-old not equipped with twenty years of personality-typing knowledge, I had to rely on my intuition, and what it was telling me was that all Dan needed was an opportunity to shine. Much to the dismay of the older leaders, both adults and fellow Scouts, I started to give him more leadership responsibilities, and I encouraged him to speak his mind when he disagreed with a course of action. In turn, he became far more receptive to instruction, and he started to realize that discipline was not an enemy to risk taking but an assurance that, whatever risks were taken, they would not be taken in vain.

This is the growth arc for the Hunter. I like to refer to it as the Tom Cruise Arc. Think about it. In almost every one of his movies, Tom Cruise—I mean his character, of course—goes through a similar growth pattern:

1. A cocky, talented risk taker with a penchant for recklessness.
2. Constantly ignores warnings about his character flaws.
3. Tragedy or failure befalls him.
4. A period of despair humbles him.
5. With the help of a supportive friend or lover—almost always a Gatherer— he regains his strength.
6. Confident again but now more open to learning from his mistakes, he succeeds where he once failed due to a new technique or tactic he learned in the process.

In a much broader and expansive way, this arc holds true for all Hunters. It's about identifying what their craft is and being open to stretching the boundaries of that craft. It's about *nana korobi ya oki*: "falling down seven times, getting up eight." That's why Hunters need to be encouraged to take chances. If they don't learn how to grow from adversity when they're young, imagine the price they'll pay when they're older and the consequences of failure are more severe. With "proper failure," there's no limit to the number of techniques a mature Hunter can add to their repertoire; think of a chef who travels to China to make hand-pulled noodles, or a musical artist practicing a new instrument. All that's needed in the maturation process is a little blood, sweat, tears, and the humility to realize as early as possible that they might be good but not as good as they think they are.

Four Questions for Hunters

1. What is my craft?
2. What are my skills?
3. What is my role in the world?
4. What is my flaw?

The role of Hunters in society is an interesting study in demographics. They make up about a third of the population, which is much closer in size to the Gatherer plurality than the less plentiful Shamans and Smiths, but their laissez-faire temperament stands in stark contrast to the occasionally overbearing social sensibilities of the Gatherers. On the flip side, Hunters are dynamic when it comes to their craft, and this boldness in whatever field or endeavor they pursue can give them a rather oversized social presence that can cause ripples to reverberate across the landscape like a cultural shock wave (see figure 4.1 at the end of this chapter).

THE FOX

Cocky, sly, smooth, and charming, Foxes, like all Hunters, have a natural confidence and grace. From the outside, it's a common mistake to confuse them with a Peacock, their equally performative Hunter sibling. Contrary to the Peacock, however, who works hard for the attention they so desperately crave and are unafraid of showing a little sweat if it gets them Instagram likes, Foxes seem to attain their popularity effortlessly. In fact, everything about a Fox seems effortless, making them the perfect embodiment of cool.

The Improviser

Hokey religions and ancient weapons are no match for a good blaster at your side, kid.

–Han Solo (Lucas, 1977)

What is your primary talent? Ask a Fox that question, and they'll have difficulty coming up with an answer. Not out of humility, mind you, but from the sheer difficulty in singling out one thing that they do better than everything else. They're liable to just say, "Everything!" and call it a day, though the humble ones (i.e., mature) might just refrain from answering the question entirely. The reason is, a Fox's primary talent, the ability to improvise, is predicated on the belief that they have the capability to be good at anything at any moment. This confidence is their trump card; their ace in the hole; the play that, when the situation is most dire (it's no surprise that the Fox is the quintessential quarterback), the Fox undoubtedly pulls out at the last moment to achieve victory.

Informed by their experiences—what younger Foxes lack in number they make up for in variety—Foxes' visceral instincts are second to none. There are very few scenarios they have not seen, very few types of people they have not met, and very few situations they cannot escape from at a moment's notice. Foxes are skeptical of abstract theory, as they prefer to place their trust only in things that they themselves have seen or experienced. Because of this, the standard classroom setting holds very little interest for them; they prefer learning from the "school of life." Nonetheless, just as it is for the Peacock, school can be a pleasurable experience for the Fox, and they frequently use it as a training ground to practice the charm and wit they'll need to survive in the real world. Foxes generally become popular among their classmates, and despite their penchant for mischief and fidgety classroom demeanor, they usually avoid the wrath of their teachers, who view them as entertaining scoundrels.

The Dealmaker

They worship at other shrines; profess another creed; observe a different code. They can no more be moved by Christian pacifism than wolves by the bleating of sheep. We have to deal with a people whose values are in many respects altogether different from our own.

—Winston Churchill (1937)

The best networker of all the types, the Fox, unlike the relentless yet sometimes graceless Killer Whale, is an effortless schmoozer who takes it upon themselves to meet all types of people and not just those who could be future assets. This egalitarian openness is communicated subconsciously, and it enables Foxes to be everybody's best friend and essentially the hub of a vast and diverse human marketplace. They regularly broker deals; introduce future partners, both business and romantic; and connect buyers to sellers, employers to employees, and everyone in between.

During personal interactions, Foxes are masters of the perfect line, their cognizance of an individual's body language and microexpressions allowing them to identify exactly what a person wants to hear at the given moment. This knack for swift, observation-based action and reaction is also why Foxes excel at making risk/reward determinations, calculating them at a speed that surpasses all other types. With their network of connections and shrewd gambling instincts, it's no surprise that Foxes frequently find themselves in such industries as politics, management consulting, real estate, and stock trading.

The Madison Avenue Marketer

What else is there for me to conquer? Hopefully my ego. How will I know when I've succeeded? When I stop caring what anyone thinks.

—Madonna (quoted in Q *Magazine*, 2008)

The same instinct that enables Foxes to be hypercognizant of how others appear causes them to be even more conscious of their own appearance. They realize that their cool factor relies heavily on a mixture of confidence and perceived effortlessness, and they make painstaking preparations behind the scenes to keep up this facade. This can lead to an enormous amount of pressure when in competition; not only do they have to win, but they also have to make it look easy. Like Peacocks yet far more disciplined, Foxes spend hours crafting their physical appearance, whether they're body sculpting at the gym or testing out different wardrobe combinations in front of the mirror.

Unfortunately, a Fox's desire to always say the cool thing or be perceived in the best possible light can lead to a great deal of irritation for the people around them, who may begin to view the Fox as disingenuous. When this occurs, a Fox most likely doubles down on the charm, hoping that it is enough to reestablish their identity as a dashing and debonair expert on beautiful cocktails, beautiful people, and contemporary style at large. Regrettably, this only damages their reputation further, causing them to appear ingratiating and borderline sleazy, more into self-promotion than establishing authentic and genuine relationships with others.

The Adventurer

To me a heaven would be a big bull ring with me holding two barrera seats and a trout stream outside that no one else was allowed to fish in and two lovely houses in the town; one where I would have my wife and children and be monogamous and love them truly and well, and the other where I would have my nine beautiful mistresses on nine different floors.

–Ernest Hemingway (2003)

Foxes love to explore. New things equal new sensations, and to be in an unfamiliar scenario encourages the improvisation they so obviously cherish as an inescapable part of themselves. Foxes try everything. It is common when speaking to an older Fox—and perhaps a not-so-old Fox—to be regaled with fantastic stories of all the crazy experiences they've had in their lifetimes: going salmon fishing deep in the Alaskan wilderness, sliding across an Arctic ice sheet, running with the bulls, or maybe even discovering the New World.

That might be the reason Foxes, when compared to the other sixteen types, are the most likely to jump from job to job or have a career that involves moving from project to project. Become a taxi driver? Awesome! What better way to learn how to navigate a city and scour its nooks and crannies for the best places to eat. Work as a location scout? Did someone say free travel? It is this explorative spirit that sets the Fox apart from some of the other aggressively ambitious types, like the Stag or Killer Whale. Success for a Fox is not measured by how high you can climb on the social ladder or sustained dominance in your professional field; it's based on pleasure. And if you ask any Fox, they'll assure you that pleasure is fleeting, and if you want it to continue, you have to chase after it.

THE SHARK

Sharks are the most active of the sixteen types, which, considering their blisteringly active Hunter siblings, is saying something. Few would mistake them for the equally laconic yet gentle Butterfly, nor would the clever, bend-the-rules mentality they share with the Fox ever be enough to confuse the Shark's verbal conciseness with that of the Fox's verbosity. The aggressive, physical nature of Sharks is so pronounced that it makes them the easiest animal type to identify, their actions speaking louder than any words might.

The Specialist

I am not sick. I am broken. But I am happy to be alive as long as I can paint.

–Frida Kahlo (quoted in *Time*, 1953)

The most noticeable trait of Sharks is their unparalleled facility with tools. Therefore, they learn best when engaged kinesthetically. They want to touch things, manipulate them, and have an immediate impact on the world around them. In the hands of a Shark, a simple tool is elevated to its fullest potential: Picasso's brush, Miles Davis's trumpet, or nunchucks wielded by Bruce Lee. This virtuosity doesn't come easy. Sharks spend hours practicing until they fully master whatever tool they choose. It's a phenomenal talent to have but one that can easily wither away in an occupation that does not utilize it; put a Shark in a cubicle, assign them a stack of paperwork, and they are likely to smash one and burn the other.

For this same reason, Sharks commonly struggle in school. Forcing a Shark to sit and listen to a lecture on political upheaval in pre-Elizabethan England is like putting them on the torture rack itself. They don't want to memorize facts about combat; they want to engage in it. For those Sharks who are academically gifted, school is tedious but doable, though even those few rarely choose to pursue postgraduate study. This could possibly explain the dearth of qualified surgeons in the world; surgeons are basically master tool users (it's not a coincidence many of them choose such tool-based hobbies as golf and fishing), making Sharks the type most equipped to excel in the job and the type least likely to go through all the academic requirements to achieve it. School can be grueling for Sharks, and it is not out of the ordinary for them to misbehave. And unlike their Hunter siblings, the Fox and the Peacock, who also have a habit of disregarding rules, Sharks lack the requisite charm required to avoid punishment from their teachers. However, put a tool in their hands, whether it's a ball, wrench, paintbrush, or scalpel, and watch them become a star.

The Hunter

I wanted to play it with an economy of words and create this whole feeling through attitude and movement. . . . I felt the less he said the stronger he became and the more he grew in the imagination of the audience.

–Clint Eastwood (quoted in McGilligan, 1999)

In words and actions, a Shark chooses carefully. There are neither extraneous sentences nor wasted movements, as a Shark, when focused, can be extremely precise and patient, like a predator waiting for the perfect time to strike. Yet because of their penchant for reflexive action, these traits usually go unnoticed; there is a common misconception that Sharks are incapable of forethought. In actuality, a Shark's tendency to throw themselves into a situation with reckless abandon is merely a reflection of their ability to scan the environment and gather an incredible amount of information in the limited time before they feel they must react—Sharks do not sit idly by during times of action.

What seems like recklessness is more an indication of the Shark's ability to react faster than others. More cautious types view this lightning-fast decision making as rash behavior brought on by immaturity and impatience. The truth is, the difference between an inexperienced Shark and an experienced one is not discretion. It's ability level; immature Sharks haven't misjudged the situation as much as they've misjudged their own ability to handle it. Mature Sharks, however, are keenly aware of their own skill level and the work it took to get there, with the speed at which they pounce on their prey only masking the hours spent hiding in the bushes.

The Aggressor

It was not my intention to do this in front of you. For that, I'm sorry. But you can take my word for it; your mother had it coming. When you grow up, if you still feel raw about it, I'll be waiting.

–Beatrix Kiddo (a.k.a. the Bride; Tarantino, 2003)

There is absolutely no subtleness to the Shark. They tell you what they think when they think it. This bluntness is one of the few things they share with Smiths. However, whereas a Smith is often oblivious to the offense that might be taken due to their forthrightness, a Shark really doesn't care if they hurt someone's feelings. They hate when people mince words. It's almost as if the Shark interprets verbal discretion as an expression of fear, and if it's one thing Sharks want everyone to know, it's that they're not afraid of anything.

When problems arise, Sharks like to meet them head on and aggressively, favoring the "might makes right" approach that usually allows them to get their way in most confrontations. Nevertheless, this approach can be problematic in situations that require more nuance and tact. It can also be disadvantageous when combating other aggressive types, as Sharks frequently find their straight-line approach outmaneuvered by wily Foxes or strategically overwhelmed by Killer Whales. Regardless, Sharks are widely respected for their confident, attack-first mentality, and it would be wise to remember this: They make loyal friends and vicious enemies.

The Action Hero

[Jerry Krause] said organizations win championships. I said, "I didn't see organizations playing with the flu in Utah."

—Michael Jordan (2009)

Sharks live for the pressure. Nailing a shot at the buzzer? Got it. Scaling a rocky cliff sans harness? Piece of cake. Performing emergency transplant surgery? Scrub up. Sharks are addicted to the adrenaline rush that comes with having to block out all other distractions, including family, friends, and teammates, to succeed at a singularly vital task. This ultrafocus can cause them to appear callous and arrogant, sometimes making it hard for them to lead colleagues and coworkers, even when the collective objective is clear.

They have very little patience for the weaker members of the team and, when push comes to shove, prefer to do a task themselves rather than delegate it to a person of lesser ability. A Shark would argue it's just them leading by example. Other types commonly view it as the actions of a prima donna. Either way, whether their teammates love them or hate them, there's no one those same teammates would trust more to take the last shot.

THE PEACOCK

There is no animal type that shines brighter in the spotlight than the fun-loving, gregarious Peacock. All Hunters love to be excited, but there are two who stand out for their capacity when it comes to fully appreciating the world's sensory pleasures, and no one would ever confuse the flamboyant Peacocks with the gentle Butterflies. Peacocks demand to be seen and heard, and with their audacious performing talents, they rarely have a problem achieving either.

The Performer

I'm a failure as a woman. My men expect so much of me, because of the image they've made of me—and that I've made of myself—as a sex symbol. They expect bells to ring and whistles to whistle, but my anatomy is the same as any other woman's and I can't live up to it.

—Marilyn Monroe (quoted in Brown and Barnham, 1992)

At face value, the attention-starved Peacock's performative talent can seem a tad superficial, especially when compared to the sometimes transcendent, artistic powers of the equally sensitive Butterfly. However, Peacocks are no slouches in the creativity department, and unlike the Butterflies, who are allowed to retreat to their creative cocoons to compose art on their own schedule, Peacocks are usually expected to—by virtue of their exhibitionist nature—create art on the spot. Even when it appears like Peacocks are just hamming it up for the audience, it goes beyond that. They don't want attention; they want immortality. They want to be remembered. They want each glorious moment of their life, of which there are many, to be catalogued, examined, and then overexamined. And to do this, they need to be larger than life, a symbol, an icon, an image for an ordinary person to aspire to. They have a feel for the dramatic that is second to none, and this ability is expressed in the way they dance, sing, or go about their everyday business. It's not unusual to encounter a Peacock dancing or whistling while they work.

The boldest of the Hunters, Peacocks throw themselves completely into whatever they do. Their courage surpasses even that of the aggressive Foxes and Sharks, both of whom are quite familiar with taking calculated risks but generally do so in situations where the outcome is determined objectively. Peacocks, though, are usually required to subject themselves to the mercy of a fickle and subjective audience. Maybe this courage is what makes Peacocks so irresistible. Contrary to Butterflies, who are free to hide behind their art, there's no such luxury for Peacocks because they are the art. And to constantly open themselves up to scrutiny and rejection time and time again is not only a boldness that transcends the mere desire for attention but also a requirement for immortality.

The Life of the Party

Hey guys, there isn't gonna be a Plan B. You called me in to bring the thunder and that's what I'm going to do.

—Jack Black (2006)

Peacocks love to have fun and spread that good cheer to their loved ones, their coworkers, or random strangers they just met on the subway. Warm and full of life, their energy can be infectious in social situations. The same over-the-top expressions that make them such entertaining performers also make Peacocks one of the more engaging types to interact with. Their idea of comedy is filled with slapstick, well-practiced impressions, dirty jokes, and bodily humor. It's not uncommon to hear them let out a huge belly laugh or giggle uncontrollably; when a Peacock feels a certain way, you'll know it, as will everyone within a hundred-foot radius. Be it a party, club, bar, or church picnic, the Peacock is usually the center of attention.

Unfortunately, their fun-loving demeanor can sometimes take on a "look at me" vibe that alienates friends and irritates people who might've just been laughing at the Peacock's jokes moments earlier. What was once hilarity turns into loudness. That pearly white smile? Narcissism. At the end of the day, however, these foibles are usually laughed off as harmless and, when considering the Peacock's big heart, irresistibly endearing.

The Acrobat

Everything is about your movements and precision and timing, which is what gymnastics is about.

—Shawn Johnson (2012)

Of all the types, Peacocks are the most in touch with their physical bodies. Differing from Sharks, who, with workmanlike precision, practice their superior hand-eye coordination to perfection, Peacocks revel in their gross motor skills: dancing, skating, running, and just plain moving through the physical space of our concrete world with an effervescence that defines beauty in motion. This is not to say that they're unwilling to practice. Quite the contrary, with their grace and clearly visible joy, Peacocks have a way of making practice appear so fun that everybody wants to participate.

Sharing the pleasure of physical touch is important to Peacocks. They're the most touchy-feely of all the types and a constant initiator of both bear hugs and trips to see HR. If Butterflies are the maestros of figurative balance, then Peacocks are the maestros of actual balance, the connection between their mind and body so finely tuned they're capable of executing all manner of flips, twirls, jumps, and pratfalls. Whether it's in dance; physical comedy;

or such competitive sports as gymnastics, diving, and figure skating, Peacocks always move with such poise and fluidity that it makes other types appear almost clumsy; the intuitive types, by comparison, look physically inept.

The Hedonist

Today me will live in the moment, unless it's unpleasant in which case me will eat a cookie.

—Cookie Monster (2020)

There is a tragic irony in striving for immortality in a moment; regardless of however many times a Peacock basks in glory, the moment never lasts as long as they want it to, and there are always other people (i.e., other Peacocks) seeking the spotlight. To compensate for any lost attention, Peacocks resort to various forms of consumption. Unfortunately, they soon realize that the satisfaction gained from these coping mechanisms is as fleeting as the spotlight, which inevitably leads to a vicious cycle of overconsumption as they lustily feed their habit.

Vices, like overeating, alcoholism, drug abuse, gambling, and sex addiction, can turn the Adonis- and Aphrodite-like figures of the Peacocks into shadows of their former selves: the former high school quarterback who's now overweight, jobless, and reminiscing about the good ol' days or the diva, past her prime, who must wear more and more make up to conceal an aging process sped up by cocaine and years of self-neglect. Fortunately, mature Peacocks learn to harness their need for attention in a way that doesn't lead them to self-destruct in a blaze of hedonistic glory, and in the process, they teach the rest of us how to enjoy life.

THE BUTTERFLY

One part gentle, one part easygoing, with more than a splash of space cadet, the Butterfly can defy all misconceptions of what it means to be a Hunter. In fact, from the outside, they can seem far more akin to their distant Shaman cousin, the solitary Humpback Whale. Not as kinetic or aggressive as the Foxes and Sharks or as dramatic as the Peacock, the Butterfly is a more delicate breed of Hunter, relishing the simple pleasures of life as they come to them.

The Free Spirit

Some say cavalry and others claim
infantry or a fleet of long oars
is the supreme sight on the black earth.
I say it is
The one you love. And easily proved.

—Sappho (1971)

The Butterfly surpasses all types in its appreciation and sensitivity for beauty. They can see splendor in a blade of grass, hear complexity in a simple note, and taste perfection in a freshly brewed cup of tea. For Butterflies, life is a breeze of fresh air, cool and evanescent, and to harbor any negative energy toward anything would be to squander the moment. Because of this, Butterflies are naturally inclined to avoid conflict at all costs, opting to smile through most volatile situations. While their natural preference is to experience new things, Butterflies are not as demanding for novelty as their Hunter siblings the Foxes and are quite content to enjoy the same sensations over and over again, frequently mining them for new pleasures in the process. Decision making can be both an easy and difficult process; Butterflies are highly adaptable to the consequences of most decisions, but their tendency to refrain from taking a hard and fast stance on anything can be a detriment when they're the one having to decide.

The one area in which Butterflies deviate from this optimistic indecisiveness is their respective artistic field; whether it's within their job or hobby, Butterflies always find a way to express their creativity. That's when the free spirit morphs into the insightful but fastidious critic, pointing out the slightest errors in all manner of compositions: pasta that's not al dente, a stitch that's out of place, a minor chord that should've been a diminished chord. Interestingly, Butterflies don't view this critique as a matter of voicing a subjective, contrary opinion as much as righting an objective, artistic wrong. Just as they appreciate the variety of styles in which beauty can be achieved, Butterflies also believe there are a variety of mistakes that can offend the senses; they'll scrub the graffiti off a wall to make room for the spray-painted mural.

The Master of Harmony

It's pronounced wee but spelled O-U-I. It's all you'll want to say when you're sitting at one of the thousands of little cafes that line the streets and you're looking at a menu full of foods you just want to eat for days. And then you wake up early, and the sun is rising in shades of pink over the white buildings as you make your way through the sleepy streets until you're upon the fresh markets!

–Giada De Laurentiis (2013)

Unlike the Shark, the master of tools, the Butterfly specializes in balancing the various elements of a craft to achieve creative harmony. As chefs, Sharks master the knife, the crepe griddle, the wok burner, the broom-handle-like rolling pin. Butterflies, however, are virtuosos of the pantry and larder, with extensive knowledge of spices, fresh herbs, and various other ingredients. Such artistic elements can be dangerous in the hands of non-Butterflies, as the possibility of overdoing it is quite common. Who hasn't overused a favorite ingredient before or worn too much of a favorite color? When it comes to fashion, no type is more equipped—and more likely—to compose a stylish ensemble from a bucket of spare parts: the designer scarf, the shirt purchased at the Phoebe Bridgers concert, the slacks from the thrift store around the corner.

For Butterflies, style is not about being cosmopolitan. It's about balance and nuance, two things their Hunter siblings the flashy Peacocks occasionally have difficulty grasping. The Peacock might make a great model, but it's the Butterfly you want designing the clothes. Not only are Butterflies gifted at blending artistic elements, but many of them also have an innate ability to blend their sensory perception. It's not out of the ordinary for Butterflies to taste colors, see melodies, touch flavors, smell textures, or hear fragrances, a phenomenon known as synesthesia.

The Sensitive Pushover

It's like all my life everybody keeps telling me that I'm a shoe. You're a shoe, you're a shoe, you're a shoe! But what if I don't want to be a shoe anymore? Maybe I'm a purse, or a hat.

–Rachel Green (Burrows, 1994)

Although on the outside they might appear like doppelgängers for the equally sensitive Humpback Whales, Butterflies are inwardly distinct, their carefree, epicurean style diverging greatly from the pensive meditation of the Humpback Whale. In social groups, it's not unusual for Butterflies to be fairly quiet, just happy to be in the mix of things. At their worst, however, Butterflies can be extremely susceptible to social pressure. It's almost impossible for them to say no, their experience informing them that, whatever new adventure is presented to them, they are more likely going to enjoy it than not.

It could be said that Butterflies are regularly coaxed into doing things against their better judgment, but that would be assuming that Butterflies have a clear sense of judgment in the first place. The reality is that, especially with immature Butterflies, they would prefer to have their decisions made for them; if you command a Butterfly to go down a certain path, don't be surprised if they thank you for giving them directions. When they do act defiantly, it's often in a passive-aggressive manner; an irritated Butterfly might withhold sex from their partner because they're "tired" or promise to attend social gatherings they loathe, only to flake when the time comes.

The Artist

I am a writer an a singer of the words I write I am no speaker nor any politician an my songs speak for me because I write them in the confinement of my own mind an have t cope with no one except my own self.

—Bob Dylan (1963)

Lacking the easy charm of Foxes or the bravado of Peacocks, Butterflies prefer to work outside the spotlight. However, this in no way means that they dislike attention. Like the Sharks, who practice their craft for days on end, Butterflies hole themselves up in their creative space (studio, kitchen, office, etc.) until they have completed a work of art worthy of admiration. This process can be grueling, and there is the danger that the Butterfly, not really known for their determination and focus, could become distracted by other sensory pleasures, such as an invitation to lunch, finally uncorking that Pinot they've been saving, or a random frisbee flying past their window.

For Butterflies, much like it is with their similarly (but to a much greater degree) hedonistic siblings the Peacocks, there's always a delicate balance between consumption and production. To tip the scale too much to one side might lead to sloth; too much to the other side, boredom. Nevertheless, Butterflies are no strangers to the idea of balance, and once they've discovered that perfect harmony between work and play, creating and consuming, they are free to live a life filled with beauty—savoring it and creating it.

	What is my craft?	What are my skills?	What is my role in the world?	What is my flaw?
Foxes	The Dealmaker	The Improviser	The Adventurer	The Madison Ave. Marketer
Sharks	The Specialist	The Hunter	The Action Hero	The Aggressor
Peacocks	The Performer	The Acrobat	The Life of the Party	The Hedonist
Butterflies	The Artist	The Master of Harmony	The Free Spirit	The Pushover

Figure 4.1 Hunter Roles

CHAPTER FIVE

THE SHAMANS

"LET ME SEE YOU STRIPPED DOWN TO THE BONE" (GORE, 1985)

Shamans and Smiths often grow up thinking that they're a bunch of weirdos. When you only make up about 15 percent of the population combined, your two packs are most assuredly living the life of outsiders. And society, being the generous sort, tends to punish those on the fringes by labeling them as "weird," a pejorative that Shamans and Smiths inevitably grow to believe. Thus, perception becomes reality. Smiths, God bless them, couldn't care less. You tell them they're in the minority, and they'll say, "Fuck the majority, and I said it with authority!" like it's their own NWA anthem. Immature Shamans, though, don't have it in them to fight back. They like people too much and love themselves too little, and that makes for a rather tumultuous path to "normalcy." It's only by searching for what's normal do they find the truth within themselves, or to paraphrase one of the writers on the Youtopia Project website, discovering as an adult that she was a Shaman reassured her that she was not of some alien species. The search for self-knowledge, above all other things, is the quintessential Shaman growth arc.

So much of a Shaman's life is spent trying to assimilate to the values of the most populous pack, the Gatherers, who prize duty, family, and the security that both of those things bring. Natural dreamers, Shamans envision a domestic future that would make a Lexus commercial envious: a beautiful, uniquely designed home by the ocean; a lucrative job that empowers their creativity; an equally successful spouse; and a few precocious kids as well dressed as their adoring parents. Of course, this paradise is an illusion. Not that the goal is unachievable, but any attempt to turn their dreams into reality inevitably leaves the Shaman with a nagging feeling, like an emotional hunger pain, reminding them that, no matter how much they consume on the outside, they'll still feel hollow on the inside.

Having a guide who understands this plight is vital, which is one of the reasons Smiths make the best mentors for Shamans; as fellow abstract types, they communicate on the same wavelength, not to mention that a Smith's antagonistic relationship with Gatherer society helps strengthen a Shaman's resolve, like a trainer yelling at their boxer to not fear their opponent's punches. Mature Shamans, those who have been through this hell of self-doubt and come out the other side, also serve their Shaman pupils well. On the *Late Show with David Letterman* (Letterman, 2013), during an interview, Jennifer Lawrence was lamenting the pressures of Hollywood and the various social obligations that are required, after which they cut to commercial, and when they came back, a hot mic caught Letterman, in a rare candid moment, advising her, "They need you a lot more than you need them!" Much-needed advice from one (more grizzled) Shaman to another. Of course, this is not to say that Gatherers and Hunters can't be helpful teachers to Shamans, though it does take an ample amount of skill and experience for them to suppress their concrete bias or even acknowledge its existence at all. And take my word for it, it exists.

This is a Gatherer and Hunter world—together they constitute around 85 percent of the world population. Think of the stereotypical dichotomy we see in pop culture. It's always some version of the Odd Couple—or Bert and Ernie for all my fellow Gen Xers and those who came after. On one hand, you have the organized and responsible but rigid and dull Bert. On the other hand, you have the messy and careless but fun and spontaneous Ernie. Look, I don't want to get in the weeds here. I know this section is supposed to be about the Shaman growth arc, but to truly understand a Shaman's quest for self-knowledge, we must first understand its impetus.

Throughout their entire lives Shamans are inundated with images and ideas of what it means to be normal. And when they're not being hit with those influences by the various multimedia conglomerates, they're often being pummeled by them at home. The odds for a Shaman child having a Gatherer parent are high; aside from their aforementioned population numbers, Gatherers place a strong emphasis on family, so it makes sense that they would be the most likely type to become parents. Once again, I can't repeat the disclaimer enough: Any type can understand another if they're mature enough. That being said, in my experience observing and working with children and their parents, I've found a consistent tension arises between Shaman children and their Gatherer parents. Whereas Hunter parents, who may not fully understand their Shaman children and might wish they were a little cooler, tend to be fine with them due to the Hunter's generally laissez-faire parenting style, immature Gatherer parents can be extremely overbearing. They can do this with hard power—the rigid taskmaster—or soft power— the parent who keeps applying "gentle" pressure on you to get married and start a family like your more "normal" cousins.

At this point, it probably seems like I'm just shitting on Gatherers right now, though it's worth mentioning that shit usually funnels down, and any shots taken at those poor, unfortunate Gatherers is clearly punching up. For their part, Gatherers have the best intentions. Sure, there are those few assholes who really do just want to make people's lives miserable and de- rive an inflated sense of self-worth by bossing around the sensitive kid who always seems to be reading Neil Gaiman or playing *Magic: The Gathering*, but the same could be said for the other packs. We can all be fantastic and horrible; we just do it in our own way (I go over this in chapter 13, "Deviant Roles"). In the typical Shaman-Gatherer scenario, we can observe how a Gatherer's desire for security can conflict with a Shaman's intuitive idiosyn- crasies. When a Gatherer parent sees their Shaman child veering toward the fringes of society, their instinct is to bring them closer to the center of town, where it's safe.

A perfect example of this dynamic can be found in Peter Weir's (1989) *Dead Poets Society*, a film that's the epitome of Shaman-Gatherer, student- teacher, child-parent conflict. Here's a personality type–flavored logline: Rich high school kids in a Gatherer haven (a.k.a. a New England private school for boys) are encouraged to find themselves by their new Shaman teacher, much to the chagrin of the headmaster, teaching staff, and parents, who are all—you guessed it—Gatherers. Clearly, there's a slight Shaman bias in the movie. I won't delve much further aside from one specific scene, as I'm one of those people who detests spoilers, even for a movie released in 1989, and this chapter is on Shamans and not just characters from *Dead Poets Society*— though any confusion between the two is understandable because there are a lot of Shamans in this movie.

Anyway, the scene happens at the end of the movie, so minor but I promise not game-changing spoilers ahead. Neil, a Shaman student (a Dolphin, to be specific) who dreams of being an actor, has a confrontation with his Gatherer (Stag) father:

FATHER: We're trying very hard to understand why it is that you insist on defying us. Whatever the reason, we're not going to let you ruin your life. Tomorrow, I'm withdrawing you from Welton and enrolling you in Brighton military school. You're going to Harvard, and you're going to be a doctor.

NEIL: But that's ten more years! Father, that's a lifetime—

FATHER: Oh, stop it. Don't be so dramatic. You make it sound like a prison term. You don't understand Neil. You have opportunities that I never even dreamt of and I'm not going to let you waste—

NEIL: I've got to tell you what I feel—

FATHER: What? What? Tell me what you feel. What is it?

NEIL: ... (Weir, 1989)

Neil never tells his father what his feelings are. He never tells him how much the life his father has planned for him makes him feel trapped and inauthentic or how much acting makes him feel truly like himself. He's too afraid. Not only does he have little faith that his father would understand, but he's also not even sure whether he's doing the right thing in the first place. It's hard enough to take the "road less traveled"; try doing it with a backseat driver who keeps reaching over your seat to take the wheel. We can't blame Neil for his self-doubt. He's young and malleable, and at this point, his dad has shown very little evidence to assuage his fears. Unfortunately, this is a situation that Shamans know all too well.

EXPAND YOUR SENSE OF SELF

The first step for a Shaman to not feel like a weirdo is to accept that much of what they're taught to value at an early age as being "normal" is merely a social construct. It doesn't really exist in any substantive way. It's a facade: a beautiful Victorian from the front but a Pick-Up Sticks tangle of rickety beams holding it up from behind. For concrete types (a.k.a. around 85 percent of the world), there's nothing wrong with surface pleasures. Just because marriage is primarily a legal contract, one that enables you to save money by filing joint tax returns, it doesn't deny the existence of love within the marriage itself. The pageantry of the process, the formality of the commitment—these are all essential to the majority of people. However, it's worth noting that they aren't essential to *all* people. Shamans, by and large, find very little inherent joy in the trappings of success, aside from that which they've been pressured to accept as normal. And even then, there's always that voice in their head, guilting them for the inauthenticity of it all. I imagine it sounds much like Robert Mitchum, a legendary actor, when he whispered into Nick Nolte's ear at the Academy Awards, "Just remember, kid—it's all bullshit" (quoted in Leary, 2008).

As a Shaman matures from childhood to adulthood, they must remember exactly that: It's all bullshit. They must learn to tear the facades down within their own lives, especially those that have stood erect for years. All the things they've learned they must start reexamining for meaning and not assume someone else's priorities as their own. If a Shaman's lifelong quest is to attain self-knowledge—and trust me, it is, even if some don't know it yet—then they must begin the painful and arduous task of reassessing their identity, discovering what is essential, and stripping away all the details that are merely distractions on the path to wholeness.

This journey is exemplified in the following Buddhist tale (retold in Salinger, 1963, and now retold by me, like a rapper reusing that Keni Burke "Risin' to the Top" bass line for the umpteenth time):

Duke Mu of Chin said to Po Lo, "You are now advanced in years. Is there any member of your family whom I could employ to look for horses in your stead?"

Po Lo replied, "A good horse can be picked out by its general build and appearance, but the superlative horse—one that raises no dust and leaves no tracks—is something evanescent and fleeting, elusive as thin air. The talents of my sons lie on a lower plane altogether; they can tell a good horse when they see one, but they cannot tell a superlative horse. I have a friend, however, one Chiu-fang Kao, a hawker of fuel and vegetables, who in things appertaining to horses is nowise my inferior. Pray, see him."

Duke Mu did so and subsequently dispatched him on the quest for a steed. Three months later, he returned with the news that he had found one. "It is now in Shach'iu," he added.

"What kind of a horse is it?" asked the Duke.

"Oh, it is a dun-colored mare," was the reply.

However, someone being sent to fetch it, the animal turned out to be a coal-black stallion! Much displeased, the Duke sent for Po Lo. "That friend of yours," he said, "whom I commissioned to look for a horse, has made a fine mess of it. Why, he cannot even distinguish a beast's color or sex! What on earth can he know about horses?"

Po Lo heaved a sigh of satisfaction. "Has he really got as far as that?" he cried. "Ah, then he is worth ten thousand of me put together. There is no comparison between us. What Kao keeps in view is the spiritual mechanism. In making sure of the essential, he forgets the homely details; intent on the inward qualities, he loses sight of the external. He sees what he wants to see and not what he does not want to see. He looks at the things he ought to look at and neglects those that need not be looked at. So clever a judge of horses is Kao that he has it in him to judge something better than horses."

When the horse arrived, it turned out indeed to be a superlative animal.

Four Questions for Shamans

1. What is it that fuels me?
2. What is my "normal" role.
3. What is my superpower?
4. What is my flaw?

Perhaps it's due to the Shaman's abstract nature, but their growth arc is quite a departure from the previous two concrete packs, the Gatherers and Hunters. If we were to visualize Gatherer growth, it would be as a bubble slowly expanding outward. Hunter growth, however, would be a jagged line graph, with so many ups and downs it resembles the stock chart for a rising tech company. Shaman growth, though, would be something else entirely. I imagine it'd look a lot like watching Bob Ross paint: the outlines and hues of a Shaman's identity gradually drawn right before our very eyes. But in this case, just before Bob starts shading in the highlights and shadows, he takes the painting, tears it to shreds, and starts anew. It's a painful but necessary decision. It makes me think of the scene from Martin Scorsese's *The Departed*, when Captain Queenan (played by Martin Sheen) asks Billy Costigan (Leonardo DiCaprio), "Do you want to be a cop, or do you want to appear to be a cop?" (Scorsese, 2006). Eventually, every Shaman must make that decision (see figure 5.1). Do you want to be happy, or do you want to appear to be happy?

THE DOLPHIN

What sets Dolphins apart from their Shaman siblings is the ease with which they can assimilate into society. This is not to say that it's any better or worse for them in terms of emotional health, but externally, the popular Dolphin is a paragon of social excellence. And unlike the moody, puckish otherworldliness of a Baboon, a Dolphin's idealism is grounded in community, teamwork, and an emotional candidness that makes them the most likable and personally accessible of all the types.

The Community Organizer

Standardized personality differences between sexes are of this order, cultural creations to which each generation, male and female, is trained to conform.

—Margaret Mead (2003)

Vocal but not aggressive, sociable but not oppressive, Dolphins use their substantial interpersonal skills to build authentic communities where individuals can be themselves without fear of social reprisal. As group leaders, Dolphins have no equal when it comes to eliciting the intimate thoughts and feelings of other group members, encouraging each individual to share past mistakes, present-day anxieties, and future dreams. During brainstorming sessions, Dolphins ensure everyone has the opportunity to speak and be heard, frequently abstaining from voicing their own opinion until the very end. As a Shaman, Dolphins are always wary of exerting too much pressure from their position of authority. This also allows the Dolphin who might not have prior experience in a particular situation to pool the best answers from the group, eventually leading to an ideal solution; a Dolphin need not know the way in order to lead the way.

This style of direction can be baffling to other, more authoritative types (I see you Stags and Killer Whales), who view the Dolphin's leadership style as the sort of "leading from behind," overly democratic idealism that pervades leadership conferences and sells books but is ineffective in the real world. Dolphins can only laugh at the irony: two of the most aggressive types bending to the will of others. To a Dolphin, the world is what we make of it, not the other way around, and the only reason such antiquated concepts as gender, racial, and sexual stereotypes continue to permeate society is because they continue to be indoctrinated as reality. A Dolphin's main purpose in life is to create a better reality alongside all the people who live in it.

The Teacher

The outstanding coach is a teacher that gets all of his squad to accept the role that he considers to be the most important for the welfare of all.

—John Wooden (quoted in Rose, 2010)

Like all Shamans, Dolphins are superb at connecting with a wide variety of personalities, age groups, ethnicities, and the like, communicating and sharing ideas on an emotional level. The major difference is, as a Shaman who prefers to work within systems of people, a Dolphin's energy is focused on crafting their message to each individual member of the team, class, or organization. Whether it's a superstar shooting guard in dire need of a lesson in humility (can anyone say Hunter?) or an entitled, apathetic American middle school student guilted by the story of Malala, those under the tutelage of Dolphins benefit from their outside-the-box teaching methods in a way that no amount of heavy-handed discipline (i.e., the traditional method) could match. The end result is that every member of the group feels accepted as an individual, and it's that sense of self-worth that inspires instant cohesion and a dedication to the greater welfare of all.

The TMI Guy—or Gal

Oh, the cops. I can't believe this is my life. Oh my God. I'm gonna have to send my SAT scores to San Quentin instead of Stanford.

—Veronica Sawyer (Lehmann, 1989)

Dolphins can be incredibly open about sharing their feelings, an important distinction from their equally expressive siblings the Baboons, who mostly share their ideas and opinions while keeping their deepest feelings under wraps. This leads to Dolphins being perceived as spirited yet grounded—emotions being far more accessible to concrete personality types than abstract convictions—a major reason for their immense popularity. They are the cool, unpretentious homecoming king or queen or the former student body president and valedictorian whom, in a recurring dream of your parents, you bring home for Thanksgiving.

The downside to a Dolphin's limited verbal discretion is that, by revealing so much private information (sorry Dolphins, but not everybody needs to hear about your incontinence issues), they can make others feel uncomfortable. This can also make them appear overly sensitive and emotionally needy. And at those times when appearance and reality coincide, Dolphins begin to view the popularity that came to them with such ease through a prism of neurotic paranoia, irrationally agonizing over whether everyone hates them or not.

The Diplomat

For a new type of progress throughout the world to become a reality, everyone must change. Tolerance is the alpha and omega of a new world order.

–Mikhail Gorbachev (quoted in Apple, 1990)

It's interesting to compare Dolphins with Butterflies. While the two types could not be farther apart in many ways, they do share an essential trait: an instinct for creating harmony. However, instead of blending notes or colors or flavors, Dolphins create harmony among people. They are the alleviators of social discord, the peacemakers and conflict breakers. And while peace may come at a cost (Dolphins often find themselves in the precarious position of standing, sometimes figuratively, sometimes literally, arms outstretched between two raging opponents, taking punches from both sides), they do it with such humility that it's almost impossible for the warring sides to be hostile to them.

Unhealthy Dolphins might mistake acquiescence with peace and, most commonly in romantic relationships, use a quick-fix method of avoiding conflict by repressing their own needs. A mature Dolphin, in contrast, realizes that actual conflict resolution cannot be achieved without confrontation and that diplomacy is truly a long game, one in which, with their vigorous emotional endurance and strong leadership abilities, the Dolphin is an ideal player. *La ciencia de la paz es paciencia*: The science of peace is patience.

THE GIANT PANDA

Disclaimer: Pandas do not have a monopoly on alienation. Every type, depending on the context, has probably felt a minor twinge of persecution in their life. Unfortunately, that's also the primary reason so many individuals tend to mistype themselves as Pandas—a thousand Pandas' ears are ringing with the thought "Someone wants to be me?" The same things that can riddle a Panda with self-doubt—their underdog status, humble romanticism, and pragmatic idealism—can also turn non-Pandas green with temperament envy.

The Neurotic

Maybe I'll share my life with somebody; maybe not, . . . but the truth is, when I think back to my loneliest moments, there was usually somebody sitting there next to me.

—Ally McBeal (D'Elia, 2000)

It might seem offensive and a bit out of the ordinary to start off the Panda's description with a negative trait, but as with most types, strengths derive from weaknesses and vice versa, and to fully understand the Panda, you need to know this first and foremost: They feel alone. A Panda's purpose in life, like all Shamans, is to discover their inner self and help others do the same, and much like their Shaman sibling the Dolphin, they prefer to accomplish this by working within a structured organization of people, such as the education system, the health-care system, or the government. Unlike the Dolphin, though, Pandas usually don't have a deep reservoir of extroverted energy, and instead of appearing spirited, they are frequently perceived as deeply guarded, an oddity among Shaman types.

Without the benefit of social popularity, the Panda's genuine idealism often falls on deaf ears or, worse, faces extreme opposition; they're the teacher who tries to change the grading system, the therapist who strays from DSM orthodoxy, or the politician who rails against corruption. It's this struggle against the establishment while still working within the establishment that can leave a Panda feeling alone, trapped, and ultimately doubting their own convictions. On the bright side, if a Panda's ever able to overcome the social restraints and figure themselves out (with their natural intrapersonal intelligence, most do), watch out! Their combination of altruism and pragmatism makes them a perfect conduit for real change.

The Bookworm

To me who dreamed so much as a child, who made a dream world in which I was the heroine of an unending story, the lives of people around me continued to have a certain storybook quality.

—Eleanor Roosevelt ([1960] 1961)

Perhaps it's the Panda's analytical nature and reserved demeanor that causes people to mistake them for their Smith cousins. Or maybe it's their insatiable reading habit. Fiction and nonfiction, literature and poetry, physics and history—all have a habit of appearing on a Panda's reading list. Consuming the written word is their way of interacting with ideas without the pressure of the external world; a teacher won't be jumping out of the pages to lecture them on how they're doing everything wrong, like some horrifying pop-up book from Shaman hell. A Panda's mind is a sanctuary filled with ideas and emotions they're unwilling to share. Pandas, unlike the emotionally available Dolphins, fear vulnerability (a common Panda anxiety is the belief that, by expressing their true self, they will most undoubtedly scare everyone away), so books act as virtual sparring partners, preparing the Panda for a fight they feel destined to have.

When that fight does happen, it'll usually happen on the page. Pandas make excellent writers, and it's not only due to their heightened emotional sensitivity and gift for metaphorical language, as all Shamans share those traits in some form or fashion. It's mainly because, when compared to other Shamans, Pandas are more cautious than Dolphins, more emotionally stable than Baboons, and more focused than Humpback Whales, all traits that foster good writing. A good percentage of their literary capabilities can also be attributed to the aforementioned feelings they've been bottling up inside; for the Panda, writing is an exercise in catharsis, and the more words they peddle from their creative Peloton, the better emotional shape they'll be in.

The Counselor

When people who don't know me well, black or white, discover my background (and it is usually a discovery, for I ceased to advertise my mother's race [white] at the age of twelve or thirteen, when I began to suspect I was ingratiating myself to whites), I see the split-second adjustments they have to make, the searching of my eyes for some telltale sign. They no longer know who I am.

–Barack Obama (1995)

A positive repercussion of experiencing emotional turmoil is that a Panda is well equipped to recognize and understand the pain in others. This is not just because they've suffered. It is because, of all the types, the Panda is the most self-aware and thus the most likely person to fully understand the source of their own suffering. This intrapersonal intelligence can be an incredibly powerful tool, as revealing relevant details from their own past allows them to connect on a personal level with their patients, students, or whomever it is they've chosen to mentor.

This sort of confessional therapy is normally frowned upon by the establishment for two reasons. One is the fear that the practitioner, by making things personal, will leave themselves emotionally vulnerable. The second is that, by admitting to their own personal struggles and flaws, they have relinquished their professional authority. When it comes to showing strength and establishing authority, Pandas couldn't care less. Their only concern is what method is most efficacious, and they are willing to take great emotional and professional risks to help others. The rest of us should feel quite fortunate to have their courage in the world.

The Resolute Decision Maker

If the idea is to drive them out with firearms, let every Indian consider what precious little profit Europe has found in these.

—Mahatma Gandhi (1909)

Pandas have an incredible capacity to endure. Contrasted with the Gatherer Bear, who can withstand immense physical pain, the Panda can sustain itself under enormous emotional pressure, an ability that's best attributed to their unparalleled strength of will. And unlike the Humpback Whale, whose idealism tends to venture more into self-sacrifice and voluntary exile, the Panda is not interested in leaving society. They know that being in the thick of things, even though it may be a situation they despise, gives them access to the people they want to help; sadly, it's these same people who are frequently exerting emotional pressure on Pandas in the first place.

True to their diplomatic nature, Pandas usually choose the path of compromise or passivity, which can sometimes alienate their more Shamanic—some might call them idealogue-leaning—siblings the Baboons and Humpback Whales. This moderate position is one from which the Panda makes decisions every day of their life, decisions that can be excruciatingly difficult because, due to the nature of compromise, nobody's ever 100 percent satisfied. Thankfully, Pandas are pragmatic and disciplined, and like a doctor treating a petulant child, they seek to alleviate society of its ills, whether society likes it or not.

THE BABOON

At first glance, a Baboon's neurotic zaniness might seem like showmanship and thus lead observers to mistake them for their distant cousin the Hunter Peacock. It's only upon deeper inspection that one finds their motivations to be entirely akin to their other Shaman brethren, and what was once perceived to be an uncontrolled excitability of the body is actually the exuberant enthusiasm of the spirit.

The Herald

That some desperate wretches should be willing to steal and enslave men by violence and murder for gain, is rather lamentable than strange. But that many civilized, nay, Christianized people should approve, and be concerned in the savage practice, is surprising.

–Thomas Paine (1775)

A Baboon's sole purpose in life is to inspire humankind to action. They do this not by playing to a person's self-interest, employing strong-armed authority, or even using reason; rather, a Baboon's motivational skill derives from their preternatural ability to help others see the good and evil within themselves and to empower the former over the latter. Their mix of candor and subversiveness has a way of connecting to a crowd that is unparalleled in its capacity for revealing human pathos. Baboons say the things that other people wish they had the audacity to say. They eviscerate bullies, empower the bullied, and preach to the faithless.

Of course, this would all seem massively sanctimonious if it wasn't for the fact that Baboons tend to do it with a wink and a smile, as they're among the most humorous of the types; along with Chimpanzees, they make up a good portion of the world's stand-up comedians. While Hunter types focus primarily on entertaining the audience, Baboons strive to expose human foibles and contradictions through irony, satire, and impersonation. Their vocal inflections can be abundant, but unlike the precise affectations of Peacocks and Foxes, Baboon impersonations are less technical, not particularly specific, and more concerned with expressing personal insight and absurdity than a demonstration of skill.

The True Believer

I always knew that I was going to be famous. I honest to God don't know how else to describe it. I used to lie in bed and wonder, "Am I going to be a local TV person? Am I going to be a motivational speaker?" It wasn't a vision. But as it's kind of happening, you have this buried understanding: "Of course."

–Jennifer Lawrence (quoted in Van Meter, 2013)

Baboons are highly adaptable people who certainly think well enough of themselves to point out such gifts. This is usually unnecessary, however, as such Baboon talents as articulation, interpersonal connection, and improvisation are easily observable. For this reason, starting at an early age, their teachers, peers, and parents frequently laud Baboons, as their gifts can be both flashy and academic; it's no wonder they genuinely believe that they're good at everything. Along with Chimpanzees, Baboons are the most likely type to be recognized as gifted.

This outward precociousness, along with the Baboon's seemingly flippant self-assuredness, can generate resentment from other less-vocal types. However, mature Baboons have a knack for using their charm and charisma to make amends with one essential truth: Baboon confidence is not borne out of an egotistical drive to dominate as much as an abundance of faith in their own intuition. They believe their success to be predestined, taking great risks and placing a tremendous expectation on themselves because they feel their natural gifts obligate them to do so. This strange phenomenon—where Baboons revel in their talents but take no credit for them—can be seen when giving a Baboon a direct and genuine compliment; most are rendered speechless, which is no small feat.

The Fickle Friend

Imagination is a strong, restless faculty, which claims to be heard and exercised: are we to be quite deaf to her cry, and insensate to her struggles? When she shows us bright pictures, are we never to look at them, and try to reproduce them?

–Charlotte Brontë (1847)

With their ideas being evanescent in nature, Baboons regularly flit from one project to another, feeling passionately about an idea in one moment and then forgetting about it in the next. Unfortunately, this behavior can also manifest itself within their relationships, especially those of a romantic bent. It's not that they don't care; it's just that their imagination is fueled by both spontaneity and romance, and Baboons often fear that to lose either one would endanger their creative engine, as if to not follow their muse—figurative and real—at any given moment is the equivalent to abandoning them forever.

Baboons want to be involved in everything, frequently overcommitting themselves to the multitudinous tasks they find interesting. Smoke a fifteen-hour brisket on the weekend? Sure. Learn how to flawlessly play all three of Satie's Gymnopédies? No sweat. Cowrite the script for a friend's short film? Let's get to outlining. If Baboons aren't careful, they might find themselves in a time crunch that drains that distinctive Baboon enthusiasm—otherwise known as the reason they chose to commit to so many endeavors in the first place.

The Revolutionary

When a man is denied the right to live the life he believes in, he has no choice but to become an outlaw.

—Nelson Mandela (1995)

In most social situations, Baboons can appear to be fun loving, easygoing, and (dare it be said) somewhat reserved. However, don't let that fool you. Replace the concrete setting with a conversation on abstract ideas, and you'll find that Baboons have a plethora of opinions on virtually everything. Ask them what their feelings are on a controversial subject, and you might find yourself on the receiving end of one long, albeit probably hilariously charming, monologue about recycling, the looming danger of overpopulation, or how franchise adaptations killed the feature film. They preach to you about the best films to see, best vinyl record store to go to, and best hole-in-the-wall restaurant to get authentic anything; just don't expect to be allowed back into the conversation without some effort on your part.

More aggressive than their fellow Shamans, a Baboon's fervor can often overflow to the point where it borders on zealotry. If the "road to Hell is paved with good intentions," then you can be assured that a Baboon has tread that path before. They can feel so strongly about their side of an issue that they forget to acknowledge or consider the other side. In moments like these, they can be demanding, forceful, and violent to friend and foe alike, and their heightened intensity and oft-accompanying hyperbole frequently gets them into trouble. However, the more mature a Baboon is, the easier it is for them to navigate the tumultuous waters of their own convictions, and society, more often than not, finds itself thankful for their revolutionary spirit.

THE HUMPBACK WHALE

The eyes that appear to be staring intently at nothing in particular, the quiet strength found in the bending but not breaking tremor of their voice—these are the marked traits of the Humpback Whale. From the outside, these re-served individuals are hard to distinguish from their Panda siblings; they're even hard to distinguish sometimes from their distant cousin the Hunter Butterfly. But upon speaking with a Humpback Whale, especially on a topic that matters to them, you'll find that the illusion quickly dissipates, and that timid, distant space cadet you initially thought was a dwarf star has now ex-ploded into a full-on supernova.

The Old Soul

I need to have something besides a husband and children to devote myself to! I don't want to have lived in vain like most people. I want to be useful or bring enjoyment to all people, even those I've never met.

—Anne Frank ([1947] 1995)

It always seems like Humpback Whales know more than we do and infinitely more than they let on. Perhaps it's because they're not tethered to society as so many of us are. Like their Baboon siblings, Whales prefer to work outside the social system, commonly as writers, poets, artists, spiritual healers, and small business owners. However, whereas the Baboon needs constant human interaction (some would say attention) to function, Whales are quite content to spend their time in deep introspection with their books and insights to keep them company. It is this robust inner life that frequently gives the im-pression that a Humpback Whale, when interacting with the rest of society, is a philosopher among a confederacy of dunces.

The Humpback Whale's natural inclination to look past surface appearances and expectations usually leads them to being the first person to recognize a moral dilemma plaguing society. For Whales, a corrupt status quo is something that needs to be purged, not always through revolution (as a Baboon might recommend), but through self-reflection. For a Humpback Whale, there is no great calamity occurring outside ourselves that cannot be fixed by looking inside ourselves. In times of war, they sue for peace. During a period engulfed in materialism, they preach emotional well-being. When school and education become merely a truck stop on the highway to gainful employment, Humpback Whales encourage students to take the road less traveled.

The Dreamer

As for me, I lost everything: my wife, my book, my job, everything that I thought was important. But I finally knew where I wanted to go.

—Grady Tripp (Hanson, 2000)

The most disconnected of all the Shamans, a Humpback Whale lives a fantasy-filled childhood that usually extends to their life as an adult. Though daydreaming is vital to their emotional health, the practical manifestation of imagining alligators dancing with hippos while on a conference call with the boss or envisioning, from their number-crunching cubicle, a swashbuckling exit out the window and an escape to a life less ordinary never goes well.

It's imperative for Humpback Whales to find professions or hobbies that give them an opportunity to use their powerful imaginations. Otherwise, they might find themselves meandering aimlessly through life like an emotional vagabond, devoid of purpose and forever journeying to parts unknown, in both the physical and spiritual world. This could be inevitable, however, because, despite their best efforts to ground themselves, there is always a little chaos in the life of a Humpback Whale. With their eccentricity, spontaneity, and openness to new experiences, accidental adventures are bound to happen.

The Outcast

The wisest of all, in my opinion, is he who can, if only once a month, call himself a fool—a faculty unheard of nowadays.

—Fyodor Dostoyevsky ([1873] 1946)

The easiest way to distinguish a Humpback Whale from the Giant Panda, the other reserved Shaman, is their noticeable disregard for societal norms, such as the education system, typical nuclear family values, and conventional standards of fashion and beauty. Most Humpback Whales also frown on "commercialized" entertainment, as they feel its only purpose is to prop up and justify the artificial values they so despise. This puts them squarely at odds with society in general, and unlike Giant Pandas, Whales do not compromise their values to better integrate themselves within the social structure. This can force them to the outskirts of society, persecuted and alone. Or worse yet, the Humpback Whale succumbs to the social pressure and begins doubting their convictions while simultaneously kicking themselves for not being authentic enough.

For this reason, it's not uncommon for Humpback Whales to take part in hobbies that help guide them through their spiritual confusion, like yoga (though they wouldn't be caught dead in Lululemon) or meditation; that these activities have found their way into the mainstream says a lot about how the Humpback Whales' authenticity is commonly appropriated into cool culture. Communing with nature is another sanctuary for them. There's a definite realness to hiking through a dense forest of pines or relishing the way a cool stream of water feels on the feet, and nature, in all its unpretentiousness, seems to give the Humpback Whale not only a sense of peace but also something far better: a renewed confidence in their own authenticity.

The Hero

I do not fear men-at-arms; my way has been made plain before me. . . . For that am I come!

—Joan of Arc (quoted in France, 1909)

One of the more intriguing facts about Humpback Whales is that they're the archetype for the mythological hero. They are who Joseph Campbell was writing about in *The Hero with a Thousand Faces*, though there are plenty more than a thousand Humpback Whales walking among us. From fictional stories to nonfictional accounts to fictional accounts of nonfictional stories, human history and pop culture are filled with soulful, self-sacrificing Humpback Whales like King Arthur, Frodo Baggins, Harry Potter, Luke Skywalker, and Joan of Arc.

A Humpback Whale might appear to be an odd choice for a hero. On average, they're not physically imposing, nor are they quick on their feet—literally or figuratively. What they do have is a humble heart, an open mind, and a self-assuredness that whatever is happening to them is happening for a reason. It is that faith that gives them not only the confidence to take on the most demanding of challenges but also the strength to see them through.

	What is it that fuels me?	What is my "normal" role?	What is my super power?	What is my flaw?
Dolphins	The Community Organizer	The Teacher	The Diplomat	The TMI Guy–or Gal
Giant Pandas	The Bookworm	The Counselor	The Resolute Decision-Maker	The Neurotic
Baboons	The True Believer	The Herald	The Revolutionary	The Fickle Friend
Humpback Whales	The Old Soul	The Dreamer	The "Hero"	The Outcast

Figure 5.1 Shaman Roles

CHAPTER SIX

THE SMITHS

"HAVE YOU EVER SEEN A HUMAN HEART?" (NICHOLS, 2004)

"They're like my minions. I can use them to do my bidding." A James Bond villain? Maybe a galactic conqueror in the latest Marvel movie? Nope. Try a twelve-year-old girl.

She was a student of mine for several years, though she said this during our first tutoring session in response to my question, "What do you like most about your friends?" The remarkable—and maybe not so remarkable—thing about a life spent studying different personalities is that, when it comes to people, nothing surprises me anymore. Normal doesn't exist, at least not in the way I used to assume it did. I learned the hard way, as I'm sure most do, what happens when you assume.

The *Oxford Dictionary of English* defines *normal* as

1. conforming to a standard; usual, typical, or expected
2. the usual, average, or typical state or condition

Basically, if you have a population of people, *normal* can be used to describe the standards that many in that population ascribe to. Pretty simple. Purely a numbers game. If you have a hundred people and eighty-five of them are right-handed, then we can say that the "usual, average" person in that group is right-handed, which, for those playing at home, is not the same thing as saying, "Let's beat the crap out of the other fifteen until they learn how to use their right hand better than their left." Somehow the idea of being normal has become conflated with being ideal, as if a poor village kid growing up in the Ivory Coast would ever describe their "typical state or condition" as being anything close to ideal. When we start viewing normal not as an idea that defines some element of reality, like gravity or relativity, but by its actual written definition, we become more accepting—and observant—of the various idiosyncrasies, large and small, our fellow humans possess.

Upon hearing my student describe her friends as "minions" there to do her "bidding," I, of course, couldn't help but ask the logical follow-up question:

ME: What exactly do you make them do for you?
HER: Well, if I don't like someone, I have them do stuff to that person.
ME: What kind of stuff?
HER: I don't know. Maybe say mean things, annoy them a little—or a lot.

I was intrigued. It's very rare that you get to hear such misanthropy said out loud, let alone by someone too young to know what that word means. It was refreshing in a way. It was as if years and years—twelve of them to be exact—of being pummeled by Gatherer orthodoxy had had little to no effect on her. She is, without a doubt, a Smith and, even more importantly (as I'm considering the potential moral judgment of the reader), a fantastic kid who enjoys acting, reading science fiction, and all the other things a girl her age might like. There's no cruelty in her. I know this because one time, in an attempt to be the kewl adult, I mentioned to her that I was a fan of Billie Eilish. She responded, quite matter-of-factly, "Oh yeah, she's cool. All the girls in my grade like her." Yep, it always feels great to be told you share the musical tastes of a twelve-year-old girl. And yet, she took no glee in my humiliation. She didn't even realize there was cause for it. To her, Billie Eilish was a cool musical artist adored by the girls of the seventh grade. Objective fact. Embarrassment had nothing to do with it—a lesson we should all learn from Smiths.

A lot of people might frown upon anyone, let alone a tween girl, viewing their friends as useful minions. Actually, that might be an understatement. If she had said this to one of her teachers, she'd be more likely to receive a reference for a psych eval than respect for her idiosyncratic perspective. I think my exact words were, "That's a lot of power to have." Smiths should count themselves fortunate that, by and large, these kinds of conversations with their teachers don't come up too often. Usually strong students, Smiths can progress through the education system with little trouble, so long as they keep their mouths shut when it comes to their ambivalent (they would call it objective) view of the world. It's like when the North Carolina–bred, deeply

Baptist Madison Bumgarner was a star pitcher for the San Francisco Giants. Liberal Bay Area fans didn't ask him for his political beliefs, and he wisely didn't share them. Instead, he brought them three World Series titles.

In much the same way, Smiths stand to benefit when their accomplishments, not the motivations and ideas behind those accomplishments, take center stage—another reason people are always telling Elon Musk to shut the hell up. However, this is a delicate balancing act. Smiths, unlike the assimilation-obsessed Shamans, don't care whether society accepts them or not. Of all the types, Smiths have the strongest sense of self, a self-knowledge and self-assurance that often expresses itself at an early age. They know who they are and are not inclined to keep their opinions to themselves. Their honesty is both a strength and a burden, as other types are quick to admire Smiths' refusal to equivocate but are also quick to cast them as weird, antisocial outcasts or cold, domineering sociopaths; they're either planning the next Columbine or the next Third World coup.

My student was neither. She wasn't dreaming of ways to shoot up her school; it's worth mentioning that society frequently—and unfairly—equates Smith social awkwardness with violence, ignoring the fact that many perpetrators of domestic terrorism are motivated by anger at not fitting in, an anxiety that is foreign to most Smiths. And regardless of how she led her friends, my student also wasn't devoid of feeling. When I asked her about her sister, who was leaving for college that year, she teared up at the thought, both surprised at her own tears and unable to express clearly how she felt. Behind her playful machinations was a wellspring of suppressed emotion just waiting for the maturity to articulate itself. This is the real Smith. And unlike the fiery tempers of the Hunters or the churning passions of the Shamans, the emotions of the Smiths are like cold lightning: direct, arriving without warning, and unable to fully control its power.

EXPAND THEIR SENSE OF HUMANITY

The search for information is at the heart of the Smith growth arc—*heart* being the appropriate word. So much of what Smiths try to do is eliminate the human factor when collecting knowledge; personal feelings become collateral damage as they battle for objective truth. The problem is, they could win battle after battle and find themselves losing the war. We have feelings for a reason. When we start becoming detached from those, we begin to lose the context of any knowledge we might gain and its implications on our world and the people we love. I always think of J. Robert Oppenheimer, the father of the atomic bomb, quoting from the Bhagavad Gita after watching a nuclear test: "Now I am become Death, the destroyer of worlds" (quoted in Freed and Giovannitti, 1965). Knowledge without context comes at a cost.

It's not that Smiths are incapable of understanding context; it's just that, for a Smith, understanding humans, a necessity when gaining context, is a messy affair. We are often an irrational species, driven by feelings and fancy and deceptively good at deceiving others, especially ourselves. Ideas, though, are a source of comfort. Gravity, like love, is a powerful force, but it won't drunk-dial you at 3:00 a.m. after you've already moved on to the Heisenberg uncertainty principle. Abstract concepts are a wonderful thing, and there's no doubt about their tangible impact on the concrete world. And yet there's a restrictive quality to their impersonal nature, as if the ivory tower serves as both intellectual sanctuary and cloistered prison. The following conversation was between a Smith friend of mine and my younger brother, who was playing *Final Fantasy XI*, an early-aughts massively multiplayer online role-playing game (MMORPG) precursor to *World of Warcraft*: basically, a game where you interact, via digital avatar, with thousands of people in a fantasy world:

MY FRIEND: How often do you play?
MY BROTHER: Eh, an hour a day. You thinking about playing?
MY FRIEND: Oh no, I can't play games like this.
MY BROTHER: Why not?
MY FRIEND: They're too fun. I'll play forever. And when your make-believe life becomes more fun than your real life, that's when you need to stop.

That stoppage, preceded by the awareness of the potential danger, is essential to a Smith's growth arc. Mature Smiths know when to, from time to time, rejoin the actual people in their life so that they might understand them better because there's wisdom in knowing people, too, as Einstein, an obvious Smith, demonstrated in a conversation he had with an attendee at a conference at Princeton in 1946:

ATTENDEE: Dr. Einstein, why is it that, when the mind of man has stretched so far as to discover the structure of the atom, we have been unable to devise the political means to keep the atom from destroying us?

EINSTEIN: That is simple, my friend. It is because politics is more difficult than physics. (Dora Dore, Ku, and Jackson, 2014)

Four Questions for Smiths

1. How do I understand morality?
2. How do I express my creativity?
3. How do I serve humanity?
4. What is my flaw?

The Smith growth arc is almost like the Shaman arc in reverse. Smiths already start with a strong understanding of themselves; what they don't have is the Shamans' readiness to let others in. They frequently mistake the self-knowledge they possess as a certainty, a mistake they rarely make when delving into more objective ideas where, in the words of another Smith, Nobel laureate Richard Feynman (1964), "people search for certainty, but there is no certainty." And it is that disconnect wherein lies the problem. Immature Smiths tend to see objective knowledge and knowledge of people as mutually exclusive, usually praising the former and devaluing the latter.

If we were to visualize the Smith growth arc, it would be (much to a Smith's delight) one big brain. However, this brain has been cleft in two, with the logical left hemisphere severed from the emotional right. To fully mature, a Smith must learn to bridge the gap between the two (see figure 6.1). Fun fact: A postmortem study of Einstein's brain found that the only significant physical anomaly was an abnormally large corpus callosum, the part of the brain responsible for integrating information between both hemispheres. Instead of viewing their emotions as incomprehensible urges that need to be suppressed, mature Smiths come to realize that delving into the complexities of their feelings is the best way to harness their power, bringing agency to the Smith's ingenuity. After all, it's not impossible to control cold lightning; just ask Edison.

THE KILLER WHALE

There are several personality types who like to work behind the scenes, humbly avoiding the spotlight whenever possible. The Killer Whale is not one of them. Well known for their natural drive to lead, Killer Whales, as opposed to the similarly commanding but far more authoritarian Stags, derive their power from the force of their intellect, convincing their followers, in a not-so-subtle way, that they're the smartest person in the room, and as such, to follow another would be folly.

The CEO

I started questioning gender-based assumptions a long time ago. When I was eight, I was confused at being called "bossy," because I wanted to direct the plays that we would put on for our parents—but the boys were not.

—Emma Watson (2014)

Among all the types, Killer Whales are one of the most exceptional students, exceeded only by their Smith siblings the Spiders. Nevertheless, when compared to a Spider, what a Killer Whale lacks in patience and intellectual fastidiousness they more than make up for in ambition. They don't want to be in charge; they expect it, considering their leadership role to be the inevitable result of their superior drive and vision.

Like all Smiths, Killer Whales have strong analytical skills, but they readily accept that their skills pale in comparison to the innovative Chimpanzees and theoretical Owls. What they do not capitulate on is control. In their minds, there are only two types capable of taking all the impractical, disjointed, and speculative ideas of the Chimps and Owls and transforming them into a real, meaningful product, and the Spiders' caution is more likely to lead to the spinning of wheels than the creation of a successful company. Once the necessary information has been acquired, Killer Whales act decisively, recruiting qualified allies and finding optimal roles for them. It is no surprise that a substantial number of CEOs are Killer Whales; their ability to identify and use a person's unique talents is a necessity for organizational success.

The Commander

The object of all work is production or accomplishment and to either of these ends there must be forethought, system, planning, intelligence, and honest purpose, as well as perspiration. Seeming to do is not doing.

–Thomas Edison (2016)

Their knack for recognizing strengths and weaknesses, while beneficial to their allies and followers, can make Killer Whales dangerous opponents. Whether it's a head football coach devising special blitzes to take advantage of a slow-footed quarterback or a general planning troop movements based on deficiencies in the enemy ranks, Killer Whales always come prepared with a plan of attack. They specialize in coordinating multiple concurrent actions, the power of their strategy deriving not from any specific part but from the overwhelming sum of the whole plan. These strategies are always developed over time, and it's not unusual for a Killer Whale to possess a playbook—literal or figurative—from which they regularly work.

Like Spiders, Killer Whales prefer to rely on plans that have a proven track record of success (usually their own success) and likewise are quick to abandon a strategy if it proves to be ineffective. Unlike a Spider, whose contingencies are tailored to respond, a Killer Whale enjoys forcing the action. This is not to be confused with recklessness, as every move is done with a great deal of forethought. It's just that Killer Whales would rather not hide in the shadows; it's much harder to target the bull's-eye on their backs when they're running roughshod over you.

The Dominator

I would have you, right here, on this desk, until you begged for mercy . . . twice.

–Irene Adler (McGuigan, 2012)

The forceful nature of the Killer Whale makes them just that: a force of nature. And while tremendously powerful, like any natural disaster, an intense amount of destruction can occur. To put it bluntly (they would), Killer Whales can be emotionally insensitive control freaks at their worst, however not in the cold, indifferent way commonly associated with Smiths. In fact, Killer Whales might be too intense, the hunger to achieve their desired end becoming so overwhelming that they begin to disregard the very allies helping them reach that goal. The same analytical prowess that enables a Killer Whale to make objective, strategic decisions can also render them, at best, unaware to the various societal elements involved in an endeavor (social norms, prevailing protocols, personal feelings) and, at worst, dismissive of them.

Understandably, this aggressive behavior, even when motivated by altruism, like Hermione Granger scolding a less-than-studious Harry Potter, can cause a Killer Whale to upset their friends, colleagues, and family members. Never one to be unsuccessful at anything—including relationships—Killer Whales work to mend the bonds that have been broken. Unfortunately, this often leads to them adding more fuel to the fire, as their controlling albeit well-intentioned pleas come off more as manipulative power plays than expressions of remorse. However, mature Killer Whales come to learn that you can't force a person to feel anything. And for the lucky people who are wise enough—and brave enough—to see past the Killer Whale's surface aggression, they will find no friend more loyal, no lover more affectionate, and no opinion more truthful.

The Cynical Pragmatist

No public man in these islands ever believes that the Bible means what it says: he is always convinced that it says what he means.

—George Bernard Shaw (1932)

Despite the occasional lapse into dictator mode, Killer Whales are usually capable of conferring power to others within the group. But make no mistake: This act of deference is more a reflection of their pragmatism than any sense of humility. They realize that the most effective strategy for keeping a complex machine running smoothly is to make sure all its myriad parts are greased. Because of this, Killer Whales tend to be quite cynical when it comes to issues of morality; the visibility of any leadership position they might hold frequently causes mature Killer Whales to avoid controversial subjects altogether.

With a Killer Whale, their public opinion might differ from their private one, as opposed to a Spider, a fellow cynic who regularly chooses to express no opinion at all. This mixture of cynicism and pragmatism is also what enables Killer Whales to be such astute judges of talent. By stripping away such surface traits as gender, sexuality, race, and nationality, Killer Whales can single out individuals for what really matters: the skills and knowledge they can provide to the organization.

THE SPIDER

If life is, in the proverbial sense, like a game, then the Spider seems to be playing chess while the rest of us are playing checkers. Not only do they always have a plan, but they usually have multiple contingencies if something in that plan were to go awry. And as opposed to Killer Whales, Smith siblings who willfully show their motivations like a poker player slamming their winning hand onto the table, the serious and reserved Spiders very rarely reveal the personal agenda that drives their farsighted machinations.

The Empiricist

All the reason which made the initiation of physical force evil, make the retaliatory use of physical force a moral imperative.

—Ayn Rand (1964)

If research is a god, consider the Spider a true believer. More studious than Killer Whales and more grounded than Chimpanzees and Owls, Spiders rely primarily on empirical evidence to power their reasoning. Thus, they're commonly perceived to be the most reasonable of their Smith brethren. Spiders place a greater emphasis on the application of theory than the creation of it, a trait they share with Killer Whales, though Spiders are far more detail oriented. They have the uncanny ability not only to follow all the various twists and turns a complex theory can take but also to develop a system in which these ideas can flourish in the real world. Spiders view knowledge as a means of reaching an objective, one that can hopefully change the world for the better.

Much of this work is performed behind the scenes, as a Spider, on the outside, can seem similar to the introverted Owl and their Shaman cousin the Giant Panda. However, unlike those types, who tend to be pacifists, a Spider is not opposed to war in and of itself. Like all things in their sphere of understanding, war is just an abstract concept, the virtue of which is dictated solely by practicality and context. After all, to a Spider, ideas are primarily vehicles for tangible impact, and to automatically judge something as being positive or negative without understanding its context in the real world is prejudicial. In this manner, Spiders are quite objective, expressing an enormous amount of skepticism when it comes to such value judgments as good and evil. Though to accuse them of not believing in such things would be an overreach; they're merely agnostic, trusting the data they've been compiling—a lifelong enterprise for most Spiders—to lead the way.

The Reserved Contradiction

I don't open up very easily to people. In high school, I came across as a snob. Well, I am sort of a snob. I'm not very nice to people, because . . . well, I'm just not. I can come across as mysterious.

—Kristin Kreuk (quoted in Hedegaard, 2002)

Spiders are a living oxymoron. On one hand, they're industrious, career-minded individuals. On the other hand, they create systems with the expressed goal of avoiding doing more work than they deem necessary, and career ambition as a means to material success is an anathema to them. They can be terse in general conversation, but if asked about their current project, they will ramble on and on about every detail. Their thoughts are methodically collated. Their workspace is a cluttered disaster. A Spider uses an online system to schedule a meeting that perfectly fits every attendee's schedule, a meeting in which they will present the intricate details of a plan they have meticulously crafted, and just prior to said presentation, they proceed to accidentally run into a pole on the way to the office.

The most tragic contradiction: Spiders are frequently viewed as cold and indifferent despite the wellspring of intense emotions bottled up inside them. Perhaps it's their desire to always be in control of a situation (only the Killer Whale is a bigger control freak) that causes a Spider to repress their feelings for fear that expressing them might leave them vulnerable. A Spider might choose to just shut most people out entirely, which invariably decreases their interpersonal skills, as their insight into people would then be limited to what books they could research on the subject. Thankfully, mature Spiders are able to relinquish the need for absolute control, opening up to a small selection of trusted individuals.

The Contingency Planner

Let's set the meeting. Get our informers to find out where it's gonna be held. Now, we insist it's a public place, a bar, a restaurant, some place where there's people, so I feel safe. They're gonna search me when I first meet them, right? So I can't have a weapon on me then. But if Clemenza can figure a way to have a weapon planted there for me, then I'll kill 'em both.

—Michael Corleone (Coppola, 1972)

The master of the algorithm, it's not unusual to hear a Spider using conditional statements like "If this, then that" when devising a strategy. Spiders pride themselves on always being three steps ahead of everyone else; don't be surprised if you find out that a Spider has already prepared plans B and C for the fifth-likeliest outcome of a given scenario.

Long-term planning is common for the objective-minded Spider. Days, weeks, years, even decades could pass before a Spider gets what they want (every Spider would've passed the marshmallow test). This is not evidence of fear or dispassion but merely the patience to wait until certain conditions have been met and the Spider's goal is ripe for the taking. Unfortunately, there can be negative consequences to such narrow-minded dedication, as Spiders are not the most self-aware individuals, and the vigilance they devote to their plans doesn't always extend itself to their emotional well-being. A Spider might find themselves in a situation where they've spent years of planning to achieve an outcome that they're just beginning to realize they don't want.

The Efficient Problem-Solver

Just in terms of allocation of time resources, religion is not very efficient. There's a lot more I could be doing on a Sunday morning.

—Bill Gates (quoted in Isaacson, 1997)

The Spider's gift is their ability to integrate a myriad of disparate, even discordant, ideas into a harmonious web of synchronicity, an elegantly practical, working system that solves an existing problem or fulfills a foreseeable need. For a Spider, the beauty of the design lies in its tangible efficiency, a strong departure from the other Smith designers, the fanciful Chimpanzee and speculative Owl. The Spider's plan is always to minimize input and maximize output in a way that can be easily incorporated into the general operations of the company or institution they work for.

Because of this, it's common to find Spiders in fields that possess a strong need for structural precision, such as corporate business, education, software design, and academic research. Whether they're devising a hostile takeover, a curriculum, an SaaS platform, or an experimental study, Spiders work tirelessly to create a system that, at worst, will increase productivity and, at best, will revolutionize their respective industry.

THE CHIMPANZEE

A Chimpanzee in a nutshell: innovation for innovation's sake, cleverness for cleverness's sake, and a wink and a nod to those too slow to keep up. Eschewing the pragmatic goals of the Killer Whale and Spider and far flashier than the understated Owl, Chimpanzees view themselves as a different breed of Smith. They are highly skeptical of both specialization and laughter-less rooms, making them the most versatile and mischievous of all the types.

The Troubleshooter

If Edison had a needle to find in a haystack, he would proceed at once with the diligence of the bee to examine straw after straw until he found the object of his search. . . . I was a sorry witness of such doings, knowing that a little theory and calculation would have saved him ninety percent of his labor.

—Nikola Tesla (quoted in *New York Times*, 1931)

The versatility of the Chimpanzee derives from their relentless desire to discover—perhaps invent—new concepts in a variety of fields. Differing from the controlling Killer Whales and Spiders, Chimps are rarely fazed when not possessing all the answers. In fact, it's more fun for them when they don't. Ironically, this is why they're such ingenious troubleshooters. If the meticulousness of a Spider makes them the master of creating strategies toward achieving long-term goals, then the creativity of a Chimpanzee makes them the master of creating innovative solutions for immediate problems. Unbound by practicality and proven results, the experimental style of Chimpanzees enables them to suggest solution models that no one in their right mind would ever propose—ideas that the Chimpanzee most definitely spouts off in rapid-fire succession.

After all, troubleshooting is just a natural extension of the Chimpanzee's penchant for tinkering. Anything that can be tested, refined, retested, and then rerefined falls into the realm of the Chimpanzee. Regrettably, female Chimps face tremendous social pressure, normally learning from an early age that it's not appropriate for a girl to be trampling around in the mud collecting snails. Perhaps it's the brashness and danger associated with being a Chimpanzee; girls are expected to act "properly" and let the boys do the dangerous work. STEM fields, areas of work where male Chimpanzees are prevalent, have historically been misogynistic, and even now, the small number of women in the physical sciences is comically depressing. Because of this, they are often forced to express their innovation in occupations that are more "female" (it's no surprise that many of these are related to beauty) as industrial designers, architects, pastry chefs, small business entrepreneurs, and creative consultants.

The Practical Jokester

They made a porn movie about Sarah Palin and the same actress, Lisa Ann, played me in the porn version of *30 Rock*. Weirdly, of the three of us, Lisa Ann knows the most about foreign policy.

—Tina Fey (2012)

It's true that most Smiths put absolutely no stock in traditional societal values unsupported by logic, though each Smith deals with social pressure in their own way. The pragmatic Killer Whales and Spiders assimilate as much as they need to in order to achieve their goals. The reclusive Owl ignores them completely. The Chimpanzee, usually perceived as the boldest of the four, broadcasts their antagonistic opinions loudly, clearly, and with a subversive touch of mischief. Chimpanzees are commonly thought of as the cool rebel or the intellectual comedian, whose jokes, while critical and dismissive of society, are tempered by the fact that the Chimpanzee seems to not take anything seriously.

They are the most likely type to play practical jokes, make sarcastic comments, and tell dirty stories under their breath during formal functions (yep, they're the coworker who always seems to slip inappropriate memes into that work email thread). Of course, there's more to this freewheeling persona than just entertainment, and just like their firebrand Shaman cousin the Baboon, Chimpanzees employ comedy as a Trojan horse, a device that persuades others to buy into their argument better than any serious debate would.

The Eccentric

Hell, if I could explain it to the average person, it wouldn't have been worth the Nobel Prize.

—Richard Feynman (quoted in Faber, 1985)

To the outside viewer, the mind of a Chimpanzee can seem like a hurricane of random thoughts (Can rotors induce flight? What are the benefits of nanotechnology? Where's the best barbecue joint west of Texas?), and in the eye of the storm sits the Chimpanzee, comprehending it all in real time. Unfortunately, what occurs inside the mind doesn't always manifest itself on the outside. Lacking the patience of the Spider and the Owl, both of whom seek to present their complex ideas in a digestible manner, Chimps, who might not even have a full grasp of their own concepts to begin with, blather on in a Holmesian stream of consciousness (Sherlock himself being a Chimpanzee) that would leave the most astute audience confused. Making matters worse, the Chimpanzee looks to address the lack of understanding not by distilling the information but by increasing the speed at which it's being communicated. In the end, an immature Chimpanzee arrogantly blames the audience's apparent ignorance.

In this manner, Chimpanzees, much like their Smith siblings, seek to remove themselves from the rest of the population; the possible exception here are the Killer Whales, who are totally fine interacting with other people as long as they have a certain degree of dominance over them. This potentially harmful behavior expresses itself differently with the other three. Whereas the Spider might slam the door on others and the Owl might just leave the room entirely, the Chimpanzee perches on the highest ledge of their ivory tower, sniping at those they deem intellectually inferior.

The Inventor

Oh Monty! How many times do you think the wings can fall off a plane?

—Gadget (Kimball, Zamboni, and Zaslove, 1989)

Despite all their charisma and energy, it's in the lab, studio, or whatever work-space they use where Chimpanzees feel most at home. If they could make only one wish, it would be to live a life devoted to inventing cool things. And not just inventing but also reinventing. Whether they're building a better chair or crafting a better beer, it's in the miniscule, specific adjustments made from model to model, from experiment to experiment, where the Chimpanzee gains a greater understanding of the world.

Now this process doesn't always go smoothly, and one could even say the very boldness and disregard for practical outcomes that makes Chimpanzees' revolutionary inventions possible can also lead to their undoing. History and literature are littered with the brutal, often fatal results of Chimpanzee inno-vation: the Hindenburg, Chernobyl, Frankenstein's monster. However, this only seems to highlight the risky nature of experimentation itself, a process not for cowards. Now imagining a world without airplanes, radio, remote control, or electricity? That's scary.

THE OWL

If a Humpback Whale is the old soul of personality types, then the Owl is just old. Now this might seem insulting, but to the information-obsessed Owl, advanced age, or at least the appearance of it, is believed to be a sign of wisdom. Every tuft of disheveled hair, every imaginary gray follicle, and every mismatched wardrobe accessory—all evidence of a life spent devoted to the pursuit of knowledge.

The Theorist

Be less curious about people and more curious about ideas.
                    —Marie Curie (quoted in Thomas and Thomas, 1954)

Owls have the unique ability to analyze complex theories with relative ease. This allows them to compress said theories into simpler, comprehensible threads, with which they weave a theoretical tapestry that is both accessible and beautiful. To achieve this, Owls frequently detach themselves from the material world, thus eliminating any distractions detrimental to their search for abstract truth.

To say that an Owl seeks knowledge would not be totally accurate, and the mere mention of knowledge causes many people to mistype themselves as Owls, or Smiths in general. A more appropriate statement would be to say that Owls prize information above all other things. This includes certain earthly desires that are viewed as automatic priorities for other types, such as family, friends, or material wealth and the security those things provide. This is often misinterpreted as a simple "Owls don't care about their loved ones." Nothing could be further from the truth. It's just their idea of caring is expressed more in the perpetual curiosity they have toward their spouse or child than in any kind of obligatory and—in their eyes—superficial show of affection expected of them due to their role as partner or parent.

The Pacifist

My pacifism is an instinctive feeling, a feeling that possesses me because the murder of men is disgusting.

–Albert Einstein (2013)

An Owl is not afraid of dying. In fact, their detachment from their corporeal self makes them reasonably accepting of death's inevitability. War, however, goes against everything they believe in. While other Smiths may believe in its ability to stimulate technological advancement through the creation of new weapons, an Owl might argue that history proves war often stymies intellectual progress (there's a reason the feudal period that took place before the Renaissance is referred to as the Dark Ages). Owls view war as nothing more than the destruction of property, the misappropriation of resources, and a complete waste of time. The fact that it commonly serves as a means and justification for expanding territorial lines they deem dubious to begin with (an Owl's disregard for intellectual boundaries frequently extends to political boundaries, as well) is even more sickening.

This same attitude can be seen in social settings, where the Owl usually acquiesces to avoid group dissension, even if the peace comes at the expense of the Owl's own enjoyment. While this acquiescence can make them appear weak and, for male Owls, strangely effeminate, the fact is they just don't put much stock into the validity of societal norms, including those related to gender roles. Aside from the obvious physical differences between genders, ones that can be clearly attributed to specific biological causes, Owls view much of the assumed distinctions between men and women as merely the product of social programming. For this reason, they are the most androgynous of all the types.

The Hermit

I had rather be shut up in a very modest cottage with my books, my family and a few old friends, dining on simple bacon, and letting the world roll on as it liked, than to occupy the most splendid post, which any human power can give.

—Thomas Jefferson (1788)

It's not surprising that Owls regularly set aside time to be alone. These reclusive respites give them an opportunity to recharge away from society's constant nagging. Unlike their fellow Smiths, who generally respond with feelings of utter contemptuousness toward anyone who dares to pressure them to conform, Owls, because of their pacifist tendencies, try to preempt arguments by avoiding belligerent people altogether. If left to their own devices, an Owl seeks the sanctuary of solitude to focus on their primary motivation: coming up with cool ideas.

Minimalists at heart, the freedom of an undisturbed and unfettered mind takes priority over material goods, most of which, Owls believe, lose value the further they venture from utility; an Owl might want a functioning car and clean clothes that fit, but don't be surprised if you see them driving up to your house in a beat-up 1995 Toyota Corolla wearing a random T-shirt, cargo shorts, and socks that don't match.

The Advisor

So, what's more likely: that an all-powerful, mysterious god created the universe and decided not to give any proof of his existence or that he simply doesn't exist at all and that we created him so that we wouldn't have to feel so small and alone?

—Ellie Arroway (Zemeckis, 1997)

Their ability to detach themselves and therefore keep a safe emotional distance from any situation is exactly what makes Owls fantastic advisors. They are big-picture people who pride themselves on their willingness to ignore small details and momentary concerns. While this may cause conflict with more grounded types, who might take offense to the notion that present-day moments and the people who fill them are expendable, Owls believe that it's this discipline that powers their originality of thought. And unlike the rapid-fire volley of ideas that constitutes the brainstorming session of a Chimpanzee—the Owl's closest Smith sibling—the Owl specializes in imagining a broad, singular vision of the future. Nowhere is this better displayed than in Jefferson's Declaration of Independence, a document that has influenced hundreds of similar documents—and, more importantly, governments—throughout the world.

An Owl's method of theorizing is far and away the most intuitive of all the Smiths. Whereas a Spider designs plans revolving around various contingencies, attempting to predict all foreseeable scenarios, an Owl enjoys the mystery of not knowing, as it enables them to take theories into previously unexplored territory and completely disregard tried and true methods, even those they would agree are pragmatically effective. It's no wonder their advice is so sought after; an Owl's awkward disconnect with the past and present best empowers them to dream of a more graceful future.

	How do I understand morality?	How do I express my creativity?	How do I serve humanity?	What is my flaw?
Killer Whales	The Cynical Pragmatist	The CEO	The Commander	The Dominator
Spiders	The Empiricist	The Contingency Planner	The Efficient Problem-Solver	The Reserved Contradiction
Chimpanzees	The Practical Jokester	The Inventor	The Troubleshooter	The Eccentric
Owls	The Pacifist	The Theorist	The Advisor	The Hermit

Figure 6.1 Smith Roles

CHAPTER SEVEN

FANTASTIC PEOPLE AND WHERE TO FIND THEM

A KISS BEFORE TYPING

Synergy. Back in college, I had a screenwriting professor who must've used that word, I kid you not, about a thousand times. It was his answer to everything:

"Is it wrong to use a montage here?"
"Does it have *synergy*?"

"Should I pop in a flashback?"
"Synergy?"

"Should I introduce my protagonist earlier?"
"Synergy."

"Moscow mule or an old-fashioned?"
"Synergy!"

After a while, he started sounding like one of those political flacks who show up on cable news to make sure both sides of an issue are represented and otherwise spend most of their airtime spouting very loosely related talking points. But I do understand the essence of what he was saying. The value of an individual part, in and of itself, depends on whether it contributes to the harmony of the whole. Understanding how all the details, great and small, interplay with the larger story—that was what he meant by synergy. Either that or he was auditioning for a job on CNN.

This same process is integral to typing someone's personality. We take a mixed bag of observations and insights and then find synergy with the story of the person's life. It takes time; practice; and, most of all, an understanding that any knowledge we gain is not the end of the journey but the beginning. Speaking of which, we have *finally* arrived at the portion of the book promised chapters ago: how to type someone. Feel free to treat the following chapters like a choose-your-own-adventure book where, after the initial introductory chapter—in this case, this one—you'll travel from page to page depending on wherever your typing adventure takes you.

Be prepared to blow a goodbye kiss to all the convoluted theories (I'm looking at you, function types) and fifty-plus-question tests designed to make us feel safe and certain (I mean, it must be accurate because we were assessed using a *test*). David Ben-Gurion, the first prime minister of Israel, once described Einstein as a "scientist who needs no laboratory, no equipment, no tools of any kind. . . . He just sits in an empty room with a pencil and a piece of paper and his brain" (quoted in Jordan, 1997). The *PoP* method is much the same way. All you need is your eyes and ears, a decent memory, and a brain that need not be remotely close to Einstein's in aptitude, and by the end of this chapter, I guarantee you'll have all the tools you need to determine whether someone is a Gatherer, Hunter, Shaman, or Smith.

Fair warning: This is a long chapter that might seem never-ending, the *Les Misérables*—the novel, not the musical—of chapters. I promise, though, by the end of it, you'll know how to find out which pack (Gatherer, Hunter, Shaman, or Smith) someone belongs to without the use of some dubious, cookie-cutter assessment. And in the spirit of *Les Misérables*—the musical, not the novel—there is even an intermission, a nod to both Broadway and small bladders.

As the curtains open, you must remember this rule: It's important *what* someone does, but it's even more important *why* they do it. Look for concrete, observable actions; then interpret them in an abstract way. You're probably thinking, "What the hell does 'interpret them in an abstract way' mean?" Essentially, I'm saying you can't always take what people do or say at face value. There's almost always something more to it hiding underneath the surface. I'd call it subtext, but that would give it an air of complexity that's not always the case; stupid people can be duplicitous, too. It's like when people tell you, "Have a nice day!" or "Keep your hair long. It looks awesome!" They don't *really* mean it. The former is just their way of being polite and spreading a nondiscerning, general cheer into the ether. The latter is just their way of surreptitiously making you look like your sister. Whatever the case, it's in this interpretation or bullshit-o-meter, whichever term you prefer, where most of the personality-typing work is done.

As for the person's actions and words themselves, it's best to examine them as a set of choices. It's not so much that a person chooses to do something as much as they choose it as opposed to doing something else. If we were to try to analyze the action purely by itself, it would be equal parts obscure and vulnerable to broad interpretation. For example, the fact that a person talks about starting a family doesn't particularly stand out, especially in a Gatherer world, where the idea of family reigns supreme. So how are we meant to interpret marital and parental inclinations without other priorities to compare them to? It's incredibly difficult to determine and understand distinguishing personality features without some kind of juxtaposition. Ever watch an NBA game on TV? Basketball players look average-sized—until you see them standing next to the ref.

There is an economic theory called revealed preference that asserts that the best way to determine the preferences of a consumer is to observe their choices when given a set of options (Tipoe, Adams, and Crawford, 2022). A person's choice to buy vanilla ice cream when there's no other option is not indicative of any preference, but if they choose it over chocolate, rocky road, and quarterback crunch? Revealed preference also allows room for deviation due to budgetary restraints: Hmmm, let me see, a four-dollar pint of Ben and Jerry's or the Safeway version for ninety-nine cents?

Personality typing is the same. We need to consider the potential for deviations caused by many of the things mentioned in chapter 2 (parental influence, immaturity, etc.), but all things being equal, the preferences a person reveals when choosing from a set of options inevitably leads us to their personality type. And for all those "open-minded" people who reflexively criticize the process as putting individuals into boxes, I refer them to their latest Google searches or their Netflix viewing activity or their Amazon browsing history as a reminder of how, every day, we put ourselves into boxes with each decision we make. There's a reason you keep getting pop-up ads for furry porn, and it's not because you've been buying Sesame Street socks (or maybe it's *because* you've been buying Sesame Street socks).

Let's go back to our personality-as-story metaphor. If we think about typing someone in the same vein as watching a movie, then we begin to see how each new scene builds the integrity of the story. The more information gathered about a person, the more rounded and defined they become. But it can be messy. Like a Tarantino or Iñárritu film, we're tasked with taking a jumble of scenes and precise yet fragmented details to derive an individual's story arc and, in the case of personality typing, their animal type. Sometimes, certain decisions a person makes can eliminate an animal type entirely from contention, like a scene ill fitted to a certain genre. Most of the time, however, each new bit of information merely adds to the larger narrative, either confirming what you originally thought or steering you toward another, albeit similar, animal type.

Warning: There will be some facts and observations that act as red herrings; just as it is with certain stories, individuals are more complex than they let on. There might also be misinformation; even fantastic films have bad scenes [e.g., that scene in *Pulp Fiction* when Bruce Willis goes down on his girlfriend (Tarantino, 1994). I get it. She's pregnant. Can we move on to the "Zed's dead" stuff already?]. But take heart. Overall, you'll find that, if you put in the work, most of your observations will match up, most stories will make sense, and a person's personality type will express itself so clearly and elegantly that you'll almost take its discovery for granted, as if you always knew it. In that way, everyone's story has synergy.

BREAKING DOWN A "SCENE"

Now that I've spent a lot of time going over the general philosophy of interpreting personality-typing information, I need to explain how to harvest that information. I know "harvesting information" sounds, at worst, like every dystopian sci-fi sentient machine nightmare and, at best, terribly inhuman in that Mark Zuckerberg, I-want-to-let-the-world-devour-itself-cuz-I-never-got-laid-in-college kind of way, but I assure you that the *PoP* method is as organic as your local farmer's market. And like a spoiled Californian—of which I include myself—you can reap its fruits all year long.

First things first, I'll need to introduce you to a couple of basic techniques that I've adopted from mentalists, fortune tellers, and clairvoyants, a professional class of which opinions range from admiration to dubiousness. Regardless of whether you believe they possess magical powers or think it's all one big con (granted, those two things aren't mutually exclusive), I think we can all agree that they have extremely powerful skills of perception and emotional intelligence, honed by years of experience reading into the hearts and minds of complete strangers. It only makes sense that we should adopt some of their methods as we attempt to do the same.

Basic terminology:

- **a read:** a piece of information obtained through various means
- **thin-slicing:** finding patterns of behavior based on narrow windows of experience and information, popularized in Malcolm Gladwell's (2007) *Blink: The Power of Thinking without Thinking*
- **a hot read:** information gained about someone before interacting with them, either through prior research or passive observation
- **a cold read:** information gained about someone while interacting with them, either through active observation or by their responses to specific questions or statements

The difference between a hot and cold read is pretty simple. I use online dating as an example. Let's say you're on Hinge looking for a date, and someone's thirst-trap pic catches your eye. A hot read would entail all the information you can thin-slice about said prospective partner from their profile: how they love cats and dogs equally, play the bass for a local prog-rock band, their likes, dislikes, interests, and hobbies—other than flexing in the perfect lighting of a half-naked selfie. A cold read would be when you meet them at your local Applebee's, and in response to a question about whether they think it's weird to eat French fries with mayonnaise, they proceed to go on a fifteen-minute rant about why the price of gas has skyrocketed the last few years.

Out of the two, cold reads require more skill, as you'll be in the line of fire and will need to adapt to the situation quickly. Hot reads, though, are far and away, the easiest potential source of information. It's like in the film *Léon: The Professional*, when Léon (played by the underrated Jean Reno), an assassin, tells his surrogate daughter (played by a young Natalie Portman) that, the closer you get to the target, the more skilled you need to be; the sniper rifle is the first thing you learn, and the knife is the last (Besson, 1994). One could imagine a less-proficient hitman—a B/C student in the professional-killing world—playing it safe and using a sniper rifle for the entirety of their career and not much harm being done (to them at least). Likewise, hot reads are the equal-access personality-typing tool used by people daily. In fact, I would bet a million dollars of the money I don't have to wager that you've already performed hundreds of thousands of hot reads in your life. Of course, experience doesn't always translate to skill (someone could make scrambled eggs the wrong way for their entire life). You'll need to hone your hot-reading skills. Once you do, you'll find that oftentimes they'll be all you need to type someone. Now for the obvious disclaimers (see figure 7.1).

I knew that button would come in handy. But seriously, a lot of these hot reads will not always fit. Just because a person's bossy like a Stag doesn't mean they're a Stag. And just because a person isn't bossy doesn't mean they're not a Stag. And there are plenty of traits that aren't listed here because, honestly, I probably forgot them. So don't take these things like they're some hard scientific theory or mathematical proof. There are no epistemic certainties. With personality typing, it's less "if . . . then" and more "if . . . then maybe?"

Figure 7.1 Big Ass Reminder

TRUST THE PROCESS

The first step to typing anyone is to find out in which pack they belong: Gatherer, Hunter, Shaman, or Smith. My initial guess is always Gatherer, and the reason is pure math. They make up around half the world's population, so my odds of being right without a shred of evidence are still at a respectable coin flip. Take it from me: Assume everyone is a Gatherer until they prove otherwise. When it comes to Hunters, that proof is not hard to find. Hunter traits don't introduce as much as announce themselves and are generally quite distinguishable from those of Gatherers. This makes Hunters some of the easiest people to type.

Think of a typical kindergarten class. Everyone knows that you always have half the class patiently sitting and listening to the teacher's instruction, while a third of the class fidgets, pokes other students, or possibly runs in circles around the classroom. Those are your Gatherers and Hunters in a thin slice. Of course, that leaves around 17 percent of the kids in a sort of personality no man's land, harder to type though clearly not in either the Gatherer or Hunter trench. These are your Shamans and Smiths, and as I've written many times, they frequently choose to hide. Because of this, their traits are less obvious at first glance.

I've met a few Gatherers and Hunters who dislike this setup. They think that describing their characteristics as transparent is the same as accusing them of being simple. I interpret said transparency as them being confident enough to show who they really are. Plus, Coco Chanel said, "Simplicity is the keynote of all true elegance," so take it as a compliment (quoted in *Bazaar*, 2017). You don't really want to lie in that anonymous grass on the other side, especially because Shamans and Smiths are commonly seen as awkward, less polished versions of their more populous, concrete cousins. Let's face it, Gatherers and Hunters, if it weren't for this book, you might not know Shamans and Smiths even existed at all.

So, the question remains, How do we find Shamans and Smiths? Not to sound all Taoist—especially because everything I know about the religion comes from reading the *Tao of Pooh* (yep, *that* Pooh; Hoff, 1982)—but the key to typing Shamans and Smiths is to try without trying. They'll eventually show themselves to you. If you observe certain people carefully enough, you'll begin to see them do things that seem, for lack of a better term, a bit off. I've already broken down the definition of *normal*, so I feel totally comfortable and nonjudgmental in saying that Shamans and Smiths frequently do things that are abnormal. For example, most people know that, when a woman asks you how her outfit looks, unless you're on her payroll—or maybe because you're on her payroll—you should always say, "It looks great." Or you can have a conversation like the one between a Smith friend of mine and his girlfriend:

GIRLFRIEND: How does this dress look?
SMITH: It makes you look fat.
GIRLFRIEND: What?!
SMITH: You asked me how you looked! I was just being honest.
GIRLFRIEND: By calling me fat?!
SMITH: Technically, I didn't say that. I said the dress made you look fat.

I think we can all guess how the rest of that conversation went.

First Impressions

First impressions are the cornerstone of hot reading. The directness and sparseness of their information is a boon, helping to prevent us from the overthinking that often occurs with too much information. No distractions, no rationalizations, no making excuses or bringing up obscure reasons why a person is the type you want them to be. It's like when Maya Angelou said, "When someone shows you who they are, believe them" (quoted in Winfrey, 2011). There's a certain purity when meeting someone for the first time. Even when they lie, it's with the pure, unadulterated amateurishness of someone who doesn't exactly know how to lie to you. And how could they? I think we sometimes forget that, when we meet someone for the first time, they're meeting us for the first time, too, which makes it difficult for them to adjust their personality to ours if that is their wont.

Think of it like being introduced to characters in a movie: Indiana Jones's thrilling boulder escape with a stolen artifact in his hands, Darth Vader choking out a rebel soldier as he lifts him off the ground with one arm, the underlying mistrust hidden in the friendly banter of the bank robbers in *Reservoir Dogs*. Whichever traits the filmmaker chooses to emphasize first are usually a good indicator of who the character is. The same is true in real life. First impressions have a way of crystallizing certain traits that can direct you toward a person's personality type. The next time you meet a person for the first time, notice what characteristics stand out the most. Once, when a friend brought up the topic of MBTI for the first time, and she declared that she was an INTP (the MBTI version of an Owl). I laughed almost instinctively:

ME (involuntarily smirking): You're not an Owl. You're a Peacock.

PEACOCK: You can't just say I'm not that! It's what I got on the test!

ME: The test is wrong.

PEACOCK: I've taken like two tests! They both said I was an INTP!

ME: Nope, pretty sure you're a Peacock.

PEACOCK: Why would you say that?!

ME: Cuz you're loud.

PEACOCK: I'M NOT LOUD! Okay, I'm loud. But there's more to me than that!

ME: I know. But your loudness is the easiest thing to notice. I can't say for sure whether you're a Peacock because there are other loud types, but I can definitely say you're not an Owl.

I was lying. With her bright, fluorescent wardrobe; flashy scarves and headwear; and love of dancing and partying—all hot-read information—I was absolutely sure she was a Peacock.

The following are some first impressions for each of the four packs.

Gatherer First Impressions

- Responsible
- Grounded
- Socially aware
- Embodiment of the Boy Scout Law (trustworthy, loyal, helpful, friendly, courteous, kind, obedient, cheerful, thrifty, brave, clean, reverent)
- Tough
- Realistic
- Respectful
- Might hold back what they're thinking or feeling
- Comfortable with formality and social etiquette
- Strong sense of authority
- Conservative

- Rigid
- Smothering
- Not particularly adventurous
- Hesitant
- Cautious
- Family: at a certain age they almost always are married and/or have kids; younger ones want to be married and/or have kids
- Has an overwhelming sense of "normal"
- Steady energy
- In social situations: focused on social standing (i.e., Are they acting the proper way?)
- Well-behaved students
- Views society like a custom-tailored jacket that fits perfectly, with a sense of certainty ("This is the way things are")

Hunter First Impressions

- Flighty
- Fun
- Spontaneous
- Counterculture
- Extremely open to trying new things
- Restless energy
- Expressive boredom
- Flashier wardrobe (especially women)
- Gravitates to tools and other concrete objects
- Reckless
- Competitive
- Prone to taking up physical challenges (bikes, skateboards, tricks, jumps, etc.)
- Consumptive
- Loves playing games
- Gets injured a lot (especially when they're young)
- Kinetic energy
- In social situations: focused on appearance (How do things look, sound, smell, etc.?)

- Kinesthetic learner as a student
- Views society like the jacket's too tight, and they're just waiting to take it off so they can dance around without tearing it, Chris Farley–style

Shaman First Impressions

- Sensitive
- Imaginative
- Daydreamers
- Impractical
- At worst, an idealogue
- Insecure
- Moody
- Hypersensitive
- Empathetic
- Might appear like they don't fit in
- Some might be in a crowd but look alone; others might be off to the side, literally alone
- Must fully believe in something to participate in it
- Views their actions as a representation of themselves
- Good listeners (especially when learning about people)
- Passionate
- Inner turmoil
- Spiritual energy
- In social situations: focused on how people in the room are feeling
- As a student, they favor subjects like the humanities, history, and art
- Views society like the jacket doesn't fit, and they're skeptical that it ever will

Smith First Impressions

- Might not be aware of or care about social etiquette
- Indifferent
- Calculating
- Analytical, always thinking
- Socially awkward: either quiet, abrasive, or arrogant
- Insensitive
- Might seem like they're on the spectrum

- Intelligent
- Knowledgeable
- Honest
- Reverent to the truth
- Objective, usually expressing opinions without bias
- Direct
- Easily disinterested in things they view to be superficial
- Not always concerned with physical appearance
- Cool energy
- In social situations: focused on fully understanding the ideas being discussed
- Hot and cold students: some are exceptional and ambitious; others are disinterested and rebellious
- Views society like a jacket that doesn't fit, but unlike Shamans, they're more skeptical of the jacket itself

WHAT DO YOU DO? DO YOU LIKE IT?

Technically speaking, hot reading doesn't generally include the asking of questions, which tends to fall under the purview of cold reading. However, we're not trying to be clairvoyants here, possessors of seemingly hidden knowledge; we're trying to personality-type people, so direct questions of the unintrusive variety still qualify as hot reads in my book—literally. And the number 1 question to ask a person when attempting to type them is "What do you do for a living, and do you enjoy it?"

In the right circumstances, an individual's occupation can be a perfect window into who they are. In many other cases, however, a job is just a job. It pays the rent and keeps the lights on, a means of survival more than a reflection of personality. It's like in Chris Rock's stand-up special *Kill the Messenger* when he joked, "Some people have jobs, some people have careers, and the people with careers need to shut the fuck up when you're around people with jobs" (Callner, 2008). Even for those with careers, we shouldn't always presume satisfaction. Some people choose their careers for financial reasons and, prophetically, find that the money isn't enough to buy happiness. Others find themselves cowing to familial pressure (*Dead Poets Society* déjà vu). And then there are some of us who find that, while our choices were well-meaning and entirely of our own volition, the careers we chose don't fit us as well as we thought—or hoped—they would.

For those who actually do enjoy their current profession, it's very likely that the requirements of their job match well with the skills and interests inherent within their personality type. However, there's quite a bit of overlap, as plenty of jobs are appealing to people from different packs. What distinguishes a person's type is not the job itself but what they like about it. These preferences tend to be explicit. What aspects do they prioritize? Are there certain areas they gravitate to? Are there certain areas they avoid? How do they play to their strengths and hide their weaknesses? Teaching and writing, for instance, draw individuals from all over the personality spectrum: Gatherers, Hunters, Shamans, and Smiths.

As Teachers . . .

- **Gatherers:** Dominate the elementary school level, where they enjoy the opportunity to create a safe space in which they can provide structure and teach students how to navigate society.
- **Hunters:** Commonly teach such subjects as art, PE, and trade skills (woodwork, metalwork, etc.), where they focus on the mastery of technique and craft.
- **Shamans:** Lean toward areas that focus on human development (social sciences, humanities, etc.), where they can use their interpersonal skills.
- **Smiths:** Frequently found at the university level, where they use their vast wealth of knowledge to stimulate the free exchange of ideas.

As Writers . . .

- **Gatherers:** Masters of society at large, they elucidate the intricate details, subtle manners, and unspoken rules that govern all societal systems (Austen, Updike, Clancy, etc.).
- **Hunters:** Sensation junkies, they favor lush imagery and visceral storytelling, regardless of whether they're describing a bull fight, listing their sexual exploits, or typing out a good old-fashioned crime noir (Hemingway, Pushkin, Sand, etc.).

- **Shamans:** Natural empaths, they delve into the inner workings of the soul, often choosing melancholic flights of fancy and elements of neurosis over exciting narratives or complex plot structure (Salinger, Tolstoy, Brontë sisters, etc.).
- **Smiths:** Theorists and skeptics, they examine ideas and conceptual structures in the search for truth; their stories are the abstract come alive (Rand, Orwell, Atwood, etc.).

SEVEN SKILLS

When it comes to how people behave in a work scenario, there are three traits that stand out above all the others:

- **Leadership:** What is their specific leadership focus?
- **Intelligence:** What is their intellectual advantage over another type?
- **State of being:** How do they perceive the world?

Each of these traits relies on a specific skill unique to a person's pack. Those three skills feed off each other, creating a foundation from which all the other skills derive. Appropriately, they create a triangle, illustrating how strong and vital these foundational skills are.

Whether you're a company employee, an independent contractor, or self-employed, there is a certain area of competence you rely on when you need to marshal resources to accomplish a task. This is true even in non-work-related activities. Take the Beatles, for instance. Each member had their own role within the band. George was its empathetic, spiritual core. John was the skeptic who analyzed world affairs. Paul was the craftsman who seemingly composed melodies out of thin air. And Ringo was the grounded guy who helped keep them all together. Or for those not yet at retirement age, there's always the Teenage Mutant Ninja Turtles: Leonardo (the organized leader), Michelangelo (the guy who throws himself into a fight), Raphael (the brooding emotional rebel), and Donatello (the scientist). Once you've discovered a person's foundational skills and organizational focus, it's easy to see how the remaining four subset skills relate. It's even easier when you have a diagram like figures 7.2–7.5.

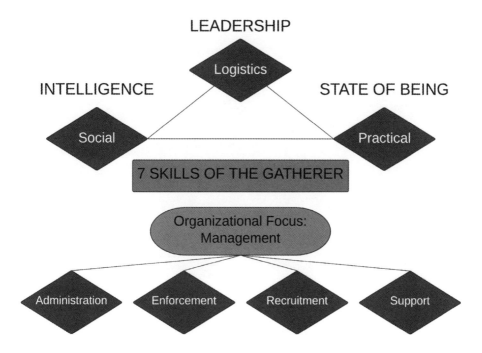

Figure 7.2 The Seven Skills of the Gatherer

The Seven Skills of the Gatherer

Foundational skills:

- **Logistics:** Masters of the supply chain, specializing in resources (acquisition, storage, transportation, and utilization)
- **Social intelligence:** Possessing tact, common sense, and a supreme knowledge of society's ins and outs
- **Practical:** Concerned with the actualities of a scenario; looking for concrete, feasible solutions to problems

Organizational skills (management focus):

- **Administration:** Directing and supervising daily operations
- **Enforcement:** Compelling compliance with rules and regulations
- **Recruitment:** Enlisting new members and aid
- **Support:** Ensuring proper upkeep and health maintenance

Figure 7.3 The Seven Skills of the Hunter

The Seven Skills of the Hunter

Foundational skills:

- **Tactics:** Virtuosos of the spontaneous maneuver, specializing in action, reaction, and putting out fires
- **Spatial intelligence:** Possessing the ability to visually manipulate objects in space along with enhanced recognition of fine details
- **Mindful:** Concerned with being in the moment, attuned to the present and not distracted by past regrets or future worries

Organizational skills (operations focus):

- **Promotion:** Marketing, sales, and networking
- **Advanced tool usage:** Applying practiced precision and technique
- **Performance:** Exhibiting concepts with grace and flair
- **Aesthetic design:** Composing beauty for all five senses

Figure 7.4 The Seven Skills of the Shaman

The Seven Skills of the Shaman

Foundational skills:

- **Diplomacy:** Natural mediators and counselors, specializing in bringing people together, either at the external social level or the internal emotional level
- **Emotional intelligence:** Possessing deep empathetic capabilities that enable them to see into the hearts and minds of individuals, even complete strangers
- **Empathetic:** Concerned with the emotional temperature of the room, constantly measuring the feelings of others and themselves

Organizational skills (HR focus):

- **Team building:** Coaching teamwork and self-improvement
- **Counseling:** Empowering individuals' emotional growth
- **Communication:** Championing and spreading ideals unequivocally
- **Healing morale:** Alleviating emotional and spiritual wounds

Figure 7.5 The Seven Skills of the Smith

The Seven Skills of the Smith

Foundational skills:

- **Strategy:** Thoughtful architects of the big picture, specializing in future projections and grand schemes over present, everyday concerns
- **Logical intelligence:** Possessing a logical prowess and adherence to reason that they use to break down complex ideas and systems
- **Objective:** Concerned with determining and examining abstract truth free from emotion and any other distractions of the concrete world

Organizational skills (analytics focus):

- **Executive coordination:** Marshalling forces toward a singular task
- **Organizational design:** Creating systems of efficiency
- **Product design:** Inventing new models, innovating old ones
- **Research:** Investigating for fresh concepts and conclusions

POSSIBLE OCCUPATIONS

A Stag friend of mine was talking about how he wasn't happy in his current job as an auditor. He said he hated waking up at some god-awful time, still dark outside, and driving for an hour on a traffic-infested 405 freeway just so he could cram himself into a 5 × 5 cubicle and crunch numbers for the remainder of the day. At the time, I was busy navigating the morass of building my education company, no small task for someone like me, who had no idea what I was doing. Even so, I cherished the hours; I got to wake up whenever I wanted. My friend was envious. He said he was considering starting his own CPA firm, to which I so elegantly exclaimed, "Dude, it's so awesome. You can wake up whenever you want, make your own hours, and buy a bunk bed so you can sleep on the top bunk!" Okay, maybe not the last part, but at the time, owning my own business sure made me feel giddy and free like Tom Hanks in *Big*. I even made sure to have one of my old Transformers toys, Shockwave ('80s kids know how *kewl* he was) on my desk at all times.

The reason I'm telling this story isn't to mock my immaturity back in the day (it's far easier to mock my immaturity in the *present* day) but to illustrate that, while our occupations may change, our personality types don't. My friend left to start his own business, and guess what? Instead of waking up at some god-awful time to sit in traffic on the way to cubicle hell, he woke up at some god-awful time so he could sweat through a daily exercise regimen *and* then work:

> ME: What was the point if you're just going to wake up at the same time?
> MY STAG FRIEND: Yeah, but now I have more time during the day to get stuff done.

I should've known. He's a Stag. Stags love waking up early "to get stuff done." A Stag wakes up; runs a mile; gets in early to the office; finishes all their work for the day at such a quick pace that they can leave early, guilt-free; shops for groceries; and then calls their friends to brag about how productive their day was. My friend might've gone from auditor to accountant, but he's still a Stag, and that organized, responsible, detail-oriented spirit translates to both professions.

Keep that in mind when you read the following lists of possible occupations. There are thousands of jobs that an animal type might enjoy. There are thousands of jobs that are not on any of the following lists. Don't curse me out at the top of your lungs just because your job isn't on there or because it's on another pack's list. Occupations are a generally low-risk, high-reward proposition when it comes to personality typing. Either they'll help you type someone in seconds, or they'll act as a mere footnote in a much longer story. Regardless, very little effort is needed to obtain the information—the beauty of a hot read.

Possible Occupations for Gatherers

- Education: teachers, administrators, aides, support staff (cafeteria, clerical, and janitorial)
- Finance: auditors, accountants, loan officers, financial advisors, actuaries
- Health care: doctors, pharmacists, nurses, office staff
- Military and law enforcement
- Supply-chain logistics
- Engineering, especially structural and mechanical engineers
- Law, specializing in contracts, regulations, and policy, usually working for a large firm or the government
- Government
- Religion: members of the clergy, worship leaders, support staff

Possible Occupations for Hunters

- Finance: stockbrokers, investment bankers, venture capitalists
- Entrepreneurial enterprise
- Professional trade: welders, carpenters, plumbers, masons
- Entertainment
- Artistic design: graphic designers, interior designers, industrial designers, photographers
- Culinary arts: chefs, pastry chefs, bartenders, sommeliers
- Marketing, promotion, and sales: salespeople, real estate agents, business brokers
- Service industry: hospitality managers, waitstaff, massage therapists
- Law, specializing in trial law and litigation

Possible Occupations for Shamans

- Education, usually preferring a more flexible curriculum, often education professors and counselors
- Academia, specifically in the humanities or social sciences
- Writers: novelists, screenwriters, long-suffering copywriters
- Mental health: therapists, counselors, social workers, psychiatrists
- Small business ownership
- Spiritual guidance: religious leaders, fortune tellers, motivational speakers
- Comedy, specializing in satire and stand-up comedy
- Nonprofit work
- Law, specializing in constitutional law

Possible Occupations for Smiths

- Tech sector: project managers, software designers, coders
- Academia, specifically in the sciences or mathematics
- Corporate: chief executive officers, operating officers, financial analysts
- Research and development
- Technical design: inventors, product testers, city planners
- Engineering, specializing in architecture and computer science
- Data science and analytics
- Law, often legal scholars and judges
- Government, specializing in policy creation

INTERMISSION

As promised! You have fifteen minutes to "hit the head" (as Gatherers are so fond of calling it), pop that popcorn, and uncork your best pinot noir. Curtains open promptly folks.

THE PEPSI CHALLENGE

For any kid who grew up in America in the '80s, the Pepsi challenge was a ubiquitous feature of malls, theme parks, and wherever else a large congregation of willing participants could be found. I have fond childhood memories of going to Wild Rivers, a water park located in Irvine, California, and between going down twisting slides that would make a personal injury attorney salivate and firing supersized water cannons at innocent inner-tube loungers, sidling up to the Pepsi challenge booth (basically a folding table and a high school kid whose only job responsibility was to pour and ask one question) to get my two free sips of soda and give my opinion on which one was better. As a rather talkative nine-year-old, I'm not sure which of the three appealed to me more. When it came to the taste test, I chose Pepsi every time. Little did I know that there was a trick.

Detailed in Malcolm Gladwell's (2007) book *Blink: The Power of Thinking without Thinking*, the purpose of the Pepsi challenge was to take advantage of an individual's first impression. Pepsi had discovered that tasters, when given a sip of two separate beverages, generally preferred the sweeter of the two (Pepsi). However, when given that same choice over the course of an entire can, tasters usually chose the less-sweet option (Coke).

Personality typing is the same. First impressions can be indicative of a person's animal type, but too often, we make final conclusions that are disproportionately weighted toward them. We need to give a person more time to reveal themselves. The fact that to this day I prefer Pepsi validates my initial first impression, but I still had to drink an entire can—thousands of them—to confirm this. And to be honest, I'm not sure *when* I was sure. Was it after the first can? Was it after the 440th? When exactly did I reach my caffeinated epiphany? Thankfully, I have a better memory when it comes to people. Later in this chapter, when I begin to use juxtaposition as a personality-typing technique, I go over specific times—"Pepsi challenge moments"—when the personality types of an individual I knew well (or in some circumstances barely knew at all) were crystallized for me. Kind of like the epiphany I had drinking Crystal Pepsi for the first time: "Wait, Pepsi and Coke are actually clear?!"

COLD READS

As a teacher working with kids on a one-on-one basis, the first thing you learn (aside from the fact that kids have no semblance of age—no matter how old you are, you're old) is that, the more questions you ask, the less likely they are to answer honestly. It's like you're interrogating a suspected felon; the more direct your approach, the more they clam up and smugly ask for their lawyer. (Of course, I'm an expert on police interrogations because I've watched a lot of *Law and Order*—at least all the Jill Hennessy episodes.) Adults can be cagey too, but unlike kids, most of us don't get a whole lot of attention anymore and, whether we care to admit it or not, are dying to answer questions about ourselves. Kids are usually so exhausted from having to deal with their prying parents that they have no desire to appease another nosy adult rummaging through the adolescent detritus in their head.

This is where cold reading comes in handy. It's a way of relaxing a person's defenses; they're far more likely to give away information as a response to an indirect stimulus than they would to a direct question. Cold reads are a subtle way to close the distance between you and the person you're trying to type, though they can be difficult to master (remember my fanboyish reference to *Léon: The Professional*—it's so much safer to use a sniper rifle than a knife). Whether the distance is physical or emotional, the closer you get to a person, the more vulnerable you both become. But like most things in life, if you want the truth, you can't be afraid of taking a few risks and getting your hands dirty. Think of cold reading like a sharp blade: If used correctly, it can cut deep down into the bone without the person feeling a thing. There are two cold reading techniques that, when slightly modified, can be used to great effect when personality typing.

Shotgunning

This is where the reader uses broad claims that can apply to a large majority of people to gain a "psychic" connection:

- "I'm sensing that you've lost a significant person from your life."
- "Your energy shows that you've had a recent conflict with an authority figure."

Statements like these can apply to most people most of the time (a recent break-up, a lost friendship, a death in the family, arguments with their parents or boss; Rowland, 2002).

In much the same way, we can use shotgun statements to read someone's personality. Talking about a topic that most people can connect to on a casual yet personal level is a useful method of eliciting a response. It could be an opinion, an observation, or even a joke, though it's most effective if delivered in a way where the true intent—getting information—is far from sight. My tried-and-true shotgunning method when working with students was making fun of my mom. Technically speaking, everyone has a mother, and savoring jokes at her expense (which, after being raised by a mischievous Chimpanzee father, isn't hard to do) is not only fun but also bound to get a reaction. The key is how to interpret the reaction for signs of personality type.

In my teaching experience, if a student seemed anxious or taken aback by the dig at my mother, then there was a strong likelihood that they were a Gatherer. Adult Gatherers, though, are more likely to respond with judgment than fear. Gatherers respect authority, so much so that they can't help but defend any mother under attack by an ungrateful, disrespectful son. Hunters, for the most part, have no problem laughing at a parent's expense—even if the joke isn't funny, the sheer audacity of it lights up a Hunter's limbic region like a Christmas tree. As with any imperfect but pleasantly surprising gift, it's the thought that counts. Shamans and Smiths generally react in a pensive, thoughtful way, though a Smith is more concerned with what information they can derive from the joke, while a Shaman's mind immediately wanders toward thoughts of the relationship they have with their own mom. Either way, the response of the other, non-Gatherer packs is not always consistent when it comes to this shotgun statement, so I treat any reaction different from the Gatherer response as a less-specific confirmation of the person's non-Gatherer status.

Barnum Statements

Barnum statements (a.k.a. the Forer effect, a.k.a. the personal-validation fallacy, a.k.a. the Pollyanna principle—I know, this cold-read technique has more aliases than Daenerys Targaryen—the Khaleesi effect—this name sounds so much better) is when the practitioner makes broad, complimentary claims about an individual that are often quickly confirmed as being true. The key, of course, is that the statements are, like shotgun statements, broad enough to be applicable to most people. The big difference here, however, is their complimentary nature. Barnum statements tend to work because people want to believe positive things about themselves, and as long as they don't stray too far from reality (e.g., stating that a painfully shy person excels at public speaking), an individual often goes to great lengths to fill in the blanks for you where they see fit (Dutton, 1988).

Mention leadership qualities, and they might hearken back to their days as student body vice president; allude to natural athletic talent, and they'll pull a Bundy (as in Al from the classic sitcom *Married with Children*) and regale you with the time they scored four touchdowns and led their high school football team to the city championship. To really sell the trick and assuage skepticism, you can use noncommittal words like *oftentimes* and *occasionally*, a technique that can even have the most out-of-shape person agreeing to your claims of their athletic talent and reminiscing about "that time I ran a 5K with a couple friends."

This is a common problem with most personality-typing systems (Enneagram, MBTI, etc.). Too many of the descriptions focus entirely on positive traits. The result is that people frequently mistype themselves as they fill in the blanks. Look, if you tell someone that they're a natural leader who has supreme powers of ingenuity, toughness, and flight and can shoot laser beams from their eyes, how do you think they're going to respond? "Oh no, I'm just an ordinary person with mediocre talent and mundane dreams"? However, there *is* a way that Barnum statements can be used to increase the accuracy of personality typing and not just for ego fluffing. Two ways, to be exact.

I call the first method the Costigan variant, after Leonardo DiCaprio's character in *The Departed*. Anyone who's seen the movie probably remembers the moment when Billy Costigan, interviewing for a job as a state trooper, is harshly interrogated by his would-be superiors. Hidden among the jibes and insults is a pertinent question (mentioned previously in this book): "Do you want to be a cop, or do you just want to pretend to be a cop?" (Scorsese, 2006). The implication is that many applicants want the power and authority of being a cop without understanding the seriousness of the responsibilities. They rightfully deduce that Billy doesn't have the stomach for law enforcement but instead possesses the intellect and complexity for undercover work.

The goal of the Costigan variant is to test a person's commitment to a trait, like having them dress in ill-fitting clothes and checking themselves out in the mirror. Case in point: I know an Owl who was trying to convince me that she could be a Chimpanzee. When I said that Chimpanzees are much more aggressive than Owls (think Tony Stark vs. Bruce Banner), she claimed that she, too, was aggressive. Instead of disagreeing, I tested her aggression in the form of a hypothetical: "If someone cut you off on the freeway, would you change lanes so that you could drive up beside them, honk your horn, flip them the bird, and then proceed to cut them off?" The horror on her face gave me her answer: not a Chimpanzee. As a side note, I don't know too many Chimpanzees who would do that, either, but the reaction from the mischievous Chimpanzee would be entirely different—they might scheme a better form of revenge—from the pacifist Owl.

As discussed earlier, individuals are quick to claim personality types based on a whole description, especially when it's positive. The Costigan variant isolates a singular trait of a type and uses an extreme scenario to test a person's commitment to that trait and, consequently, that type. Therefore, it works best when you suspect a person has mistyped themselves, and your goal is to eliminate that specific personality type from consideration.

The second method is negative confirmation or, perhaps an easier term to remember, the Idlewild variant, named after Outkast's 2006 album. *Idlewild* was, to put it generously, not a great album, especially following the mainstream success of *Speakerboxxx/The Love Below* and the pure awesomeness of *Stankonia*; even the greatest of groups can have a bad day. In fact, it's almost a scientific certainty that they will (okay, probably not a scientific certainty). Michael Jackson had *Michael*, the Beatles had *Yellow Submarine*, and even Fiona Apple had—no, wait—Fiona Apple has never had a bad album. Though you get the point. These things happen, and it makes more sense for an artist to accept the low points in their discography as part of the creative process instead of pretending like they never happened. In some cases, it's empowering to embrace it. The most ardent fans, channeling their inner "contrarian is cool" hipster, frequently hail those albums as the best (I admit, I do love Weezer's *Pinkerton*).

The Idlewild variant exists with this supposition in mind: If the average person is eager to take on *any* positive traits, as seen using typical Barnum statements, then the reverse can be said for negative traits; they shun them at all costs. However, like the musical artists mentioned previously, common sense and/or humility requires the average person to own up to at least a few negative traits. And just like it would be shocking to see Snoop Dogg take the blame for Kanye's *Jesus Is King*, most individuals are loathe to adopt someone else's weaknesses; if they're going to admit to flaws, then those flaws might as well be theirs. A Peacock, for example, is far more likely to accept the accusation of being an attention hog over that of being an anal-retentive rule follower. Likewise, a Beaver, but in reverse order.

More confident personalities, essentially ardent fans of themselves, embrace their inner Idlewilds. Case in point: I had previously written a series of satirical descriptions—featured in a later chapter in this book—detailing each personality type's deviant role, a glimpse into a type at their worst. One of my students, a mature, serious-minded Stag, insisted on reading her deviant role (spoiler alert: it's called the Fascist), and upon reading the line "putting you in charge of [the world] would make the planet a little closer to Nadia Comăneci and a little less like a society run by a motley crew of imbeciles, lechers, and weaklings," she laughed and exclaimed, "People *are* stupid, and it pisses me off when they don't listen to me!" That's the beauty of negative confirmation. Not only does it allow for a person to declare their type with their own words, but it also acts as a measuring stick for their maturity. The more developed we are, the more we realize that our strengths exist not in spite of our weaknesses but because of them; a Stag's youthful rigidity and bossiness often blossoms to forthrightness and strength. It's like when Nietzsche ([1886] 1998) said, "The great epochs of our life come when we gain the courage to rechristen our evil as what is best in us."

CONTEXTUAL JUXTAPOSITION

At this point, you should be able to roughly identify a person's pack based on initial impressions (observed traits, their job, and other hot-read-obtained info) and cold reads. For example, let's say you know a graphic designer who loves hiking in their free time, is passionate about Shibari (the ancient Japanese art of rope bondage), and belly laughs every time you tell your version of the barrel joke. All those initial signs scream Hunter. However, you want to be sure you're taking a nuanced approach to the final confirmation, and contextual juxtaposition enables you to do exactly that. It is a method based on revealed preference. You remember that economic theory I described what seems like ages of info dumps and random asides ago? Revealed preference involves choosing between a set of options: in this case, between two competing packs. You might think your graphic designer friend fills all the Hunter boxes, but what if, upon comparison, their traits bear a closer resemblance to a Smith? Their love of hiking could be fueled less by a desire to immerse themselves in the woods and more by a desire to catalogue the animals that reside in those woods. Perhaps it's not the sensation of the ropes but the psychological effect of being tied up that piques their fancy. And the barrel joke? It's just funny. Juxtaposition has a way of illuminating personality traits to the naked eye.

Gatherers versus Hunters

As an unapologetic enthusiast of '90s cinematic schlock, I wholeheartedly claim that the best portrayal of the difference between Gatherers and Hunters can be found in the opening scene of *First Knight*, a Merlin-less (i.e., drab) retelling of the Arthurian legend starring Sean Connery (Arthur), Julia Ormond (Guinevere), and Richard Gere (Lancelot). The scene features Lancelot, a vagabond with Van Halen locks and Zatoichi sword skills, dueling and besting overmatched challengers. When a defeated opponent asks him for the secrets of his skills, Lancelot imparts advice that seems easy enough to follow. But just as he has the polite fellow thinking, "Hey, I could get there someday," his last bit of advice slams the poor guy back down to earth like a German suplex off the top turnbuckle: "You cannot care whether you live or you die" (Zucker, 1995). Those words will get a Gatherer to freeze every time. And I know you know why.

Gatherers value safety and security above all else; why in the hell would they risk their life just to win a meaningless duel? For Hunters, however, it's the risk that makes the whole proposition worth doing in the first place. Their cardinal value, excitement, is predicated on the suspense of not knowing how things are going to turn out, making a victorious outcome even sweeter. Granted, the stakes are usually not life and death, but the instinct for risk taking remains the same. Safety and excitement: These two desires are polar opposites. It's no surprise that juxtaposing them is the easiest way to determine whether a person is a Gatherer or a Hunter.

Both Gatherers and Hunters respect tried and true methods; no matter how much mature Hunters push the boundaries of their craft, in their nascent stage, they stick to the fundamentals, very much adhering to the Nietzschean adage "He who would learn to fly one day must first learn to stand and walk and run and climb and dance; one cannot fly into flying" (Nietzsche, [1883] 1961). The big difference between Gatherer and Hunter methods of operation lies in the means in which those methods have been accepted. Gatherers tend to follow techniques that have been accepted by an acknowledged authority. Hunters follow techniques that have been adopted as accepted practice. Here's where we can use a shotgun statement to bring this distinction to light.

One that I've used many times is bringing up my method for cooking rice; cooking is as practical a skill as it gets, so it usually has broad appeal among the concrete types. I tell the prospective Gatherer or Hunter, "Making rice is easy. First, pour the water. Then, stick your index finger in so that the tip is barely touching the rice. The water level should reach your first knuckle." Here are the usual responses to my shotgun statement:

Gatherers:

- "What?! How is that even a measurement?"
- "Google says we should do two cups of water for every cup of rice."
- "Who told you to do it that way? What are their qualifications?"

Hunters:

- "Ooh, let me try it!"
- "Cool."
- "Duh. I do that all the time."

This one time, I was cooking with two Gatherer friends, and of course, when it came time to make the rice, I used the finger technique. They were flabbergasted. One of them almost snatched the pot from my hands. "We need to measure it!" The only way I was able to assuage their fear of a poorly cooked pot of rice was to assure them that I saw celebrity chef Ming Tsai use the technique all the time, and he owned an entire restaurant, had French training, went to Yale, and everything. I had a similar experience when talking about barbecuing brisket. One friend, a Beaver, to be exact, was discussing his measured method of cooking ribs (using a meat thermometer), and he asked me at what temperature did I know the brisket was finished. I said, "I don't use a thermometer. I just lift it, and if it jiggles, it's probably done." The look on his face was skepticism dosed with spite. It was like I had told him he was adopted.

Another concrete topic that's useful for juxtaposition: sports. Gatherers frequently identify with the grinder athletes, the players who pride themselves on toughness, willpower, and doing all the little things—the thankless sacrifices for the team—that the average fan can't see. In football, for example, these types of players are often offensive linemen (protecting the quarterback and creating holes for the running back with little fanfare), the defensive tackles (taking on double-team blocks in the trenches), or the running back (fighting for those hard 4th-and-1 goal-line yards and popping blitzers). Hunters, though, tend to relate to the dynamic athletes, skilled players with explosive speed and power: the flashy receivers and cornerbacks or the physical freaks of nature at linebacker and defensive end.

You were probably reading that last paragraph and thinking one of two thoughts: "I hate sports and don't get what any of these things mean" or "So wait, just because I'm a Gatherer, I'm standing around with all the fat guys while the Hunters look like Adonis?" If it's the first thought, then you're really not going to get what I say next. If it's the second thought, I would say two things:

1. I would never call a man who's 6'6" and 350 pounds and who can run forty yards in five seconds "fat," especially not to his face.
2. I would remind you that, when it comes to athletic respect, money talks, and that the three highest-paid positions in professional football are quarterback (all types like quarterbacks), offensive line (more specifically offensive tackle), and defensive end (guy who hits the quarterback). Gatherers and Hunters are both getting paid well.

Speaking of money, that's another area where you can tell Gatherers and Hunters apart. First off, they both tend to enjoy handling money but in different manners. Hunters are 700 percent (exact figure, of course) more likely to talk about personal finances than Gatherers. They love the humble brag, the flex, the not-so-humble brag, and the posing-in-an-exotic-location-on-a-vacation-I-may-or-may-not-be-able-to-afford Instagram standby. Gatherers love the authority that comes with being the person "responsible for the money"; they love being the bank when playing *Monopoly*. Mature Gatherers prefer to treat their financial heft like they're George Foreman. They may smile politely and hawk grills that purportedly make a healthy burger (oxymoron?), but they're a knockout artist at heart, and if you dance and preen too much in front of them, they've got a right cross (in this case, a substantial net worth) just waiting to send you to the canvas.

The best descriptor for Gatherer financial planning is prudent. For a Hunter, it's shrewd. Both try to diversify their portfolio, spreading their investment risk across multiple financial sectors and assets, but Hunters favor a more risk-taking approach (growth stocks), while the Gatherer plan is more risk averse (dividend-yielding bluebloods). Think of it like the buy-and-sell, timing-the-market, stock-options, and short-selling tactics of a day trader versus the long-term, find-a-solid-company-and-hold-it approach of Warren Buffett. Both can be effective or ineffective, depending on the maturity and skill of the individual.

Pepsi Challenge Moment

This was a situation where first impressions seemed to be in conflict, and a simple, direct follow-up question—not even a cold read—was all the clarification needed. I was attending a friend's birthday dinner where the topic of personality types came up (I swear it wasn't me). Someone whom I had never met jumped into the conversation and insisted that I type her. It just so happened that, at that moment, we were finishing up dinner and moving on to the escape room we had reserved, so I told her to give me some time and I would type her later.

Fast-forward to the escape room; there we were, standing in a dark hallway waiting to be led into a mysterious room in which we'd be trapped for an hour like lab rats, and she came up to me again, "So have you typed me yet?" On the inside I was thinking, "Damn she's pushy," but on the outside, I relented:

Me: What do you do for a living?
Her: I own an interior design company.

Based on her job, the natural first impression of her pack, which if you read the first half of this Hugo-esque chapter should be easy to determine (I'll give you a few seconds before reading on) . . .

. . . was that she was a Hunter. More specifically, a Butterfly, given that Butterflies are the kings and queens of conceptualizing visual and spatial beauty. However, Butterflies aren't usually that aggressive or pushy, and this woman was *determined* to get the information she wanted. So, I asked a follow-up:

Me: What do you like more about your job: the design itself or running the business—you know, telling people what to do?
Her: Oh, definitely telling people what to do.

And just like that, I had a clearly delineated revealed preference. She gravitated to the supervisory role. She was blunt, aggressive, and confident when it came to reaching her objectives. She wasn't a Butterfly. She wasn't even a Hunter. She was a Stag (a Gatherer, but you should know that by now)!

Gatherers versus Shamans

One of the useful things about owning an education company at twenty-seven is that, aside from it showing you how little you really know about running anything, it brings the conflict between Gatherers and Shamans front and center. A system of education is conceptually the perfect convergence of the Gatherer desire for safety and the Shaman desire for self-knowledge, and as such, teaching is teeming with individuals from those two packs. And trust me, they don't always get along. There are huge philosophical disagreements between the two, and being a youngish business owner situated in the education field gave me a not-so-small taste (more like an entire meal, if you ask me) of the two main conflicts at the heart of the matter:

1. tradition versus intuition
2. practical versus shamanic

My company performed a lot of contractual work for public school districts, which involved attending various meetings and functions where I interacted with teachers, parents, district administrators, and other education providers (i.e., the competition). I cannot tell you the number of times I was mistaken for either a college student and/or a clerical representative of the company I owned. When it came to the signing of the actual business contract, district employees commonly gave me a look of dubiousness and frustration, as if they were already mentally preparing to reprint the contract for the person who was actually authorized to sign it. "This is for the *owner* to sign," I was told a few times. This is a great example of the Gatherer influence—or more accurately, dominance—of the education system.

Gatherers respect tradition, a value that engenders an almost automatic deference to older individuals (I'll use a more generous term and say "experienced") in the education system. The more experienced one is, the more reliable they're presumed to be, the more likely to uphold traditional methods and less likely to take unnecessary risks when educating the future of civilization. As someone who looked (another generous interpretation) like the high school kid who always sat in the back of class and cracked jokes at the teacher's expense, it was unfathomable for some district employees that I could oversee a company responsible for teaching hundreds of students a year. Shamans, though, view some of the traditional goals of education and, by extension society, with deep skepticism, as when James Baldwin (1963) remarked, "The paradox of education is precisely this—that as one begins to become conscious one begins to examine the society in which he is being educated." This often causes Shamans to buck norms and ignore rules to gain, in their minds, a greater achievement: a deeper connection with their students. Besides making a Shaman a walking lawsuit waiting to happen, this interpersonal touch enables them to rely more on their intuition when it comes to figuring out the best way to help their students grow.

Dead Poets Society is a film that perfectly exemplifies this difference in philosophy. However, it's clearly biased toward the Shaman perspective (which is why it is heavily mentioned in the Shaman chapter of this book). A good portion of the film's sympathetic leads are Shamans, and the film itself generally portrays the Gatherer characters as being obtuse, cynical authoritarians. But if we choose to use the film as a long-form sort of shotgun statement, much can be revealed by the results. Shamans *love* it, full stop. I've never met a Shaman in my life who didn't, and I've met more than the demographics would suggest. Education, personality typing, and writing are catnip to Shamans; they bring them out in droves. Gatherers tend to view the film like they do most films that challenge the education system (pointing at you *School of Rock*): with a mixture of bemusement and skepticism. Entertaining, maybe even inspiring, but not to be taken with any bit of seriousness.

This is not to say that Gatherers don't hate how they're frequently portrayed. Always playing the hard-ass can't be much fun. But if you look past the biased characterization, there is a truth that can't be ignored. When Mr. Nolan, the principal in *Dead Poets Society*, brags, "Last year we graduated fifty-one [students], and more than 75 percent of those went on to the Ivy League," its purpose is to introduce the school as a setting for cloistered and stilted elitism (Weir, 1989). But reading the statement by itself, it sounds much like the brochure of any education program, private or public, trying to appeal to new students. What parent in the world wouldn't find it enticing to send their child to a school that sends three-quarters of its graduating class to the likes of Harvard and Yale?

Contrary to popular opinion, not all Gatherers are paternal taskmasters and tiger moms; mostly they just view school as a way for their children to become better citizens. Some drive their kids hard, but most just want them to be "good kids." I found this to be the most common term that Gatherer parents would use to describe their child in my tutoring company's customary preprogram interview. Gatherer teachers, while using the grading system as a means of control, are usually more concerned with ensuring that their students are acclimated to the practical requirements of society and life in general than they are about academic achievement. They're realists at heart; they'll push the students whom they view as having superior talent, but for the majority of students, it's about teaching them how to eventually feed and clothe themselves and become productive members of society.

Shaman teachers tend to focus on more abstract goals, like self-worth and identity, and they view their role as fundamentally a guardrail against their students falling into, as Thoreau (1854) put it, "lives of quiet desperation." If it was up to them (it often isn't), the primary approach to teaching would be holistic in nature. But much like the Montessori method, this sounds good in theory (it's not a surprise that a good deal of education professors are Shamans) but is difficult to apply, as most administrators, school board members, parents, and other decision makers are Gatherers who favor the traditional approach.

Sometimes distinguishing between Gatherers and Shamans can be tricky; as mentioned earlier, immature Shamans try to assimilate into Gatherer society by painfully swallowing some of their values. However, you'll be happy to know that we have our own version of a stomach pump: a Barnum statement, Costigan style. The moment you suspect you might be talking to a Shaman in Gatherer clothing, throw some Gatherer red meat out into the conversation (marriage, weddings, family gossip, career details, etc.), and then pay close attention. If they're a Gatherer, they won't just eat it up; they'll devour it like a vegan in a tub of hummus. If the person is a Shaman in hiding, you should be able to sense a certain feeling of doubt or internal conflict, kind of like when someone tries to convince you they're into smooth jazz—*no one is into smooth jazz*. They might become visibly uncomfortable; their tone of voice might lose confidence; their opinions might become less like them and more like a Hallmark card, impersonal and so very, very standard.

Pepsi Challenge Moment

Sometimes first impressions can conflict; then there are those moments when the person we're trying to type is in active conflict with the first impressions they're giving off. I was at a bar a few years ago, discussing personality types with a Dolphin whom I knew reasonably well. Another person, whom I didn't know as well but from limited information I guessed to be a Beaver, walked over to us and wanted to know what we were talking about. When the Dolphin mentioned personality typing, the Beaver looked at me with skepticism. Beavers often dislike personality theory, feeling that the process puts people into boxes (ironic, given their preternatural talent for categorizing, organizing, and *literally* putting things into boxes). Despite his visible irritation, he joined the conversation anyway. To be honest, I think he was pretty interested in knowing about my Dolphin friend (not personality wise, but in the biblical sense, if you know what I mean) and thus tried his best to participate so that he could stay in the conversation:

DOLPHIN: Ooh, what do you think he is?
ME: Hmmm, he seems like a Beaver.
BEAVER (perturbed): What's a Beaver supposed to be like?
ME: Responsible, organized, conscientious, cautious—
DOLPHIN: That's definitely you!
BEAVER: That's not me. I take risks.

At this point, my friend and I sensed that he was a bit chafed by the description, so we changed the subject. We didn't know him well, but on first impressions alone, it was pretty clear to us that risk taking was not part of his natural modus operandi. He was probably thinking, "This guy doesn't know me," or "Get a load of this presumptuous asshole," and he was correct on both accounts. I didn't know him, and more often than not, I am a presumptuous asshole, but presumption is the nature of personality typing. You listen to your first instincts and then lie in wait for the moment when they're either confirmed or proven false. Lucky for me, I didn't have to wait long.

The topic of conversation had shifted to traveling. The Dolphin was an avid traveler (as many Dolphins are), and the Beaver, who was born in another country and had done an ample amount of traveling himself, was ecstatic to be talking about something where he felt he was on equal footing. He assumed their perspectives on traveling were aligned. They weren't. The Dolphin, in her self-actualizing Shaman kind of way, was considering living in Turkey for a year or two, a country she had never been to before. The Beaver's auto-response: "You can't do that! That's too dangerous!" It wasn't just the rapidity of the comment that caught us off-guard—the words were barely out of her mouth before he issued his edict—it was the certainty, directed at someone he barely knew. That was as good a confirmation as any.

I knew nothing about whatever risk-taking endeavors he might have in his past. What I did know, however, was that when introduced to a scenario with a degree of risk, his reflex was a Gatherer one: cautious, commanding, and vigilant. Remember, it's not what we do but why we do it that reveals our type. He could've spent time as a deep-sea fisherman or a firefighter or even served for a few years in the Marines defusing bombs in the fields of Afghanistan, and it wouldn't change the fact that his primary priority was safety. And I know you might be thinking, "No way those bad-ass dudes from *The Hurt Locker* are safety-first!" Yep, even them. *Especially* them. I mean, they turn weapons of undifferentiated destruction into harmless science fair projects. I actually know a guy who did exactly that. And guess what? He's a Beaver, too.

Gatherers versus Smiths

There's a scene in the movie *Blade* [for the comic-book-film uninitiated, it was a Wesley Snipes–starring vampire flick whose sequel Roger Ebert (2002) aptly described as a "vomitorium of viscera"], where Blade, our half-human, half-vampire protagonist whose mission is to hunt vampires to extinction, is described by the vampire antagonist as having "all our strengths, none of our weaknesses" (Norrington, 1998). And that's a perfect description of the Gatherer-Smith relationship, at least from the Gatherer perspective. As mentioned in an earlier chapter, there's a certain cross-section of the Gatherer population who misidentifies itself as having most of the Smith strengths (logical analysis, objectivity, ingenuity) while possessing none of their weaknesses (lack of interpersonal awareness, dispassion, social awkwardness). Another cross-section of Gatherers doubts the existence of Smiths entirely; a Gatherer once came up to me after one of my personality-typing workshops and asked, "Is the Smith type for real, or did someone just come up with it to give people an excuse for being assholes?" Like Blade, this incredulity can't help but cut a path toward Smiths' social extinction.

From the Smith perspective, the relationship is easier to understand: Smiths hate Gatherers. I know, I know, my second-grade teacher always used to say, "*Hate* is a very strong word and should be used sparingly" (though I still protest it's fair game for a seven-year-old to *hate* Brussels sprouts). However, in deference and appreciation to Ms. Cheng, one of my favorite teachers,

I phrase it more judiciously: Smiths spend their lives ignoring authority; Gatherers spend their lives instilling it. Resentment is baked in the cake.

Now that you've been properly comic-book-film-initiated—thank you Wesley Snipes—it behooves me to bring up a scene from Marvel's *The Avengers*, as it vividly portrays this conflict between Gatherers and Smiths. In this scene, Captain America (supersoldier, uberpatriot, embodiment of "American" values) gets into a heated argument with Tony Stark (in his own words, "genius, billionaire, playboy, philanthropist"). You don't have to be a personality-typing virtuoso to figure out Cap is a Gatherer; I mean, his "weapon" is a *shield*. And Stark, with his tech bona fides and disdain for authority, is pretty obviously a Smith (fun fact: Robert Downey Jr. based his portrayal of the character on a real-life Smith, Elon Musk—most likely a Chimpanzee). Their argument centers around this exchange:

> CAPTAIN AMERICA: The only thing you really fight for is yourself. You're not the guy to make the sacrifice play, to lay down on a wire and let the other guy crawl over you.
>
> TONY STARK: I think I would just cut the wire. (Whedon, 2012)

There's a clear distinction here between the values of Gatherers (courage and self-sacrifice) and Smiths (cleverness and problem solving), and it's only natural for people to pick a side. If you're trying to type someone and you're deciding between a Gatherer or a Smith, this scene can act like a Barnum statement; whichever side of the argument they lean toward is a good indicator of their pack.

A useful shotgunning topic when distinguishing between these two types is anything pertaining to the attainment of knowledge. Both value it but for different reasons. Gatherers want information because they believe it gives them a certain status—and moments after writing that, my ears are already ringing with the screams of Gatherers cursing me out for the insinuation that their quest for knowledge is anything but noble. And I get the anger, but that's not exactly what I said. The word *status* itself implies nobility, and in the world we live, the most practical method of reaching that nobility is by earning a degree, accreditation, license, or some other means in which society formally declares that you're not some poseur or deadbeat. Smiths, for the most part, want information because they think it's fun or because they think it gives them power, which, for specific Smiths, is pretty much the same thing as fun. A friend of mine who's an Owl hates that Owls are always stereo-typed as being geniuses (okay, maybe he doesn't hate that as much as being stereotyped as the virginal hermit who's unaware of their surroundings most of the time). He's fond of saying, "I just like to know stuff, but it doesn't mean that the information is important or that I'm smart. I know a lot about three things: massage, Air Jordans, and fantasy football. Pretty sure that doesn't make me a genius."

I've already referred to an example that can act as a Costigan variant for Gatherers versus Smiths: the question of whether a person would be willing to experiment on themselves to learn more about a drug. The proper phrasing—hyperbole being essential—would be "Let's say there's a drug that could theoretically unlock your brain's potential, but it could have dangerous side effects. If there was no other option, would you test it on yourself?" As with most Costigan variants, the interpretation of their response is just as im-portant as their answer. Did they pause to think about it? Was their reply as immediate as a Beaver being told of plans to move to Turkey? I recently dis-covered another version of this hypothetical when talking to an Owl friend. She told me she would be more than willing to go into a burning library to save the last surviving copy of a book. Either version you use, I think the set of revealed preferences is clear: safety or information.

As it relates to the things we can see, Gatherer and Smith differences are fairly transparent. Most Smiths possess an unintentionally cold veneer, not so much a purposeful poker face as much as an overwhelming feeling of ob-jectivity. Compared to this, even the toughest of Gatherers can appear warm. And the softer Gatherers? They're like oversized teddy bears. The two packs also have vastly divergent social profiles. In social situations, Smiths can fre-quently do things that, at worst, are offensive and unsettling and, at best, surprising and out of the ordinary. People commonly assume that they're somewhere on the spectrum. I was talking to the mother of a Smith student, and she both praised and lamented his brutal honesty: "When a mother asks her son how she looks, he's not supposed to say, 'You look terrible.' I love that he's honest, but could he do it in a way that didn't make me want to slap him?" Gatherers, as I've stated many times, have a natural comfort in social situations. Even if they're not commanding the room, mature Gatherers leave very little doubt that they belong there.

Gatherer-Smith interaction is not that common. Percentagewise, there are only a few Smiths to begin with, and considering the strong disagreements the two packs have on essential values, they're not exactly flocking to socialize with one another. For that reason, the most common place to see Gatherers and Smiths interact is at work, where neither type gets a choice. Despite their differences, Gatherers and Smiths frequently share the same objective (occupational success), and for the most part, if both types can avoid talking about their personal thoughts and opinions, Gatherer-Smith work relationships tend to run smoothly. Still, specific fissures can emerge, the most common being practicality versus logic.

I can't tell you how many times I've had to explain the difference between being practical and being logical. It's as if everybody met some smart person in their past who was both practical and logical, and because of that they started conflating the two as interchangeable descriptors for intelligence. Suffice to say, they mean entirely different things, and we can use this distinction to separate Gatherers and Smiths.

The shotgun statement I like to use is bringing up an excerpt from Australian philosopher Peter Singer's (1979) *Practical Ethics* (obviously a riveting dinner-conversation topic) where he writes that parents should be able to euthanize newborn babies if it's discovered they carry genetic markers for severe disabilities. The Gatherer response to this is generally quick and severe. They believe that, in theory, it's monstrous and, in practice, well, being an intellectual bedfellow of the Nazis usually doesn't lead to a good night's sleep. The Smith response is more nuanced. Even if they disagree with Singer, they're far more open to his utilitarian argument that "newborn human babies have no sense of their own existence over time" and that euthanizing a newborn destined to have a debilitating and, most likely, painful disability for the rest of their life is not only merciful but also a more efficient use of the parents' love, essentially saving it for another child who could possibly have a longer, less-excruciating life.

Pepsi Challenge Moment

Gatherers love to point out the numerous times I pick on them for making assumptions about other types, which is invariably true: They make a lot of assumptions about other types. All jokes aside, the truth is we all do. Sometimes these assumptions—especially from parents—can lead to detrimental effects on our emotional growth and feelings of self-worth. Other times, they're just funny and revealing about who we are as people.

A very close friend of mine is a Killer Whale (Smith), and this one time, we were spending a comfortable Sunday at her beachfront apartment, when she said that her boss needed to talk to her:

ME: On a Sunday?
KILLER WHALE: It's this crazy project we're working on.
ME: And he wants an in-person work meeting? At the beach?
KILLER WHALE: It's easier to discuss things in person. Plus, he might not want to have our conversation documented.

My friend has a stereotypical Killer Whale job—project manager at a major tech company—and from what she told me of her boss (hardworking, friendly, family man), I guessed he was a Gatherer. In my mind, the odds were slim to none that he would be spending his Sunday afternoon in an intense work meeting. Regardless, I got to preparing dinner, and my friend went off for her meeting, saying she'd be back in an hour or so. She was back in ten minutes, perturbed. "He was just taking his kids to the beach and thought it'd be cool for me to meet them! Like, why? I thought we were going to discuss work—stop laughing! Seriously, stop laughing, or I'll stab you in the face!"

Gatherer versus Smith is not as simple as family versus work. Plenty of Gatherers are hyperfocused, career-oriented professionals, and plenty of Smiths are loving, conscientious parents. It's more of a mindset. Gatherers view work success as a means of attaining status and security; Smiths view it as a demonstration of their substantial knowledge base. Gatherers view their children as an extension of themselves, whom they must keep safe. Smiths view them as special curiosities to be studied and then interacted with accordingly. While my Smith friend could appreciate the fact that her boss's family was important to him, they weren't necessarily important to her; the notion of meeting kids she'd probably never see again wasn't exactly exciting for the utilitarian Killer Whale. For the Gatherer, his kids were the main reason he worked so hard in the first place, so it's only natural he'd enjoy his Sunday with them and introduce them to a coworker if given the chance.

Hunters versus Shamans

There's no fight that's more pompous, more performative, or more unlikely to lead to actual punches thrown than a literary feud. Less mano a mano and more *chisme y más chisme*, when literary titans brawl, expect opinions to be sharp, compliments to be backhanded, and gossip to be on a constant stream, all mustered up with equal amounts of self-importance and self-loathing. And that's the matchup we have here today for your reading pleasure: poet versus poet; Lord Byron versus John Keats; Hunter versus Shaman.

The feud between Byron and Keats was based on a variety of factors. Byron was a tall, handsome aristocrat; Keats was a short, sickly, doctor-turned-struggling-poet. Byron's aesthetic based itself on the Augustan tradition (early-eighteenth-century classicism), favoring classical style and form; Keats's aesthetic rejected the Augustans, favoring authenticity and emotions, a style that would usher in the Romantic Era. Byron idolized Alexander Pope, the presiding GOAT of the Augustan Age; Keats hated Pope and critiqued him vociferously. And perhaps, most importantly, Byron was successful; Keats was not (Hanson 2015). Looking at these facts as a matter of history, it would be easy to ignore personality type altogether and assume that their feud was primarily influenced by differences in social standing, artistic preference, and professional success. But let's take a closer look, shall we.

Lord Byron was known for his flamboyance and wit, and he used both, along with his ancestral title, to enter the elite circles of English society. Yes, Byron was the one born with a silver spoon in his mouth, but it was these Hunter traits (self-promotion, charm, social dexterity) that made Keats, a man of lesser means, gag; Keats once commented after reading a favorable review of Byron, "You see what it is to be six foot tall and a lord!" (quoted in Hanson, 2015). Not only was Byron the talk of the town, but he also knew how to get people to keep talking; here was a man who clearly loved his own celebrity. Keats was the perpetual Shaman outsider. Critics often savaged his work; reviews of Keats's *Endymion* were so severe that they were, in all earnestness, considered to be the cause of his untimely death at twenty-five (tuberculosis was the actual culprit). If they were around today, Byron would be Taylor Swift (popular, photogenic, a closet full of awards) to Keats's Eva Cassidy (my second Eva Cassidy reference, so if you haven't Googled her, do it *now*). Not that Swift and Cassidy are feuding (kind of impossible considering Cassidy's tragically premature death in 1996 at the age of thirty-three, which you'd already know if you Googled her like I told you to), but both artists' careers share similar cultural dynamics to Byron and Keats: mainstream success versus posthumous reverence.

Even the poets' artistic styles demonstrate Hunter-versus-Shaman distinctions:

- Byron representing a Hunter's mastery of craft (technique, form, and function)
- Keats representing a Shaman's affinity toward personal authenticity (high feeling, candidness, and imagination)

At the end of the day, anyone with internet access and a pulse can read up on both men and proclaim, "Keats was just jealous of Byron's accomplishments!" But when you start really understanding the differences between Hunters and Shamans, you come to understand that these two highly passionate, creative individuals were inspired by separate muses. Like most Hunters, Byron was concerned with pleasing his audience with his best possible performance, viewing Keats's disregard for popular norms as a mixture of amateurishness and self-importance. The Shaman in Keats, however, was fueled by a devotion to principle, in this case his belief that the current classical Augustan style, as best personified by the superstar Byron, was unoriginal, overrated artifice. In their own words:

> BYRON ON KEATS: He himself, before his death, is said to have been persuaded that he had not taken the right line and was re-forming his style upon the more classical models of language ([1821] 1833).
> KEATS ON BYRON: There is this great difference between us. He describes what he sees—I describe what I imagine—Mine is the hardest task (1819).

The feud between Byron and Keats also exemplifies one of the major contrasts between Hunters and Shamans: the visceral versus the intuitive. Both packs seek pleasure—or at least what's commonly viewed as pleasure—more than Gatherers and Smiths, but for Hunters, that pleasure is usually derived from something they can access with one or more of their five senses: the gliding strokes of a massage, the sweeping arpeggios of *Stairway to Heaven*, the olfactory top notes of lavender and bergamot that reach for the sky. Shaman pleasure is frequently personal, connected to some value or dream residing within the Shaman themselves: finding a home for an orphaned yorkie mutt, discovering a new musical artist whom no one's ever heard of, falling in love—again.

The topic of traveling makes for an effective shotgun statement when juxtaposing visceral and intuitive satisfaction. For Hunters, a vacation is a tale of two extremes: outdoorsy, backpacking, extreme-weather adventuring or sipping a mai tai while getting a pedicure at some luxury beachfront resort. It's all about stimulating their senses with new experiences, whether they stretch to exhilarating heights or sweep to relaxing lulls. Skydiving, surfing, and wine tasting are all common activities on a Hunter itinerary (organized fun is their favorite, and sometimes only, type of organization). Shamans generally like to travel off the beaten path; Iceland and India are far more likely Shaman travel destinations than the typical American standbys of France, Italy, and the United Kingdom. Their primary goal is to digest, both literally and figuratively, the culture of wherever they are. Through homestays, native guides, and sometimes just randomly meeting the locals, they seek an authentic experience—or at least something they believe to be authentic—because discovering and understanding new cultural identities helps a Shaman to shape their own.

Another great shotgun topic when personality-typing Hunters and Shamans is, funny enough, personality typing. In my experience, the majority of Hunters have no interest in the subject; for those Hunters who are reading and, more importantly, have purchased this book, you can disregard the last sentence or consider yourself part of an extremely special minority. Perhaps it's the way personality theory is often discussed, *theory* being the quintessential Hunter boner killer (lady boners, too!). Personality typing, by definition, is a system of categorizing people, and any conversation that revolves around a person's inherent skills and weaknesses is bound to be seen by Hunters as a direct assault on their belief that they're capable of doing anything. Of course, there are practical uses for personality typing in which Hunters might find interest: sales and marketing for Foxes and Sharks and romantic compatibility for all Hunters (to be honest, all types are interested in romantic compatibility).

Shamans, to put it mildly, love personality typing like a junior high crush, vacillating between feelings of maddening, unfulfilled obsession and euphoric, incomprehensible rapture. What do you expect when you're talking about people whose primary desire is to understand their place and purpose on the planet? When distinguishing between a Hunter and a Shaman, one of the easiest techniques I use is a simple Costigan variant: I mention that they should take the personality test on my site. Talking about personality typing is one thing, but actually spending the time to take a test is not how most Hunters roll. Being the accommodating sort, they generally say all the right things, the usual variants of "This test sounds interesting," but when push comes to shove, they usually end up "forgetting" or avoiding it entirely. You never have to ask a Shaman to take the test; they'll ask you where they can find it.

Important reminder: The purpose of this book is for you to learn how to become the test, so really, after reading it, you should never have to ask anyone to take the test again.

Pepsi Challenge Moment

Hunter-Shaman relationships can be fraught with deception. I suppose that's what you get when you mix a Shaman's need for emotional connection with a Hunter's tendency to modulate their behavior to match whomever they're around.

It reminds me of when I was in college and a Shaman friend asked me to type a guy she had been seeing for a few weeks. At this point, I had already been in a conversation with him for a good fifteen minutes, so I had a pretty good idea of his type. When I told her he was a Hunter, she didn't believe it. She insisted he was, like her, a Shaman and beseeched him to take the test so he could prove me wrong. He was hesitant (see earlier) and tried to stall as much as he could, but she was relentless. I'll admit, I'm not always right on these things (in my twenties, I made plenty of mistakes, and some even had to do with personality typing), but in this specific scenario, I was pretty certain I would be proven right. And I was. He eventually wore down and took the test, and his results were just as I predicted they would be. When my friend asked me how I knew, I gave a less than insightful answer:

ME: Well, he's pretty laidback.
SHAMAN FRIEND: Was that all?

Perhaps not. Perhaps I was withholding. Perhaps in my early twenties, I didn't really know how I knew. Perhaps I didn't want to unload a bunch of pseudo-psychoanalytical bullshit on a friend who was so desperate to feel a connection to this guy, and then I end up looking like Phoebe's boyfriend on an episode of *Friends*. You know, the guy, played by Fisher Stevens without the *Short Circuit* brownface, who keeps psychoanalyzing—albeit accurately—and annoying everyone to the point where Phoebe dumps him (Myerson, 1995). The correct answer is probably all the above.

In hindsight, there was a specific detail that led to my read on him. During our conversation, he was friendly but cautious, calibrating his words carefully; he avoided stating any opinions that might be deemed mildly inflammatory, waiting for me to say them (sorry, but Beyoncé is overrated, even back then) so that he could tepidly agree. He also showed absolutely no interest in personality typing, which stood out in stark contrast to my Shaman friend. It's worth mentioning that he was an immature Hunter, so in no way am I implying that all Hunters strive for false conversational concurrence or avoid the introspection that personality typing requires. But even the most mature Hunters care less about authenticity and empathy than the average Shaman, so comparing respective enthusiasm levels for those two values is the easiest way to tell Hunters and Shamans apart—an important thing for Shamans to remember, given their habit for projecting their own values onto Hunters, who are easy targets due to their conflict-avoidant tendencies.

Hunters versus Smiths

"Maybe I could be a lawyer!?" Seriously, I don't think I've ever seen my mother happier, at least when it comes to things *I've* said or done, than when I said those enthusiastically noncommittal words—instead of apathetically noncommittal, which was my norm at the time. I had been a graduate of UCLA for more than two years and spent most of my week working as a starter at a nine-hole executive golf course. It was fantastic. I would play nine holes every morning with the weekday regulars, check in for work around noon, and spend the rest of the day sitting at the front desk and perfecting the art of collecting green fees and announcing the next group up on the first tee. During lulls, I even found time to write two feature scripts that eventually had the pleasure of being rejected by Brett Ratner (insert sexual misconduct joke here).

So, of course, I never ended up going to law school. In fact, I never even applied. A friend of mine was attending law school at the time, and she flat out said, "Don't do it. We have similar personalities, and I *hate* it." But I still ended up taking the LSAT because, well, I had already paid for it, and I'm a sick human being who actually thinks taking tests is kind of fun. Which, in the most roundabout way—even for my standards—brings me to the reason I bring this all up in the first place. There was an essay question on that LSAT that, to this day, I remember and use as a perfect illustration of the difference between Hunters and Smiths.

The question was whether one form of intelligence is better than another. Take, for instance, the act of shooting a basketball. While a person with logical/mathematical intelligence might be able to calculate the precise angle and force needed to make the shot successfully, a person with kinesthetic intelligence would be able to pick up the ball and make the shot while barely having to think about it. The essay's supposition, that the latter intelligence is clearly superior, was a bit of a cheat because, technically speaking, the second person would be blending two forms of intelligence (kinesthetic and spatial). Of course, that was not the answer the esteemed makers of the LSAT were asking for. My fellow test takers and I were asked to take a side, so I, being the extremely brave soul that I am, decided to hedge my bets (i.e., totally cop out). I wrote that neither is superior, as it depends on the context—which just so happens to be my go-to response to most questions regarding personality typing, including the inevitable "No, really, which type is the best?" No matter what side you take, the argument introduced by the essay is a relevant one. Practice versus theory, technique versus technology, instinct versus reason—these are the elements of the prototypical Hunter-Smith divide.

For anyone who loves to cook, eat, or just pretend to do both well, there's *The Chef Show* on Netflix, hosted by writer-director-actor Jon Favreau (a.k.a. the guy who saved two pop culture franchises: *Marvel* and *Star Wars* from the creative brink) and Roy Choi of Kogi Tacos fame. In one episode, Roy Choi, a Hunter, is having a difficult time figuring out how to pop the lid off a fancy new blender due to an unfamiliar mechanism, basically a plastic hook that's there to, ironically, make the blender easier to open. He explains his difficulty by saying that chefs are essentially cavemen, preferring simple methods over unnecessary accoutrements that only complicate the process (Favreau, 2020). This gels with his Hunter modus operandi. As opposed to Smiths, who are always looking to create tools to increase efficiency (technology), Hunters focus on mastering their skills with the tools they have (technique). It's like the relationship between Q and James Bond, tool builder versus tool user.

On a deeper level, a lot of these Hunter-Smith distinctions can be attributed to their differing perception of time: Hunters zoom in; Smiths zoom out. It reminds me of the short film *Powers of Ten*, which begins with an aerial shot of a couple having a picnic at a park and then zooms out ten meters. It repeats this zoom out, each time increasing the degree by a power of ten, eventually taking us into our solar system, the galaxy beyond, and finally the edge of the known universe. The camera rests as we contemplate the vast galactic swath of nothingness. Then the camera reverses course, zooming back to earth, back to the picnic, and in negative powers of ten, into the man's hand. We travel into his cells, their strands of DNA, their individual atoms, all the way down to the subatomic level (Eames and Eames, 1977)—something Dennis Quaid would refer to as *Innerspace*.

Hunters are in-the-moment, reactive hedonists whose ability to zoom in and perceive time at the microlevel enables them to act and react at an extraordinary speed. It's like that moment in *Big Trouble in Little China* when Jack Burton (Kurt Russell) catches a knife thrown at him and throws it back in a split second, finally getting to show off the quick reflexes he's been bragging to everyone about for the entire movie—so much so that no one, including the audience, believes him (Carpenter, 1986). Conversely, Smiths are big-picture, contemplative analysts whose ability to zoom out and perceive time at the macrolevel enables them to avoid the trap of momentary influences, transitory trends, and cultural fads; they refuse to be slaves to the present.

This difference of temporal orientation can be seen in a Hunter's preference for tactics versus a Smith's preference for strategy. And yes, I know those two terms are used together so much that people frequently mistake them for being synonyms (just because salt and pepper go well together doesn't mean they're the same thing!). Here's a definition that's easy to remember:

- tactics = short-term gain for possible long-term loss
- strategy = long-term gain for possible short-term loss

As you can see, *tactics* and *strategy* are obviously not synonyms. Their goals naturally conflict, meaning that, while an individual can possess the ability to use both, they always gravitate to one of them. These contrasting preferences can be seen in the famous Stanford marshmallow experiment. In that study, young children were given a choice between one small but immediate reward (a marshmallow) and two small rewards if they waited. At that point, the researcher would exit the room, leaving the child unattended. Some children would eat the marshmallow without hesitation. Others would wait for the promised greater reward. Essentially, it was a measure of delayed gratification. According to the study, researchers found that children who were able to wait longer usually had better life outcomes (Mischel, Ebbesen, and Raskoff Zeiss, 1972). Now, it's worth mentioning that the validity of the results has been challenged since then—*better life outcomes* being a hazardously subjective term—and the test's predictive power seems slightly tilted in favor of Smith long-term planning. That's why I've devised my own test; I call it the Princeton Hans Gruber test—because why not add a little Ivy League "legitimacy" to it.

The Machiavellian terrorist Hans Gruber (do I really have to mention that he was played by Alan Rickman?) is the main antagonist of the movie *Die Hard*. He has a perfect plan, intricate, methodical, well-prepared for contingencies, and it's all foiled by John McLane (Bruce Willis), a cop who's quick on the trigger and even quicker on the one-liners. I think it's fairly obvious here who's the Hunter and who's the Smith. In the climax of the film—spoiler alert—McClane bests Gruber using a tactical trick, namely a gun attached to his naked back using Christmas wrapping tape (McTiernan, 1988). Tactical heroes defeating strategic villains is a common pattern in action films. Think about it the next time you watch a Bond film or any gun-packed, fists-of-fury, popcorn flick. Analyze the plot using my Princeton Hans Gruber test, and see how it computes. Definitive Hunter bias, which makes perfect sense—these are *action* films after all. I guess that makes it Smiths: 1, Hunters: 1.

Pepsi Challenge Moment

One of the unfortunate aspects of personality typing is that it can descend into personality stereotyping, a process that's indoctrinated into us at an early age. Whether it was John Hughes or the Disney Channel, just think of all the types popular culture introduced you to as a child: the jock, the popular kid, the nerd, the rebel. At a certain point, reality begins to mirror art, and these types become so ingrained in our notion of proper society that we become our own self-fulfilling prophecies, fashioning ourselves into whichever role we feel fits best. Maybe more than any other, the Hunter-Smith relationship—more precisely our understanding of it—suffers from these superficial categorizations. It's frequently seen as a conflict between jocks and nerds or cool kids and social outcasts.

I often wonder if this dichotomy is a Gatherer construction, their attempt to understand two types of people who clearly differ from them. Hunters receive the "cool" tag due to Gatherers' admiration (Hunters might say envy) for their spontaneous nature. Smiths, though, are tagged as, at best, "misanthropes" and, at worst, "virginal weirdos" whom Gatherers perceive with a mixture of disdain and grudging respect; they appreciate the Smiths' contributions to society but abhor their methods and overall social demeanor. Despite such conjecture, what I know for sure is, as it pertains to this simplistic stereotyping, for most people a dose of reality intervenes.

It was a student, an adult in her midforties, who showed me that it's an amateurish mistake, especially for someone who prides themselves on reading people, to look at Hunters and Smiths—or anyone for that matter—as if we were all kids in *The Breakfast Club*. My director described this student's entrance into our tutoring center (in the middle of a tutoring session, I wasn't present to witness it) like she was a whirlwind, pacing back and forth, aggressively unsure and talking to herself with partially constructed thoughts. She finally got up the nerve to ask about the possibility of receiving language tutoring. She also wanted to make it clear that she wasn't an idiot. I took her on as a student and would learn a few more details about her:

- She was a software developer.
- She was socially awkward.
- She was blunt and direct.
- She wasn't particularly self-aware.

All these initial impressions pointed in one direction. I mean, a socially unaware tech nerd? It's like central casting put out a call for a Smith. And she was Asian, too—"awkward tech nerd" being one of the few roles Asians can get in Hollywood, along with "virginal martial artist" or "guy with an accent who owns the liquor store down the street." I was so convinced that she was a Smith I never considered anything else, even as new bits of information were revealed. For one, she didn't want to practice her reading. I was like, "Um, this is language tutoring. You need to be able to understand what you're reading." She insisted it wasn't important because she hated reading anyway, and to be honest, I wasn't particularly inclined to try to force a grown-ass woman who drove a Mercedes to do homework. I shifted to a vocabulary game, and she loved it. At first, I thought it was because it allowed her to avoid working on reading comprehension, which was marginally true, but she really did find the game fun. It was a mixture of drilling and play, which would normally scream Hunter to me, but I couldn't square that with the fact that she was so socially awkward *and* worked in tech. Then came the epiphany.

Long story short, she was telling me about how she recently went off on her boss over a miscommunication of project hours. Hearing the entire story, I told her that her boss was actually trying to help her by indirectly communicating how she could take time off and still get paid. I told her he was doing a "wink, wink" kind of thing, but she had no idea what that meant. It was then that I realized I was, like an idiot, ignoring an extremely important personality-typing factor staring me right in the face: culture. My student wasn't socially awkward; she was just a first-generation Chinese immigrant who had only been in this country for five years and was still getting accustomed to its cultural norms and subtleties, which is why she decided to pay for language tutoring in the first place. Yep, not one of my finer personality-typing moments. When you remove social awkwardness as a trait and add in the fact that all she wanted to do was play vocabulary games, her type was evident: She was a Hunter (a Shark, to be precise).

Disappointed but not discouraged, I took the whole situation for a learning moment, a reminder that a Hunter isn't always the cool, popular chick, and the tech sector—and the intellect we generally attribute to its members—is not purely the domain of Smiths. Oh, and I also realized that *Revenge of the Nerds* was, in fact, a comedy and wasn't really meant to be taken seriously—at least not like that documentary series, *Police Academy*.

Shamans versus Smiths

Shaman versus Smith; abstract versus abstract; or, as concrete people view it, the Battle of the Weirdos. Both Shamans and Smiths possess a heavy interest in conversing about abstract concepts (i.e., feelings and ideas). What separates them from each other is not *what* they're talking about but *how* they're talking about it. Smiths prefer to process, ponder, and express their ideas as impersonally as possible. When arguing concepts, it's not shocking for them to cite works they've read or studies they've researched. Shamans, in contrast, take those same ideas and filter them through a personal lens, preferring to use personal anecdotes or allegories to illustrate their point.

I'm reminded of reading David Byrne's (2012) book *How Music Works*. All you need to do is read his Wikipedia page to know that Byrne, front man for the legendary Talking Heads, has devoted his life to the craft of music. As such, there's a passion that's frequently ascribed to music and its practitioners, a sort of openness and exultation of the spirit that one could naturally assume permeates a book authored on the subject. But Byrne's book (which I absolutely loved, by the way) is nothing of the sort. It is no artist manifesto. It is a dry, analytical examination of the music-making process, written with Byrne's intelligent, matter-of-fact Smith voice. Instead of writing about the sheer joy of breaking into the music scene at CBGB's, Byrne brings up his band's success at the iconic venue as an example of how the acoustics of a place can help or hurt a band, depending on their style of music, an apt demonstration of his technological knowledge.

Contrast this with the Shaman approach, which is not always about the music itself but what it means to them. For example, I know a Shaman whose favorite band is Depeche Mode, and if you ask him why, his explanation always involves the same story. When he was ten years old, he heard "Enjoy the Silence" for the first time. He didn't understand how a song could be both sad and aspirational, both melancholy and romantic. In that moment, he came to learn that music, just like our emotions, can be mixed.

As with most Shamans, his insights were communicated through a personal experience. Shamans intuitively know that not only can an intimate story create a better understanding of an idea by connecting to their audience's shared experiences, but it can also create an empathetic bond, bringing people together; a Shaman's primary focus is not how people are different but how they're similar. Smiths, though, prefer objective analysis because they know that creating a wall of separation between personal feelings and information is the best way to ensure accuracy and delve deeper into topics without the distraction of social bias; they abhor such things as cancel culture and political correctness, as they tamper with the ability to have a candid discussion. A Smith's primary focus is not bringing people together through similarities but gaining knowledge of people—and pretty much everything else—through examining their differences.

Once again, personality typing serves as a useful shotgun topic. Both Shamans and Smiths tend to love the subject, making up a large percentage of online test users, much more than the approximately 15 percent of the population they comprise. However, there's a difference in how they interact with the subject matter, which is very much an extension of how the two types discuss abstract concepts in general. When it comes to personality typing, Smiths take the same view that they would of any other topic of interest, seeking to catalogue and process the information in an objective fashion. They ask questions about other types frequently, especially regarding people they work with. A Shaman's initial questions, in contrast, are almost always about themselves. When they do finally end up asking about other people, those people usually represent an extension of themselves (a significant other, parents, siblings, etc.) or their dreams (potential romantic interests). As I like to say, a Smith always reads all sixteen profiles; a Shaman always reads their profile sixteen times.

If you hearken back to Empedocles (which is what I do all the time, of course), you'll remember his theory that the universe is comprised of four elements: Earth (Gatherers), Fire (Hunters), Water (Shamans), and Air (Smiths). If we connect this concept of elemental energy to our personality observations, we'll find that the juxtaposition between Shaman and Smith energy can be a revelation when distinguishing between the two.

Shaman energy, like their element of water, is fluid. It can be as calm as a gentle stream; as tumultuous as the open ocean; or like an Icelandic geyser, simmering underneath the surface, just waiting to explode. In this way, Shamans are generally easygoing people on the outside, but on the inside, there might be a multitude of emotions swirling, some beyond the Shaman's understanding or control. All it takes is one seemingly trifling thing to set them off. Contrary to their hippie-dippie, Shamanic softie stereotype, Shaman energy can be harsh and unforgiving; as any surfer can tell you, for every beautiful, A-frame wave, there's a riptide just waiting to crush you against the rocks.

Smith energy, like their element of air, is cool, breezy, and situated somewhere up in the clouds. Smiths usually carry themselves with a certain air (pardon the pun) of indifference. This is not to say that they don't care about anything. They obviously care deeply about a great many things, but how they express that passion is more restrained than how a Shaman expresses it—Killer Whales, the most aggressive of the Smiths, might be an exception here, as their intense determination can easily mimic a Shaman's enthusiastic zeal. A Smith's ability to remove themselves from the emotional ebb and flow of life gives them an extremely measured energy; when times are rough, they're the most likely person to remind you that, if you put your situation in context, your life isn't so bad. Of course, this emotional distance can come at a cost. One must be careful, when stepping back to look at the bigger picture, not to step back so far that you're completely out of the frame. Whereas Shamans have trouble controlling their emotions, Smiths have difficulty fully engaging with theirs, being so concerned with viewing the world "correctly" that they forget to enjoy their limited time in it.

Pepsi Challenge Moment

Undoubtedly, one of the first questions I'm always asked when talking about personality typing is, "What's the perfect type for me to be with?" My reply is always the safe, applicable-in-all-circumstances, "synergy" answer (I *did* learn something from my old college professor!): "It depends on what kind of relationship you want." This kind of hedge is especially important in some of the situations I find myself in: mainly a friend who's in a committed relationship asking whether it's going to work out. I'm not in the habit of telling friends that their genuine feelings of affection for their partner are insignificant because of some theory. One, you don't really keep too many friends that way, and two, personality compatibility is a nuanced topic that should be talked about without using such terms as *perfect match* and *soulmate*. However, if we are to believe that we share consistent traits based on our personality types, then it's not a stretch to say that conflicts between personality types are also consistent, especially in the case of relationships, where contrasts in personality become heightened. This is true, even in the most theoretically ideal pairings, one of which is the Shaman-Smith couple.

Just recently, an Owl (Smith) friend of mine quickly entered—and exited—a relationship with a Humpback Whale (Shaman), a tumultuous ride that crystallizes the differences between the two types. As I said previously, the Shaman-Smith pairing is theoretically a good one, though the Humpback Whale–Owl pairing is not the best example of this. But what this situation shows is that all personalities eventually come into conflict at some point, and if you can't accept those clashes, then it doesn't bode well for the health of the relationship, regardless of theoretical compatibility.

She (the Humpback Whale) was coming off a live-in relationship with a Gatherer, and he (the Owl) was a close friend of hers. Perhaps it was the intimacy he provided; being a fellow abstract type, he was able to communicate with her in a way that her previous boyfriend could not. Or maybe she was just bored. Either way, she wanted to move in immediately. After one unintimate—you know what I mean—date. *One.* Being a Smith, he was genuinely considering the unconventional idea (a Gatherer would've been offended on principle), but her enthusiasm also scared him; after all, Owls are the masters of emotional distance, and she had managed to close that space with ease. To her disappointment, he said they should wait. So they had a few more dates, nothing consequential, and then the moment of conflict came.

They were planning on spending the weekend together, but there was miscommunication on when they would meet. She assumed the weekend meant starting Friday night. He assumed it meant starting Saturday. With that in mind, he scheduled work sessions for himself throughout Friday. By the time he got her message asking him when he'd be over, it was too late to reschedule. He ended up finishing late into the night and, exhausted, told her he'd see her early the next morning. She was hurt and accused him of not really wanting to be with her. He assured her that everything was fine and that he was just too tired and would be there bright and early the next day.

He arrived the next morning as promised, and they spent the weekend together. But her irritation—and his bewilderment at it—was underneath the surface of everything. You leave those two things unattended for very long, and they ferment into resentment and ignorance. Shamans are highly attuned to the morale of the people they're around, so in general, they're unlikely to let this kind of tension build without talking about it. However, Humpback Whales are the most conflict avoidant of the Shamans, a trait that's magnified when paired with the emotionally distant Owl; both types usually ignore the problems in the hopes that they'll just go away. Of course, they never do, and the anger that had been building up between the two of them came to a head by the end of the weekend in the form of a heated argument. She blasted him for being inconsiderate to her feelings. He accused her of being unreasonable. And like that, their relationship was over before it really began. My conversation with him shortly after went like this:

ME: You should probably just say you're sorry.
OWL: But I'm not. She is being unreasonable.
ME: From your perspective, yeah, but she's not you.
OWL: Why can't she understand that I was genuinely tired?
ME: In her mind, she would've gone if she were exhausted.

OWL: But that's not me. Why do I have to relate to her, but she can't do the same for me?

ME: I'd tell her the same thing, but I'm not talking to her. I'm talking to you.

OWL: To be honest, it irritates me to be around her now knowing that.

Knowing a person's priority values is essential to understanding—not eliminating—conflict. As a Shaman whose primary value is self-identity, the Humpback Whale viewed the Owl's inability to see things from her perspective as him being unwilling to accept her as a person, the ultimate slight. As a Smith whose primary value is reason, the Owl couldn't square his affection for her with the realization that she was judging him based on the values—her own—that she was projecting onto him, an illogical inequity. It's a cardinal Shaman-Smith conflict: Shaman purity test versus Smith indifference.

Both types might be weird, but they're weird in their own, wonderfully unique ways—as are all the types, which is why we fight so much. And just like there's no winner in the battle of the weirdos, there's no winner in any of these conflicts between types, except maybe you, me, and anyone else who, through the juxtaposition process, can distill pure and powerful character insights about the individuals in conflict. It's 180-proof personality-type moonshine.

CHAPTER EIGHT

TYPES OF GATHERERS AND HOW TO FIND THEM

Reminder: This chapter is for determining Gatherers only. Some traits mentioned may apply to other types, but this chapter is strictly for when you have already determined that someone is a Gatherer.

ONE SIZE DOES NOT FIT ALL

One of the most vital distinctions between the *PoP* method and other MBTI-based typing systems is that it eschews a "one size fits all" approach. When assessing someone's personality type, most assessors use the same questions for every single individual, without any thought of adjusting them based on a person's initial responses. What that method lacks in accuracy and awareness it makes up for in audacity. It's like asking someone out; getting flat out rejected; and then asking them, "Your place or mine?" Sorry buddy. *No* means *no.* The *PoP* method is unique in that it's modeled after computerized adaptive tests like the GRE or GMAT. The typing criteria adapt to your initial analysis of a person's type; the factors that determine a more specific personality type change based on a person's pack. For example, the traits that distinguish the different Gatherers from each other are substantially disparate from those that distinguish the different Hunters, Shamans, and Smiths (see figure 8.1).

Gatherers can be split into two separate subgroups: those who prioritize duty and those who prioritize family. This makes sense when you think about it. Gatherers want to feel secure above all else, and what aspects of life usually make us feel that way? Respect from our peers and love from those closest to us, and we get both by upholding our societal obligations and supporting our family. Of course, all Gatherers place a premium on those two things—far more than the other packs—but certain Gatherers value one more than the other.

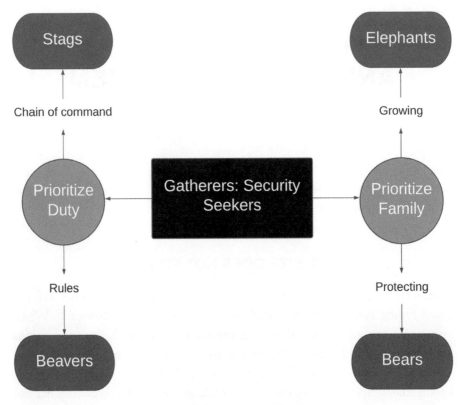

Figure 8.1 Types of Gatherers

DUTY BOUND VERSUS FAMILY BOUND

When I was young, attending parent-teacher conferences was more or less an inevitability. No matter how well or poorly (usually poorly) I was doing in school, my dad would drag me to the same place I spent most of my day so that I could hear the same reprimand I spent most of my day hearing. He must've enjoyed listening to my teachers chew me out because it's an experience we would repeat with . . . Every. Single. Teacher. It was like being at Disneyland for my dad; he didn't want to miss any rides. He told me I was lucky and that a lot of my classmates had parents who didn't have the time or inclination to go to these; apparently getting reamed by your teachers is a privilege.

I mention these sunny memories because a parent-teacher conference can reveal a clear difference between duty-bound Gatherers and family-bound ones. Now, my father was clearly not a Gatherer; his glee at my pain and embarrassment (did I mention that he made sure to introduce himself to any friend of mine we would encounter?) pretty much shows his Smith, slightly misanthropic side. Gatherers, however, are different animals. Not only do they make up half the population (I know, it's like I have that phrase on loop), but they are also the type who would make attending their child's parent-teacher conference a priority. And once they're there, how they react to their child being reprimanded is quite telling. Some parents unequivocally side with the teacher. Other parents, while not explicitly siding with their child, might fall on their sword for them by saying things like "It's my fault. I've been getting home late from work and haven't been able to keep them on task."

The first group of parents falls under the duty-bound column. It's not like they don't love or care for their child—though sometimes it feels that way to the kid—but their duty as a parent is to ensure that their child becomes a fine, upstanding citizen capable of navigating society and supporting themselves. And that means, when the teacher has a problem with their kid, Stags and Beavers have a problem, too. They're all about tough love. The second group of parents fall under the family-bound column. Elephants and Beavers also believe in teaching their child right and wrong, but they're softies at heart and can't help but rally around their kid when it feels like they're hurting.

Observing parent-child interactions is essential to finding and typing Gatherers, as they are the most likely types to have children. Chances are (and by chances, I mean approximately 85 percent) one of your parents is probably a Gatherer, too. Let's run the math (remember, these are loose, approximate figures).

If half of any given population is made up of Gatherers, let's assume that number rises to 60 percent when talking specifically about parents, which means the odds of a single parent not being a Gatherer are 40 percent. For two-parent households, that would mean multiplying that 40 percent by another 40 percent, turning it into 16 percent. That means that, if you have two parents, there's only a 16 percent chance that neither are Gatherers, meaning an 84 percent chance that at least one is. Basically, the odds are as high as Tommy Chong on a Tuesday.

If you have a family-bound Gatherer as a parent, you'll always feel loved. They take pride in creating the safest space possible for their children, where they always have enough food to eat and enough clothes to wear and always feel like their hopes and dreams are supported. However, these parents can sometimes feel smothering, especially as the child gets older. These are the parents who want their kids going to college close to home; they'll do whatever they can to prevent their chicks from straying too far from the nest. Duty-bound Gatherers might appear overly strict or even scary to their children, but by the time those kids grow older, they learn to appreciate the amount of independence—relative to Gatherers—their Stag and Beaver parents give them. Duty-bound Gatherers are careful to balance the amount of security lost when giving their children this freedom with the amount of security gained by training their children to fend for themselves. These are the parents who, when their kids come back from college on the weekend, ask, "Why are you here?"

For Stags and Beavers, much of their strength lies in their ability to be objective, even when it concerns their family. They abhor the idea of playing favorites, feeling that anything worth achieving needs to be earned the "right way." At the very least, they'll remove themselves from situations where there's a conflict of interest. The downside to this sense of fairness is that it can make them seem cold and judgmental and sometimes cause an emotional disconnect from their family and friends. Elephants and Bears, in contrast, very rarely have this issue, as they are quick to create emotional bonds with every individual in their circle of companionship. However, there are times when their constant concern is cloying, and their inability to remain impartial can be debilitating when it comes to making tough decisions concerning those they love. Nevertheless, as it is with all types, Gatherers' strengths derive from their weaknesses, and traits that might've once been seen as judgmental or smothering transform themselves into the very building blocks of a civilized society: justice and compassion.

STAGS VERSUS BEAVERS

Just as Stags and Beavers are bound to duty, the idea of duty itself must be bound to a certain moral code. Whether it's the US Constitution, the Code of Hammurabi, the twelve points of the Boy Scout Law, or the rules of Chuck E. Cheese (you can take home your leftover pizza, if you're wondering), the first law of being duty bound is to have a structure of "laws" to be bound to. And this is where Stags and Beavers differ. Stags prioritize following a chain of command, a hierarchy of authority that possesses a clear line of jurisdiction and responsibility along which orders are passed. Beavers prioritize following a set of rules. Although these two things are similar, there are nuanced differences.

Let's say an employee catches their boss disobeying company policy. A Beaver would be more likely than a Stag to report them to their superiors, understanding that rules are to be applied to everyone equally; without equal justice, we would have chaos. On the flip side, it wouldn't be surprising for a Stag to choose loyalty to the person above them. It's not that Stags don't think rules are important, but they realize that trust in the line of authority is also important; if they begin to question the authority of their superiors, then what's to stop those beneath them from questioning their authority? And on and on it goes. This is a delicate balance that's not as black and white as it seems.

One only needs to look at our judicial system as an example of the push and pull between authority and rules. Ostensibly, a court's role is to interpret the laws as written. But what happens when one court's interpretation differs from another? Which ruling takes precedence? In the United States, the judicial chain of command enables a higher court to interpret (some would argue change) the rules as they see fit. Of course, they only have this authority because of Article III, Section 1, of the US Constitution, which, in and of itself, is a rule. Like I said, push and pull.

Stags come off as bossy. They're the kid in school who always takes charge of group assignments, delegating tasks to their classmates, whether they know them or not. Beavers come off as serious. They're the kid in school who would snitch on their mother if they thought she left class without a hall pass. Granted, these are not the most flattering—or always accurate—portrayals; it's just how they can be perceived at first blush.

Stags have the luxury of being society's ideal male archetype (aggressive; confident; a strong, self-initiating go-getter), regardless of the Stag's actual gender; there are just as many Stag females as there are Stag males. This association with these "masculine" traits is usually positive. Because of this, Stags aren't particularly humble. They think everyone should be like them because, frankly, society kind of says that everyone should be like them. Beavers, paradoxically, take great pride in their humility; in a way, that kind of makes them the most and least humble of the Gatherers. A Beaver's rigid discipline, as seen in their willingness to do the proverbial dirty work in any given scenario, gives them a certain feeling of superiority—they hate asking for help. A Stag, in contrast, loves to receive help if it's for the "right reason" (mainly, their superior status) and willingly performs the dirty work in their early years in order to earn the privilege of never having to do it again.

Here's a shotgun scenario to distinguish the two: Let's say you see the person you're trying to type performing some menial chore, like washing the dishes. Offer to do it for them. A Stag almost always relinquishes the responsibility, especially if the reason you give is that they outrank you in some way (age, job status, social status, etc.). A Beaver commonly takes the offer as an insult: "Are you trying to say that you can do this better?" They actually want to do the work, as much of their ego is built on their industriousness. You want to make a Beaver happy? Thank them and tell them you appreciate all the hard work that they do and never get credit for.

ELEPHANTS VERSUS BEARS

The biggest contrast between the family-bound Gatherers is that Elephants prioritize growing their family by bringing more people into it, while Bears prioritize protecting the family they already have. If Stags are society's ideal male archetype, then Elephants are the female version: the earth-mother, queen-bee, head-of-the-PTA type. Natural herders, for them, the idea of family means everyone close to them, friends included, and they are always looking to add new people to the herd. Bears also have an archetype: the strong, silent type. Like Gary Cooper (somewhere out there, some seventy-year-old person is reading this and shouting, "Yes! Finally, a reference I understand!") or Superman, Bears are genuinely humble with a gentle disposition—but if you threaten someone they love, watch out! They'll tear your throat out without saying a word.

Both generally love the aspects of home life (cooking, arts and crafts, home improvement, etc.). Elephants crave that feeling of providing for the people they love and the people those people love and so on. They're basically that parent who's always inviting their kid's friends to stay for dinner. Their not-so-secret dream? Owning two refrigerators and two freezers. Bears, while not exactly invitation junkies, put all their heart and soul into caring for their loved ones, often in a self-sacrificing way. I had an aunt who was a Bear, and she was, without a doubt, one of the most unselfish people I've ever known. She was so devoted to my siblings and me that, when we were younger, my father had to remind us not to take advantage of her kindness because she'd probably give us anything we asked for.

Elephants come off as friendly. Bears come off as kind. Elephants are polite, socially comfortable extroverts (one of the few times where I can use that term without dumping a truckload of caveats) who make introductions effortlessly and look to bring outsiders into the circle, whether those outsiders like it or not. Bears are the steady, conscientious helper behind the scenes; at a party, they're usually the person who arrives early to help set up. When it comes to making new friends, Bears are more discerning, balancing their compassionate nature with a desire to not rock the boat and disturb the dynamic of their friend circle.

As parents, Bears can be a mixture of overprotective and permissive, simultaneously letting their children walk all over them while lashing out at anyone who might do those same children harm. In contrast, Elephants are more demonstrative when disciplining their kids—though they still can't help themselves with those hugs. More smothering than protective, Elephants are also more likely to get involved in their kids' social activities. And when those kids get older? Guess who's playing matchmaker. Of course, these traits are not exclusive to Elephants and Bears as parents. While they're easier to observe through the lens of a parent-child relationship, they can also be recognized in the way these family-bound Gatherers interact with their friends, coworkers, and classmates.

Just think of Cher (played by Alicia Silverstone) from the film *Clueless* (Heckerling, 1995) and how her Elephant nature shines through as she takes on the role of lady of the house, ensuring that her father eats right and calls his parents, while also playing matchmaker, both successfully (her teachers, one of whom is played by the awesome Wallace Shawn of "inconceivable!" Sicilian fame) and unsuccessfully (her friend Tai; R.I.P., Brittany Murphy). Or Dr. John Watson of Sherlock Holmes fame, a Bear whose loyalty and compassion are demonstrated every time he protects Sherlock's back or excuses the genius detective's eccentric, borderline sociopathic behavior.

CHAPTER NINE

TYPES OF HUNTERS AND HOW TO FIND THEM

Reminder: This chapter is for determining Hunters only. Some traits mentioned may apply to other types, but this chapter is strictly for when you have already determined that someone is a Hunter.

MISCONCEPTIONS

Unlike Gatherers, whose primary goal of security leads to their focus on duty and family, Hunters seek excitement, and as such, their priorities are focused on the differing ways they can achieve it. Unfortunately, the idea of excitement has a trivial connotation, and it's not generally seen with anything close to the seriousness as, let's say, family, but this is a misconception; I guess it's only appropriate that a superficial understanding of what it means to be a Hunter is the reason they're so often understood to be superficial. For example, saying that a Hunter focuses on excitement over family in no way makes them any less of a parent. It just makes them a different kind of parent. Whereas a Gatherer parent, especially a family-bound one, stresses the importance of keeping their children safe from the dangers of the world, a Hunter parent encourages their children to explore the world and all the excitement it has to offer.

For Hunters, the most visceral of the four packs, excitement isn't just about scanning through their Netflix queue in the hopes that watching another Christmas movie is going to cure their boredom; it's about stimulating their five senses to levels they haven't reached before. This is how they best interact with the world. This is how they know they're alive. This is how they remind other personality types that they're alive, too—and there's nothing superficial about that.

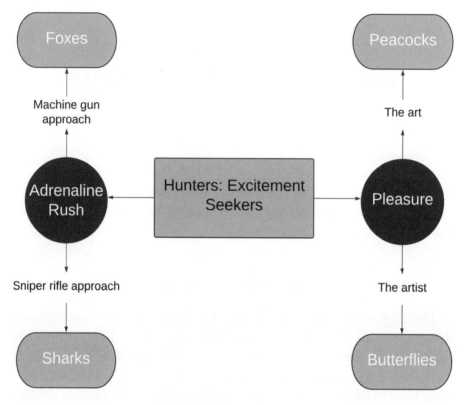

Figure 9.1 Types of Hunters

Hunters, as seen in figure 9.1, can be split into two initial groups: those who get their excitement through an adrenaline rush and those who get their excitement through pleasure. Think of it like the difference between riding a roller coaster and eating one of those fried chicken sandwiches where they use ice cream as a filling and two donuts as buns.

ADRENALINE SEEKERS VERSUS PLEASURE SEEKERS

Adrenaline seekers seek out activities where there's a certain amount of risk involved, like skydiving, racing, MMA fighting, competitive sports, and so on. These Hunters are motivated not only by the success of a triumphant outcome (a successful landing, winning the race, defeating their opponent) but also by the fear of failure. For Foxes and Sharks, the agony of defeat is more excruciating than any physical pain they could endure; one almost gets the feeling that they hate losing more than they love winning—and they love winning. The athletic brand Nike, namesake of the goddess of victory and possessor of the slogan "Just Do It," fits perfectly with the modus operandi of these highly competitive, strike-first Hunters, who are always willing to play games but readily admit that it's only fun if you're trying to win.

Pleasure-seeking Hunters are all about the sensory experience. Activities like live music, dancing, singing, a gourmet meal (I'd say sex, but then everyone's going to think they're a pleasure-seeking Hunter). These Hunters are the ultimate epicureans; if life was a Vegas-style buffet, they'd taste everything from the king crab legs right down to the not-so-gourmet, school-cafeteria-style cheese pizza.

Hunters as a whole are known for their tactical ability, a knack for determining the best course of action to take in any given scenario. It requires a quick calculation, one that differs in nature depending on the type of Hunter. For adrenaline seekers, it's all about the risk-reward ratio. For instance, when asking someone out, they realize there's more than a decent chance of rejection. But maybe a date with that person is worth the risk. Maybe it's not. Foxes and Sharks are adept at measuring whether the juice is worth the squeeze. For pleasure seekers, it's more of a pain-pleasure ratio. There's a certain amount of pain and pleasure involved with every action, and Peacocks and Butterflies excel at making decisions that minimize the former and maximize the latter (I did say they were epicureans, after all): the strenuous tediousness of exercise weighed against the beauty of being fit or the pain and *labor* of pregnancy perhaps being trumped by the pleasure of raising a child.

One of the easiest ways to differentiate between the two groups of Hunters is by their weaknesses. Foxes and Sharks are practitioners of controlled aggression. It's not just their ability to make lightning-fast, shrewd calculations but also the boldness to act on those calculations without hesitation that's the key to their success. However, for inexperienced adrenaline seekers who have not yet mastered the risk-reward ratio, this can be a dangerous proposition; if you want to climb a mountain, then you better be able to accurately assess your climbing skills. For this reason, these types of Hunters are commonly perceived as being reckless. It's no surprise that adrenaline seekers, both young and old, frequently find themselves getting injured; everyone remembers those kids in grade school who always came back from summer vacation with some sort of cast, brace, or splint on their body.

Not to be outdone, Peacocks and Butterflies are also bold risk takers, but in their case, this audaciousness is reflected in the way they pursue pleasure. Being incredibly open to new experiences, they possess a vast database of sensations (sights, sounds, flavors, etc.) that enables them to both consume at the highest level (pleasure seekers usually have great taste in art, music, and food) and create things worthy of consumption. Of course, the obvious drawback to a freely consumptive nature is the risk of overconsumption. When it comes to pleasure, too much is never enough for a pleasure-seeking Hunter, and if they don't learn to control their urges, they risk falling into a serious case of dependency, whether it's alcoholism, obesity, or an addiction to sex or drugs.

FOXES VERSUS SHARKS

Hunters are natural virtuosos with tools, so it's only appropriate that the best way to distinguish between the two adrenaline seekers is by the tools they choose and the way they choose to use them. Foxes, being instinctive improvisers, prefer to use whatever tools they have around them. Maybe that's why using people is their favorite method to get what they want; outgoing and sociable, Foxes are always around people. It's what makes them so great at sales, networking, and brokering deals. Knowing the right people is what they do best. Sharks, out of all the Hunters, are the most skilled with actual tools. Their hand-eye coordination, manual dexterity, and focus enable them to become formidable masters of artisanal crafts. That and the fact that they have absolutely no problem practicing a technique over and over and over again: The late Kobe Bryant famously shot a thousand jumpers a day as part of his offseason routine.

As adrenaline seekers mature, the divergence between their skill sets also grows. As a Fox becomes more advanced, their tool usage broadens; they begin to integrate a multitude of new and varied tools into their repertoire. As a Shark becomes more advanced, their tool usage gains refinement; they begin to delve more and more into the intricacies (Sharks love creating their own techniques) of their specific craft.

Of course, how an adrenaline seeker uses their tools is just as distinctive as what tools they use. A Fox's tool-using technique is something akin to shooting a machine gun, firing off as many bullets as they can to reach their objective—another reason they're such naturals at sales. They'll work every angle, and when that fails, they'll work every angle with another target. A Fox might go to a bar with the plan of propositioning at least ten people; even if they get rejected multiple times, the odds are in their favor that one person will say yes. Sharks, in contrast, use a sniper-rifle approach. They favor patience and precision over a Fox's haphazard (according to Sharks) approach. A Fox fires a thousand bullets to hit one target; a Shark waits a thousand seconds to hit one target.

Like all things dealing with personality type, one method isn't inherently better than the other. It just depends on the situation. It reminds me of the film *Billy Bathgate*, a Prohibition Era period piece about Billy, a young man being mentored by real-life gangster Dutch Schultz. In one scene, Billy watches two of Dutch's enforcers at a gun range. Irving takes his time, every shot hitting the same spot on the target. Lulu unloads two weapons in a matter of seconds, spraying the entire target. Dutch asks Billy who's the better shooter:

BILLY: Irving. He got 'em all in there.

DUTCH: Nah, this ain't lace embroidery. It don't have to be neat. If you got the time to set it up and you need a clean hit, you send Irving. But if you're in a tight spot, you want Lulu standing next to you. Boom, boom, boom, boom. It's all over in a couple of seconds. (Benton, 1991)

Foxes usually come off as cool. Sharks usually come off as mean. As it happens, both types are fine with this reputation. Foxes pride themselves on their supposed charm, wit, and savoir faire. Sharks pride themselves on their tough, stoic, "don't take shit from anyone" persona.

A perfect juxtaposition of a Fox and a Shark can be found in the relationship between the Marvel characters Black Widow and Hawkeye. Black Widow (a Fox), with her slick persona, varied weaponry, and manipulation of people—she is a spy—contrasts nicely with Hawkeye's gruff Shark persona, dry sense of humor, and complete mastery of the bow. It's a competitive dynamic that allows for a lot of appealing give and take—a friendship of two distinct yet extremely similar personas. At least on a subconscious level, Marvel must know this because—spoiler alert—after the death of Black Widow, Hawkeye finds himself with his own show (*Hawkeye*) and a new partner, Kate Bishop (another Fox), a gregarious, supremely confident teenager who, while being extremely skilled with a bow, also tends to use other methods to get what she wants, most notably her people skills. She even admonishes Hawkeye, telling him, "Your problem's *branding*" (Thomas, 2021; italics mine); I mean, Foxes gon' Fox.

And you want to know something even cooler? The new Black Widow (it's more of a title than an actual name because, you know, what parent would name their daughter Black Widow?) Yelena Belova is a Shark. So once Hawkeye passes the Hawkeye torch over to Kate, it'll be the same Fox-Shark, Black Widow–Hawkeye dynamic but in reverse. Just more evidence that there's an intuitive, personality-based collective unconscious. And with that, I have lost every single reader who couldn't care less about Marvel or Jung and is probably asking themselves, "Black Widow? How can a spider be a fox? How can a hawk be a shark? I'm so confused!" However, you must admit, it's kind of awesome to see how personality typing, much like the archetypes it's based on, is infused into our culture, whether we're conscious of it or not.

PEACOCKS VERSUS BUTTERFLIES

Unfortunately, there seems to be this negative stereotype that some Hunters are just a bunch of all-consuming hedonists (it doesn't help that I refer to them as pleasure seekers) who just feed off what other people produce. Nothing could be further from the truth. As much as Peacocks and Butterflies consume, they produce far more, and the thing they produce most of all is beauty.

Merriam-Webster defines *beauty* as "the aggregate of qualities in a person or thing that gives pleasure to the senses or pleasurably exalts the mind or spirit," and that is exactly what Peacocks and Butterflies seek to create: art that pleases the senses and exalts the mind and spirit. And this art can appear in any medium or form (a sculpture, a painting, a dance, a rap verse, a home-cooked meal, etc.). Of course, the use of such words as *art*, *beauty*, and *pleasure* gives way to another stereotype: that these particular Hunters are feminine in nature. I know, I know, don't get mad at me. Get mad at the society that indoctrinates us with this crap. I think we can all agree that every single one of us, regardless of our personality type or gender, can appreciate a little beauty in our lives. Simple really.

When it comes to what separates Peacocks and Butterflies, the explanation is not as simple. The easy answer would be to say that Butterflies create the art, while Peacocks are the art. Peacocks perform; Butterflies compose. Peacocks are the model; Butterflies are the fashion designer. Peacocks sing the songs that Butterflies write. Peacocks are the comic—especially broad, physical humor—the actor, the dancer, the musician; Butterflies are the chef, the poet, the choreographer, the composer. Now, as I said before, this is the easy answer, and I'd warn you not to apply this dichotomy rigidly. There's a lot of overlap. A Butterfly can go on the mic (just think of all those sensitive, acoustic-guitar-strumming singer-songwriters plying the Suzanne Vega café circuit), and a Peacock can create beautiful, artistic compositions (a lot of dancers are choreographers, too). In the end, though, it always comes down to a natural preference, and Peacocks always lean toward the spotlight, and Butterflies always lean away from it—and then maybe take a few extra steps back.

As with the adrenaline seekers, tool usage is a good way to distinguish between the pleasure seekers. Peacocks use their bodies as tools; in their prime, a Peacock might specifically craft their body for whatever purpose they need. If they're a dancer or athlete, then they'll probably be ripped. If they're a comic, a portlier figure might be more useful, especially if they "live in a van down by the river!" (couldn't help but drop a Chris Farley reference). No matter their body type, Peacocks have a natural grace. Anyone who's been on their fair share of basketball courts knows the type: the fat guy with amazing footwork who's light on his toes and a hundred times quicker than he looks. In contrast, the contents of a Butterfly toolbox depends on their chosen craft. If they're a chef, then it'll contain things like lemongrass, butter, and star anise. If they're a composer, then it'll be filled with treble clefs and staccatos. If they're an artist, then it'll feature color and form.

Peacocks come off as loud; Butterflies come off as gentle. Peacock loudness is not restricted to the volume of their voice. It can be seen in the flashiness of their clothes (more applicable to female Peacocks, in another nod to social conditioning) and the outward physicality of their movements. They have a genuinely hard time keeping still; one of the telling signs of a Peacock is their habit of fidgeting or dancing in place, sometimes even unbeknownst to them. Butterflies, however, have softer voices, their volume at times barely registering above a whisper. Their outfits are less flamboyant but can be just as attention getting. Understated but balanced to perfection.

This contrast in fashion translates well to other aspects of the Peacock-Butterfly comparison. Peacocks are much more likely to brag about or exhibit their respective skills. On Instagram, they're the people taking pictures of themselves in the most exotic places, next to the coolest cars, and always with the best possible lighting. Butterflies are more likely to post pictures of food. Granted, the food most certainly looks exotic, cool, and is shot with the best possible lighting.

CHAPTER TEN

TYPES OF SHAMANS AND HOW TO FIND THEM

Reminder: This chapter is for determining Shamans only. Some traits mentioned may apply to other types, but this chapter is strictly for when you have already determined that someone is a Shaman.

THE ADVENTURE OF LINK?

The difficulty, as any Shaman can tell you, with searching for your self-identity is that the quest can feel directionless. Where does one even start? How do you know when you've gone past the boundaries? Are there boundaries? It's not like you're in a dungeon in *The Legend of Zelda* and all you need to do is find the map, the compass, and the secret weapon (bombs were always my favorite) and then you're on your way to kill the big bad guy. Then again, maybe our self-identity is like a dungeon. There are twists and turns, secret passages to rooms you're afraid to enter, and the deeper you go, the more treacherous your journey becomes. And there are bad guys; we're just not told how to fight them—unless you were one of those lucky bastards with a subscription to *Nintendo Power*.

The point is, one can easily get lost on the way to finding themselves. It's important for Shamans to find something to hold onto, something to anchor themselves so that, even as they explore new experiences and meet new people and their sense of self matures, they won't lose sight of who they were before they started their journey; self-identity is a union of who we were, are, and have yet to become. These anchors are how we can distinguish between the two types of Shamans (see figure 10.1).

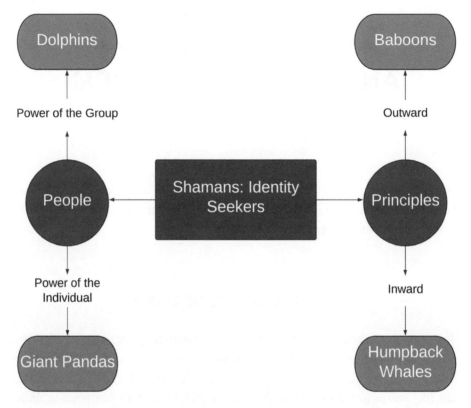

Figure 10.1 Types of Shamans

PEOPLE FIRST VERSUS PRINCIPLE FIRST

Consider this scenario: Let's say you have an idealistic, innovative teacher who genuinely believes it's their mission to develop the hearts and minds of their young, impressionable students. To do so, they're using an unconventional teaching style and curriculum, one that is individualistic and adaptable and, contrary to the teaching orthodoxy of their school, it's working. The principal of the school, a Stag—as many principals are—tells them that, while their enthusiasm and out-of-the-box thinking is appreciated, there are specific guidelines that all teachers must follow. If the teacher continues to teach in that fashion, it will be out of the principal's hands, and they'll be forced to report them to the district and recommend possible termination of employment.

This hypothetical illustrates one of the largest differences between people-first Shamans and principle-first Shamans: pragmatism. Dolphins and Pandas are far more pragmatic than their Shaman counterparts. No matter how wrong they feel the situation to be, no matter how much the situation feels like they're being wronged, people-first Shamans know that, if they were to lose their job, they wouldn't be there to help the students, and the welfare of the students comes first, period. They usually relent to the demands of authority while trying their best to integrate as much of their curriculum as possible. Baboons and Humpback Whales, however, are more likely to stick to their guns—and curriculum—and dare the school to fire them. For principle-first Shamans, their teaching philosophy and method is integral to their self-identity, and they would rather lose their job than sacrifice their integrity.

There are benefits and drawbacks to both positions. The conciliatory nature of Dolphins and Pandas usually enables them to maintain a position in which they can aid the people they care about, though caving to the institutional pressure might make them appear weak to those around them and, most importantly, themselves. Even when, deep down, they know the decision was the right one, they agonize over it anyway, subjecting themselves to an inordinate amount of self-flagellation for the sin of selling out. Taking a stand on principle makes the Baboons and Humpback Whales appear courageous, and that courage can be inspiring to others. However, chances are they'll be punished for their heresy and cast out into the wilderness—or, worse, unemployment—and from that status as an outsider, it can be almost impossible to effect the change they so strongly believe in. One only needs to watch (semispoiler alert) *Dead Poets Society* to see the exhilarating highs and tragic lows of being a Baboon teacher.

As the name implies, you'll frequently find people-first Shamans working in sectors that give them the opportunity to focus on helping people directly, such as health, education, social welfare, government service, nonprofit, and mental health; the exception here is the military, which, due to its need for conformity, is usually not an appealing organization for any Shaman to join. Because of their strong organizational skills, patience, and willingness to compromise, Dolphins and Pandas can bring forth steady, incremental change, as opposed to the incendiary calls for revolution from their more chaotic Shaman brothers and sisters (a.k.a. Baboons and Humpback Whales). For people-first Shamans, the ethical advancement of any civilization must be paced by the readiness of its citizens; true progress is not a sprint but a marathon, and one must build up their spiritual mileage (Dolphins and Pandas view themselves as personal trainers to the soul). However, the rules and regulations of any organization can be quite alienating, and it's not uncommon for Dolphins and Pandas to clash with their superiors if they feel the value system they're working under is flawed. However, these Shamans are far more likely to repress their objections, leading to a situation where they feel powerless and trapped, toiling away in a machine that both underappreciates them and diminishes them.

Power, or a lack thereof, is usually not an issue for the rebellious Baboons and Humpback Whales, as they tend to work outside the mainstream, where they're able to stretch their intuitive muscles and avoid being beholden to any sort of orthodoxy. Fueled by the strength of their convictions, principle-first Shamans seek to bring change to society by attacking it from outside its consecrated wall. They follow a creed of "You're either with me or against me"; for them, the spreading of ideals takes precedence over the will of the people. However, with their natural talent for inspiring and persuading others, Baboons and Humpback Whales commonly find success amassing followers, students, and supporters, no matter how controversial their ideas might be. They'll choose occupations that empower them with a great deal of creative freedom (writing, advocacy, etc.), or if they cannot find a field where that freedom is given to them, they'll take it for themselves, starting their own businesses, organizations, or ministries. Of course, this confidence comes at a cost; their revolutionary zeal can easily morph into demagoguery, and the spiritual isolation that comes with voicing the hopes and dreams of an entire group of people frequently leads to a state of loneliness and depression.

DOLPHINS VERSUS GIANT PANDAS

Dolphins and Pandas have the strongest empathetic abilities of all the types, so it's only natural for them to enjoy working with people. The difference between the two is not as simple as counting the numbers, but I'll be honest, numbers are what stand out first. Dolphins prefer to work in large groups. They're the person who's going to run your local AA meeting; start a vegan club at your school; or teach at a yoga studio, a reiki studio, or a university—sometimes all three simultaneously. Pandas, in contrast, prefer to work on a one-to-one basis. They make great counselors, therapists, life coaches, and Jedi masters. Dolphins have the ability to make everyone in a group feel heard. Pandas have the ability to make an individual feel that every single one of their words is being heard. A Dolphin makes you feel not only like you're part of the group but also that the group is part of you. A Panda makes you feel like the two of you are the only people who exist in the world.

Dolphins come off as popular. They have an easy sort of vulnerability, quick to divulge personal details about their life. This makes it easier for people to be vulnerable around them and feeds into their likability factor. Unlike Elephants, who rule the roost, and Foxes, who have the correct feathers, Dolphins are popular because you always feel like it's okay to be yourself when you're around them. Pandas, in contrast, come off as guarded. If a Dolphin is quick to give you the key to their emotional lockbox, then a Panda takes their key, locks it away in a steel case, locks that case away in an iron safe, and buries that safe six feet underground. They're a closed book—ironic considering how many books a Panda (a natural bookworm) opens in their lives—and only reveal themselves to a select few. This trust is based not necessarily on the length of time a Panda knows someone but on the strength of their initial connection.

Pandas tend to be better students than Dolphins (they're usually the best student of all the Shamans), but Dolphins likely enjoy school more; it wouldn't be a surprise for a Dolphin, despite their Shaman outsider status, to be elected student body president or prom king or queen. Pandas generally join a specific group, like a team sport, a service club, or the school band, a place where they can be around people but stay out of the spotlight as they all work toward a common cause.

Whether someone's a Dolphin or a Panda, they're probably going to be a bittersweet romantic, which, if personality types had a signature drink, would be the Shaman standby: one part sugar syrup, one part ice-cold vodka, and lime to taste (levels of acerbity vary among Shamans, as explained later). What distinguishes Dolphins from Pandas and vice versa is how they deal with the disappointment that society often throws at them: mainly, their sense of humor.

Dolphin humor tends to be sillier, an extension of their outwardly cheerful demeanor. They love goofy memes and lighthearted videos, believing that the key to staying the course of life, even if the journey thus far has been substantially worse than a poke in the eye with a sharp stick, is to smile and stay positive. Naturally, Dolphin popularity goes a long way toward fueling this optimism. Pandas frequently don't have this luxury. They're brooding by nature, and because of that, their humor carries more of a bite, a sort of fatalistic cynicism. They feel both a burning desire to belong and the cold, inarguable truth that they don't, and this conflicted duality is reflected in their preference for comedy that is both life-affirmingly hopeful and self-loathingly acerbic.

BABOONS VERSUS HUMPBACK WHALES

Principle-first Shamans spend their lives grappling with their constantly evolving belief system; new people lead to new experiences and new experiences lead to new spiritual awakenings. How they then apply these moral epiphanies is what helps us distinguish between Baboons and Humpback Whales. When it comes to ideas and ethics, Baboons have an outward orientation, constantly advocating for or against. Humpback Whales have an inward orientation, more interested in cultivating their value system than championing it to the masses. If Baboons are the voice to society's collective conscious, then Humpback Whales are its soul.

Baboons come off as puckish, almost always seeming younger than their actual age. They're frequent mischief makers and practical jokesters; their status as a Shaman outsider mixed with their outward orientation means that not only do they have very little interest in promoting societal norms but also they'll revel in mocking them when they can. It's no surprise that, in school (and outside school, really), many Baboons play the part of class clown. Humpback Whales, almost in direct contrast, come off as old souls, always seeming to appear older than their actual age; unlike Baboons, a Humpback Whale's response to their outsider status is to draw their thoughts inward, which often gives them the reputation for possessing profound maturity. In school, they're the daydreamer, the kid who always seems to have other, less-immediate but more-substantial thoughts on their mind.

Baboons and Humpback Whales are like two parts of the same Freudian consciousness, both fighting the same Shamanic struggle but from different parts of the iceberg. Baboons are the Shaman id: aggressive, action oriented, and more immediate in their response to their feelings. Humpback Whales are the Shaman superego: thoughtful, self-critical, and extremely conscious of the potential for self-growth from any experience. The dichotomy is like a *Calvin and Hobbes* comic strip. For those unfamiliar with the characters, Calvin is a young, imaginative boy (Humpback Whale) who finds himself in all sorts of adventures alongside his imaginary friend Hobbes (Baboon), who is literally a tiger (sorry moms, there are no tiger personality types in the *PoP* method)—if imaginary friends can be literal.

The general pattern that most of the comics follow is that Hobbes is the initiator, enabling Calvin to put his thoughts and dreams into action. Whether Calvin is a space traveler battling aliens, a hard-boiled private detective, or a masked superhero, Hobbes is constantly spurring him on and supporting him, usually by encouraging a more aggressive approach. Calvin often looks to Hobbes for wisdom; one of the best moments in the comics is when Calvin asks Hobbes what love feels like (Watterson, 1991). Either in spite of—or frequently because of—Hobbes's advice, most of the stories end in some sort of failure for Calvin. However, like any Humpback Whale, Calvin views this process (dreams to action to failure to epiphany) as an inevitability of life. This relationship pattern can also be seen in J. D. Salinger's (1961) *Franny and Zooey*, in which Zooey (Baboon) administers a dose of emotional tough love to his sister Franny (Humpback Whale), who's in the middle of a nervous breakdown, leading to epiphanies for both Shamans.

Obviously, other types have epiphanies borne from failure, but what distinguishes the Baboons and Humpback Whales is that so much of their cycle of learning is initiated by their own intuition. Instead of relying on established tradition (Gatherers); practical experience (Hunters); information that's been thoroughly researched (Smiths); or even the more measured, pragmatic approach of their fellow Shamans the Dolphins and Pandas, principle-first Shamans frequently dive into situations with nothing but the strength of their convictions. It's not as if they don't trust all those other things. They just don't trust them as much as they trust themselves. Understandably, this can also lead to plenty of negative consequences.

One of the most telling weaknesses of principle-first Shamans is their susceptibility to absolutism. The same thing that powers them—a passionate belief in themselves and their value system—can also fuel a hatred that burns like the fire of a thousand suns for anything or anyone who might contradict them. This righteous fury can lead to their downfall, much like Lucifer declaring war against heaven in *Paradise Lost* or Icarus flying too close to the sun. And if you think challenging one sun/son (if you believe Jesus equals God) is dangerous, try a thousand. Baboons and Humpback Whales can become so committed to a cause that it clouds their judgment and corrupts their actions, and they'll twist themselves into knots of moral certainty trying to justify their questionable decisions.

For the Baboon, these lapses in judgment are usually pointed outward, as they lash out with reckless abandon at anyone who crosses their belief system, like a sanctimonious crusader unaware that the "road to Hell is paved with good intentions." Humpback Whales take the same kind of certainty and point it inward, experiencing an enormous amount of physical and emotional pain as they subject themselves to a purity test of their own making. Self-immolation—both figurative and literal—is a possibility, as Humpback Whales view self-sacrifice as the utmost proof of devotion to a cause.

CHAPTER ELEVEN

TYPES OF SMITHS AND HOW TO FIND THEM

Reminder: This chapter is for determining Smiths only. Some traits mentioned may apply to other types, but this chapter is strictly for when you have already determined that someone is a Smith.

NOSFERATU

Smiths are like the vampire of personality types. From the outside, everything seems awesome. Imagine being part of *The Lost Boys*: riding a motorcycle, possessing superstrength and -speed, flying, kicking it with Jami Gertz—you know, the height of '80s cool (Schumacher, 1987). Oh yeah, there's also that immortality thing. However, these powers all come at a cost. Now, I'm not saying that Smiths must sleep during the day and come out at night (though it's surprising how many of them are night owls) or that they drink human blood (though you'd be surprised how many would consider it if they thought it might give them the knowledge of an immortal). But just like vampires, Smiths are commonly misunderstood, with superpowers inaccurately attributed to them. Just because Einstein had a genius-level intellect doesn't mean all Smiths do—I mean, genius level is kind of a high bar.

The thing we know for sure, is that all Smiths seek information. That search not only defines them but also helps to distinguish them from each other. Like with most things related to personality type, it's not what someone does but why they do it. For Smiths, the reason for gathering information differs depending on the type. As seen in figure 11.1, Smiths can be split into two groups: those who are application minded and those who are novelty minded.

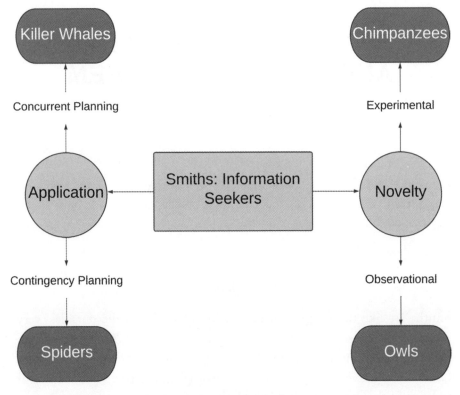

Figure 11.1 Types of Smiths

APPLICATION MINDED VERSUS NOVELTY MINDED

Application-minded Smiths, like Killer Whales and Spiders, are inherently pragmatic and, as such, seek information they can use. They view knowledge as a tool for consolidating power, and whether they're building companies or designing systems, their ability to apply the information they've meticulously collected helps them create entities that dominate their respective markets through pure efficiency. In the minds of these Smiths, every object has a true function, determined not by tradition but by effectiveness. There is a design to the world that the rest of us can't see, and Killer Whales and Spiders take pride in ensuring that everything is placed in its ideal niche.

Novelty-minded Smiths, like Chimpanzees and Owls, seek information for its own sake. For them, learning is fun, inventing is cool, and practical things are almost always created when you're not focused on creating practical things. No idea is too ridiculous; no experiment, too strange. These

Smiths delight in pushing the boundaries of intellectual exploration, devising new ways for us to understand and interact with the world around us. This open-minded, chaotic (Chimpanzees and Owls wear that word like a badge of honor) approach can lead to obvious clashes of philosophy and method with the application-minded Smiths. Take, for instance, the feud between Thomas Edison (Killer Whale) and Nikola Tesla (Chimpanzee), two titans of electrical engineering.

Edison was known for being a workhorse with a very pragmatic outlook on technology: The purpose of any invention is its practical usage and, most importantly, potential for adoption as a normal feature of civilization. He wanted tangible impact, and even though he hired Tesla as an employee (as a Killer Whale, he also knew how to maximize talent), he felt that many of Tesla's ideas were "utterly impractical" (Cheney, 2001). Being a Chimpanzee, Tesla was more interested in pushing the boundaries of innovation than corporate success. He found Edison's methods tedious at best, once remarking to the *New York Times* (1931), "If [Edison] had a needle to find in a haystack he would not stop to reason where it was most likely to be, but would proceed at once, with the feverish diligence of a bee, to examine straw after straw until he found the object of his search." Tesla continued to mock Edison's industriousness by comparing it to his own self-perceived ingenuity, saying, "I was almost a sorry witness of such doings, knowing that a little theory and calculation would have saved him ninety percent of the labor" (Doménech, 2015).

This common conflict between application-minded Smiths and novelty-minded Smiths (executive vs. analyst, corporate vs. R&D, director vs. think tank) is based mainly on their differing views of systems. At best, Chimpanzees and Owls are skeptical of them; at worst, they hate them with a passion. This can be a problem, especially because both Killer Whales and Spiders depend heavily on systems as a means of efficacy and efficiency. This reliance is a pragmatic one; like all Smiths, Killer Whales and Spiders are deeply distrustful of authority and the rigid, oppressive institutions a blind adherence to it can create. However, they also know that proper organizational structure is the only way they can achieve impact on a grand scale; for these Smiths, authority is not to be trusted unless it's their authority. Chimpanzees and Owls, in general, are chaotic types who prize their freedom and frequently balk at being in any position in which they're being dictated to. Because of these competing interests, conflict is inevitable, especially in a workplace scenario where the stakes are raised.

My Killer Whale friend who works as a project manager at a tech company (you've probably noticed I've mentioned her a couple of times now, unless you've been skipping around this book like a kid in a schoolyard) is always getting into it with her software engineers, many of whom are Chimpanzees and Owls. Her capacity is essentially an executive one; it's her job to coordinate all the moving parts to attain maximum production. Novelty-minded Smiths, however, sometimes view project managers as nagging, unnecessary hindrances, just like the project-management methodology (agile, in her case) they propagate. They might say they like it or follow it like a good soldier, but if they had a choice, they'd probably prefer to ditch the team meetings and be left to their own devices, figuratively and literally. Sometimes I wonder if it was a Chimpanzee or an Owl who created COVID just to jump-start the whole work-from-home movement.

Whichever side you fall on, it's inarguable that both Smith philosophies are necessary for not only the success of an organization or company but also civilization itself, even if the different Smith types define success in their own way. In the end, both Edison and Tesla achieved their goals. Edison became a giant of industry whose name is synonymous with lighting up the world, and Tesla became a prolific innovator; holder of more than three hundred known patents; and inspiration to future inventors, sci-fi authors, and steampunk cosplayers.

In its purest form, the divide between the two types of Smiths is an abstract one: order versus chaos. This can be seen in their differing perspectives on the value of systems, as seen here, and extends to other aspects of life. Take, for instance, their performance as students. Application-minded Smiths, while not particularly liking secondary education and the levels preceding it, realize its importance to accessing the occupational positions they desire. They're the best students of all the types—for a fun Hogwarts reference, think Hermione Granger (Killer Whale) or Severus Snape (Spider)—especially at the university level. Chimpanzees and Owls, in contrast, are hit-and-miss as precollege students. When properly engaged, they can be flashy academics (well, more Chimpanzees than Owls) and capable of demonstrating ingenuity and boldness in their unorthodox solutions to problems. Either that, or they can treat school like they treat most systems of authority: vacillating between indifference and a genuine amusement of what they view as a tedious rat race.

Like the other three packs, some of the most distinguishing features between Smiths can be found in their flaws. Application-minded Smiths, at their weakest, are overbearing and insensitive, becoming so caught up in their plans for increased productivity and performance that they forget the people who are integral to that plan, like the scene from *Game of Thrones*, where Cersei Lannister (a Stag) accuses her father, Tywin (a Killer Whale), of prioritizing the "legacy that you love so much more than your actual children" (Graves, 2013). Tywin is the most powerful man in Westeros, and yet he's ignorant of what's going on in the hearts and minds of those beneath him, including his own children, so much so that—spoiler alert—he's unable to foresee his death at the hands of his son Tyrion.

If Killer Whales and Spiders run the risk of acting like dictators, then Chimpanzees and Owls, at their worst, are only a few steps away from becoming reclusive eccentrics, so absorbed in the abstract concepts swirling around in their heads that they remove themselves from the real world. Whereas the personal relationships of application-minded Smiths may sour due to their insensitivity and bluntness, the relationships of novelty-minded Smiths are always in danger of fading away due to their indifference. If interpersonal relations were a garden, then Killer Whales and Spiders would have difficulty avoiding trampling any of the flowers, but at least they'd be able to feel the ground and smell the smashed petals at their feet. Chimpanzees and Owls might let their garden wither from lack of watering until the leaves and blossoms become so dry and odorless that they forget the purpose of having a garden in the first place.

KILLER WHALES VERSUS SPIDERS

What separates Killer Whales and Spiders from their fellow Smiths is their pragmatic approach toward information; what separates them from each other is how they put that information to use. When it comes to their modus operandi, Killer Whales use a concurrent plan of attack, marshalling forces to act simultaneously toward a prime objective. They need to always feel on top of all aspects of their life, as if every person and thing is a simple component of a complex spaceship and only the Killer Whale is capable of manning the captain's chair. Individual parts have the luxury of ignorance when it comes to the others' responsibilities; it's the Killer Whale's mastery of the whole that enables each member of the plan to focus solely on their specific task. Spiders, in contrast, are the masters of contingency planning. Not only do they make provisions for every possible—or seemingly impossible—scenario, but they also devise contingencies just in case those provisions don't work as planned, and contingencies for those contingencies and . . . well, you get the point.

Killer Whale planning is like a Kanban or JIRA board: assigning tasks, determining priorities, and monitoring progress (see figure 11.2). Spider planning is more like an algorithmic flowchart: accounting for different outcomes, specific responses to those outcomes, and then different outcomes to those responses, and so forth (see figure 11.3). Because most of this planning is abstract, it would seem like you'd have to catch them at work to see how it unfolds. However, their differing processes do translate to observable behavior outside the office. Because the nature of their planning is dependent on them taking initiative, Killer Whales are far more aggressive than Spiders. Once they have a plan, they push forward to see it through with such supreme agency and confidence that, when compared to the cautious Spider, they seem almost reckless. Killer Whales have no problem being the center of attention.

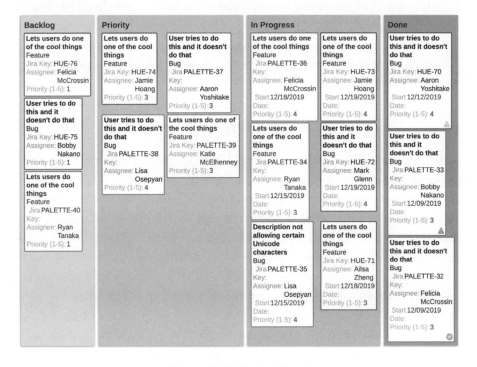

Figure 11.2 Kanban Board

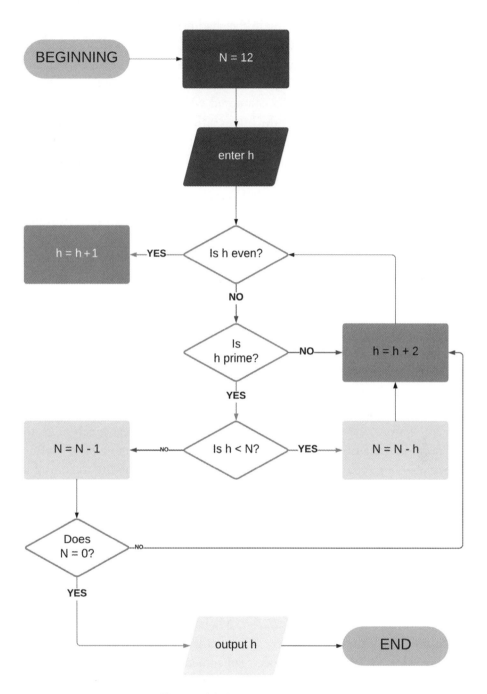

Figure 11.3 Algorithm Flowchart

Spiders tend to prefer working in the shadows. Their planning method is based less on acting and more on reacting; a Spider's patience is frequently mistaken for an inability to act. They are the most detail-oriented of all the types (even more than the fastidious Beavers), and this is a trait that can carry over in conversation. Spiders, so enamored with the details of a particular topic or story, throw them all at the listener; they're of utmost importance to the Spider, so of course, they should be to the listener, as well. Killer Whales are more direct when speaking, choosing to talk only about the details that are relevant to their audience, another reason they make good executives. Trust me, you want a Spider to plan your meeting, but you don't always want them to run it. Just like you always want a Spider to design your plan but maybe not execute it.

Killer Whales come off as dominating, though it's important not to automatically take that as a negative trait. It's just that they have very little problem throwing their intellectual weight around; Killer Whales feel like the strong, direct approach is the most effective (people usually defer to their mixture of confidence and expertise) and efficient (why waste time being polite or beating around the bush?) way to get what they want. Spiders come off as calculating robots—also not automatically negative—like all the times the director of my education company (a Spider) wished that she had a robot body so that she could be done with all the annoying physical aspects of being human. Seriously, she used to get upset when she had to eat lunch or go to the restroom because it interrupted her work. Due to their mastery of contingency planning, Spiders are incredibly confident in their ability to control a situation, but they, like the rest of us, can't always control their body: its flaws, its needs, its urges. Like Nietzsche ([1886] 1998) once wrote, "The abdomen is the reason why man does not readily take himself to be a god."

Though Smiths, in general, are known for appearing cold, Spiders appear the coldest. Keep in mind, it has nothing to do with how they actually feel; they can be just as warm and passionate as any type. But they must think about it first, and it's usually this process that the average person reads as cool calculation; I'm talking *The Godfather*, Michael Corleone (another Spider, of course), "assassinate the bosses of the other families and kill your own brother" kind of cool. Killer Whales can sometimes be an exception to the cool-as-ice Smith rule; their bluntness sometimes has them coming in hot. They're the Macbeth to the Spider's Lady Macbeth. In *House of Cards*, they're the Frank Underwood (are we allowed to refer to Kevin Spacey anymore?) to the Spider's Claire Underwood. They're Tywin Lannister; Spiders are Petyr Baelish (a.k.a. Littlefinger, a.k.a. another reference to *Game of Thrones*, with its huge cast of well-defined characters, a must-watch TV series for personality typing). All this is to say, if you ever get on either of these Smiths' bad sides, remember this: Killer Whales stab you in the front; Spiders stab you in the back.

CHIMPANZEES VERSUS OWLS

Novelty is a word that probably doesn't get as much credit as it should. Perhaps this is due to its connotation as something that is trifling, transitory, and lightweight. But to Chimpanzees and Owls, it's exactly these qualities that make novelty so vital. Things that are trifling in nature need not worry about the burden of expectations. Likewise, that which is transitory is unrestricted by changeless (and, dare I say, progress-less) permanence. And why wouldn't someone want to be light as air, unfettered by the weight of self-importance? Ideas need freedom if you expect them to fly. When it comes down to it, that's what novelty-minded Smiths want: freedom. Chimpanzees want the freedom to create cool stuff. Owls want the freedom to dream up cool concepts. And that is what separates the two.

Like all Smiths, gathering information is the most important priority. However, whereas Killer Whales and Spiders differ in how they apply the information, Chimpanzees and Owls differ in how they process the information. Chimpanzees understand the world through experimentation. They develop their theories by testing them (much respect to the scientific method) through models or experiments, and depending on the success or failure of that test, they adjust, either by creating a new and improved model or by modifying the parameters of the experiment; think Elon Musk or Benjamin Franklin. In contrast, Owls understand the world through observation. They catalog one strand of information, then another, and then another, eventually having enough strands from which they can string together a complex conceptual thread; think Einstein, Newton, or Thomas Jefferson. Because of this, Owls are the best type at distilling a convoluted idea into very few words. Chimpanzees, on the flip side, can take that same convoluted idea and present it in a style that's both entertaining and cognizant of context (Neil deGrasse Tyson, Bill Nye, Mr. Wizard, etc.).

This contrast of methodology can be seen on university campuses all over the world; it's the difference between experimental physics and theoretical physics. Basically, for anyone who's seen *The Big Bang Theory*, it would be like the intellectual rivalry between Leonard (Chimpanzee) and Sheldon (Owl). Whereas the former uses advanced tools to test specific physical phenomena, the latter uses mathematical concepts to examine the unseen relationships between matter and energy. These differences can also take place in the tech sector, though in that case, it's more hardware (Chimpanzee) versus software (Owl).

Granted, a large majority of Chimpanzees and Owls are not involved in the physical sciences or technology. For those novelty-minded Smiths, there are easily observable differences, usually still related to the contrast between experimentation and observation. Take, for example, social situations. In conversation, Chimpanzees can be the aggressor, though not in the same direct fashion as their Smith brethren the Killer Whale. Owing to their experimental nature, Chimpanzees tend to be playful, more focused on teasing out information than making an actual point. They love to test people with jokes and sarcastic comments meant to illicit a response (did someone mention cold reading?). Owls have a much more reserved approach. They can sit in a corner and quietly observe a social situation unfold for what seems like hours. They prefer this distant perch; it allows them to avoid any unnecessary distractions that actual interaction might bring.

Chimpanzees come off as the cool nerd. They cherish the seemingly random nature of their hobbies; they could cosplay at Comic-Con, play *Magic: The Gathering*, or deejay a party with equal gusto, and this confidence, when matched with their haughty disregard for the opinions of others, only helps to establish their cool cred. Owls, though, come off as distant. They, too, have a lot of interests but would prefer to keep those to themselves. It's not that Owls are afraid of people. They just, in all honesty, find people a bit boring sometimes, which is why it's not uncommon for them to zone in and out of conversation as they retreat to the sanctity of their own thoughts.

For a perfect Chimpanzee-Owl coupling, we only need to examine the friendship between Tony Stark (Chimpanzee) and Bruce Banner (Owl); you might know them better as Iron Man and the Hulk. Stark is cocky, charismatic, and never lacking for a wisecrack. Banner is reserved, thoughtful, and prefers to keep his distance from most people. However, as clearly defined as their differences are, their similarities give us even more clarity and insight into what makes these two types tick—and, in this case, gel. Their first meeting in *The Avengers* involves the two geeking out over thermonuclear physics, a discussion that, to put it politely, the other Avengers (not Smith types) couldn't comprehend even if they had it spelled out for them like Hooked on Phonics. Though for Chimpanzees and Owls, it's conversational crack cocaine. It's like inviting Kanye West to a Taylor Swift shit-talking conference; the words come out faster than the mind can organize. The two novelty-minded Smiths can understand each other (Stark even exclaims, "Finally, someone who speaks English!"). Bonding further in the lab (a place of worship for Chimpanzees and Owls), Stark encourages Banner to visit Stark Tower, describing the "top ten floors, all R&D" as *Candyland* (Whedon, 2012). If a lab is their temple, then R&D is their creed, written in an invisible language that only they can fully visualize and appreciate.

CHAPTER TWELVE

YOU ARE THE TEST

HOW TO RECAP THE LAST ONE HUNDRED PAGES

Full disclosure: I created a personality test for the Youtopia Project website. I'm not totally against online personality testing, and I'm proud of the work and thought that went into its design. But no test can replace your intuition. There's a certain nuance and feel to the human touch. It's kind of like watching those first six *Star Wars* movies and realizing how much more realistic Yoda is in the original trilogy. Regardless of the more technologically advanced CGI used to portray a more "complete" Yoda in the prequels, the original Yoda, with Frank Oz as puppeteer, always seems more real, more alive, more like an actual person reacting to the moment.

Which is why, as I mention in the preface (and probably a thousand times since), it's ridiculous to put much stock in personality tests, no matter how "official" they are. Their questions don't consider context. They don't adapt to the test taker. They don't react to the moment, nor should they be expected to. They're just words arranged in a not particularly pleasing or original way. But to think that most of the personality-typing community bases so much of their self-discovery and self-awareness on the results of what is essentially a cookie-cutter questionnaire boggles the mind. It's like taking one of those "Which Hogwarts House Do You Belong To?" quizzes and living your whole life based on the outcome. I mean, should Hufflepuff members just kill themselves now? And God forbid you get Gryffindor and someone tries to tell you different. Those be fighting words.

My favorite experience is when people tell me that the Youtopia 16 assessment (the test from my website, the Youtopia Project) is flawed because their results don't match what they got on other tests. Or when people tell me how great my test is because it does match. As if the accuracy of any test should be measured on the results of previous tests, especially when those tests center around a methodology that's more than a hundred years old. I can imagine these same people arguing against their oncologist's cancer diagnosis because they did their own research and read some apothecary manual from the sixteenth century that says their symptoms are due to an imbalance of yellow bile.

Of course, I'm not saying that my test is anywhere close to scientific, either. It's flawed in the way that all personality tests are flawed: It, too, is static and impersonal. That's why I wrote this book. So that you—yes, you—could become the test. To provide you with context, elucidate nuances, and give personal insight to ideas that are so often simplified as checklists (even worse than tests) and stereotypes to be disseminated throughout cyberspace via memes and "expert" advice.

That being said, I know that my preferred writing style featuring blocks and blocks of paragraphs with egregiously long sentences and discursive asides [in the words of EPMD (1987), "it's my thing"] might not be the first choice for any personality-typing enthusiast when it comes to ease of usage. So because I've been told that people love pictures and notwithstanding the crudity of the concept, I've added figure 12.1 as sort of a condensed version of the typing process—basically a picture worth thirty thousand words or so.

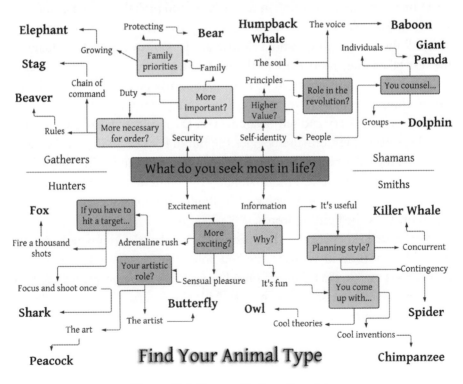

Figure 12.1 Personality Type Template

INPUT-MODEL-CHECK

As you can see, figure 12.1 is an easy-to-follow flowchart. Respond to the questions, and then follow the path created by your answers. Of course, easy as it may be, I'd be remiss if I didn't demonstrate it first; old habits die hard, and twenty years of teaching and ten years of owning an education company have ingrained in me the old, tried and true Madeline Hunter input-model-check method. Now that you've been given the input (almost seventy thousand words of it), it's about time that I model the personality-typing process.

The first step when trying to master personality typing is to practice on fictional characters. Their background history and personality traits are easily accessible to anyone with internet; the writers who conceive of them are trying, for the most part, to paint a well-rounded character; and it's not like Carrie Bradshaw is going to splash a Cosmopolitan in your face for asking too many invasive questions. Using figure 12.1, we'll type four well-known characters (if you don't know at least one of these four, you're either in serious neglect of your streaming services or you've never watched TNT in your life):

- Wonder Woman
- James Bond
- Luke Skywalker
- Hermione Granger

Wonder Woman

For the purposes of this exercise, we'll use the Gal Gadot and Patty Jenkins version of the character, as interpretations and back stories vary.

1. **What do you seek most in life?** Wonder Woman is a superhero, so it stands to reason that security, especially the security of others, is her number 1 priority. It's important to note that many superheroes, as described previously in this book, have other central values. However, in this case, there's no need to overthink it. She is Amazonian, after all—a race of women who, for centuries, thrived in the safety and security of their isolated island home.
2. **More important: duty or family?** She's an Amazon warrior committed to a code of justice. She leaves the rest of her tribe (i.e., family) because she believes it's her duty to use her powers to protect the rest of the world. Duty wins.

3. **More necessary for order: chain of command or rules?** She respects her elders, especially her mother, Queen Hippolyta, and her aunt Antiope, from whom she received her warrior training. Also, her official title is Princess Diana of Themyscira, so yeah, lines of succession and official structures of authority are a vital part of her life.

Conclusion: Wonder Woman is a Stag.

James Bond

For the purposes of this exercise, we'll use the Sean Connery version of the character, as interpretations vary.

1. **What do you seek most in life?** World traveler and super spy, with a penchant for fast cars and beautiful women (or fast women and beautiful cars). Excitement is his jam, for sure.
2. **More exciting: an adrenaline rush or sensual pleasure?** While I did just write that he loves sportscars and women, he usually ends up destroying one and ditching the other (the two terms are situationally interchangeable when it comes to Bond), all so that he can pursue the big bad guy in some death-defying scenario; the adrenaline of the chase is where Bond gets his charge.
3. **If you have to hit a target . . .** To reach his objective, Bond's going to fire multiple shots in multiple ways. Whether it's seduction, wisecracks, Q-made gadgets like rocket-firing cigarettes, or his Walter PPK, Bond tries—and tries again—every tool in his toolbox to get the job done.

Conclusion: James Bond is a Fox.

Luke Skywalker

For the purposes of this exercise, we'll exorcise any memory of how Luke was portrayed in the sequel trilogy (the last three *Star Wars* films) because, you know, they stunk.

1. **What do you seek most in life?** It helps when a character has mysterious parentage (thank you, Joseph Campbell), as everything Luke does is

centered around exploring his self-identity. He first trains in the Force to be just like his father, whom he's never met, and then later masters it so that he might save his father.

2. **Higher value: people or principles?** Luke decides to leave his friends to save his father. Tricky as it sounds, but this is Luke choosing principle (the idea that his father can be redeemed and Luke's the one to redeem him) over people (Han and Leia could've clearly used his help).

3. **Ideal role in the revolution: the voice or the soul?** It's not Luke's words that lead to Darth Vader's redemption. It's his near-death electrocution at the hands of the emperor. Luke's martyrdom reaches into the deepest parts of Vader's soul and helps him rediscover his own humanity.

Conclusion: Luke Skywalker is a Humpback Whale.

Hermione Granger

For the purposes of this exercise, we'll use both the book and film versions, as the character's portrayal is almost (did you really think they were going to give Emma Watson buck teeth?) exactly the same. We're also going to forget (clearly, I did) that I already divulged Hermione's type when I used her as an example earlier in this book.

1. **What do you seek most in life?** This one you can practically do with your eyes closed—well, not practically because you won't be able to see the chart, but you get the point. Hermione's favorite place in Hogwarts is the library. Libraries are wellsprings of information. Most of the time, two and two really does make four.

2. **Why: because it's useful or because it's fun?** The library is also Hermione's go-to when she needs to find a solution to a problem. She's an intense student who looks at school less as a fun place to learn and more as the means to reaching her ambitions. When it comes to information, she's as pragmatic as they come.

3. **Planning style?** Through the course of the series, we see Hermione devise several schemes, most of which involve multiple parts—and Polyjuice potion—moving in unison to reach a singular objective. She is a master of concurrent planning.

Conclusion: Hermione Granger is a Killer Whale.

PRACTICE MAKES PERFECT
(DESPITE WHAT ALLEN IVERSON SAYS)

It's time for the check portion of input-model-check. Kidding! It's not like I'm going to jump out of these pages like some cutting-edge pop-up book so I can check your work. Now that you have a better feel for the typing process, practice on a different fictional character. Then, when you start feeling comfortable, try typing an actual person. Finally, once you've really gotten the hang of it, use it on yourself. Before you do any of this, however, read this advice.

Go beyond the Chart

I didn't write an entire book chock full of brilliant typing insights, random personal anecdotes, and strained analogies so that you could just skip through those twelve chapters (especially the big one) like some '70s schoolgirl playing double Dutch and replace them with a chart that I designed in twelve minutes. Remember, the flowchart is like Virgil in Dante's *Inferno*. It can guide you into Hell, but reading the preceding chapters, like descending circle to circle, is the only way out the other side.

Typing Yourself Can Be Deceptive

Unless you were just rescued from a cult, you've probably known yourself all your life, and sometimes that overabundance of information can create a sort of "Where's Waldo" plethora of personal data in which defining traits hide among colorful yet irrelevant details. Plus, it's tough to understand how we truly appear on the outside because our perspective is always situated within our own headspace, often literally—kind of like how you think your voice sounds one way because you're hearing it from inside your skull, and then you hear a recording of yourself and are like, "What happened to the bass? Why don't I sound like that guy from Boyz II Men anymore?" Not to worry. There are two options:

1. As cringe-inducing as this sounds, watch videos of yourself, preferably from when you were a kid. I corrected my own mistyping of myself by rewatching old home movies. You know your five-year-old self talked a lot when you're constantly yelling at the TV screen for him to shut up.

2. Call a friend who has read this book (their own purchased copy, of course), and then ask them to type you. You'll frequently find that their observations and insights into your personality are more salient and focused than your own.

The Exception Is Not the Rule

This always reminds me of a weekly, pick-up basketball game I used to play in. There was this dude who referred to himself as Mountain Joe, on account of him being as sturdy as a lumberjack. He was strong, but more importantly, he played smart, especially on defense. There was one play when he was guarding me: I pump-faked him at the three-point line, got him to jump out of his shoes (I had made a three on the previous play), and then drove to the basket for a layup. Four full-throated profanities later, he chided himself, "One three-pointer doesn't make Eric a three-point shooter." He knew that I usually abstain from shooting the three (I prefer at least to hit rim) and that the shot on the previous play was more of an anomaly. Personality typing is the same. One instance does not make a person. Be careful not to get pump-faked.

Don't Project

The only thing worse than turning exceptions into the rule is seeking them out in the first place so you can justify your perception of someone's personality. People do this all the time, especially when it comes to romantic and parental relationships. They want so much for their partner to be the perfect match or their child to be a chip off the old block that they project character traits onto them that are either fleeting or nonexistent. Oftentimes, the appearance of these traits is an attempt from their partner or child to please them. And while behavior modification and projection are a great way to get what we want temporarily, the long-term effect is always deleterious. Beware the red-flag phrase "He/She is different when it's just the two of us." It's the kiss of death. Pretending to be something you're not is bad; pretending someone is something they're not is worse. Eventually, the truth wins, and you both lose.

CHAPTER THIRTEEN

DEVIANT ROLES

NOT FROM THAT CHLOÉ ZHAO MOVIE

I'm guessing I'm in a small minority (aside from being an actual minority, which is not a guess) in that I genuinely liked *The Eternals*, Chloé Zhao's (2021) highly anticipated, highly panned, post-*Nomadland* foray into the Marvel Cinematic Universe (MCU). The movie was ambitious and visually stunning, and its portrayal of its lead, Circe, as vulnerable, empathetic, but no less heroic (she's more Margaret Mead than John McClane) was unique for a tentpole blockbuster. However, as Rotten Tomatoes would attest, the film wasn't perfect. My biggest hang-up? I thought the movie's use of the term *deviants* for the film's—spoiler alert—purported antagonists was a bit misleading.

Hearing the word *deviant* makes me think of words like *aberrant*, *divergent*, and *abnormal*, though it's probably because I'm looking at the definition of *deviant* that I pulled up on Google right now, and those are some of the ascribed synonyms. Nowhere does it say anything about slimy, tentacled monsters who can't speak beyond a grunt or growl and, despite their celestial pedigree, more or less take on the role of the velociraptors from *Jurassic Park*, albeit with less personality. You'd think genetically engineered immortal beings from outer space would be more transcendent.

Most importantly, the main problem I have with the Deviants is that they're seen as external threats. Sure, they've been living on earth longer than the Eternals have, but because the Eternals are comprised of Gemma Chan, Kumail Nanjiani, and Brian Tyree Henry and the Deviants are basically superpowered dogs, we see ourselves in the former and view the latter as extraterrestrial, existential threats. And this is very much in line with popular, simplistic views of personality typing. We eagerly accept our virtues as being a part of us and cast out our flaws as aberrant, divergent, abnormal, and ultimately outside our normal selves. Unfortunately, this ignores a vital fact: Each personality type carries with it certain strengths and weaknesses, and these traits aren't at war with each other. They're not going to slice each other into shreds—spoiler alert—like Angelina Jolie did to that creepy Deviant during the film's climax. You can be opposites without being opposing. The capacity for incredible organizational skills does not run counter to a tendency for unbending rigidity; it feeds off it.

Take the purest ideal of each personality type, and then twist it until it's nothing more than a gnarled monstrosity of human pathos. That's a deviant role. And accepting this deviance as an essential part of who we are is vital to understanding who we are destined to become. To balance our strengths and weaknesses, we must acknowledge not only that they exist (usually not a problem when it comes to our strengths) but also that they must coexist. Jekyll cannot kill Hyde. If he did, then his true self would cease to exist. Whether you're studying Robert Louis Stevenson, Hegelian dialectics, Plato's theory of forms, or the Tao, this idea of duality, that our world is the synthesis of two opposite forces, is ubiquitous. We see it in an atom's protons and electrons. We see it in binary code's ones and zeroes. We see it in the relationship between good and evil, life and death, and light and darkness, and as "We grow accustomed to the Dark—When Light is put away," we also realize that, no matter who we are, be it a nuclear physicist, a software engineer, or Emily Dickinson herself, we are both master and servant to our dual nature (Dickinson, [1862] 1935). Plus, isn't playing the Black Swan more fun anyway?

THE DEINDIVIDUALIZERS

These are the deviant roles of the Gatherers. Their desire for security is, at its basest level, fueled by fear, and the structure and order they so desperately seek can twist into conformity and authoritarianism.

The Fascist (a.k.a. the Stag)

You're not perfect and neither is the world, but putting you in charge of it would make the planet a little more like Nadia Comăneci and a little less like a society run by a motley crew of imbeciles, lechers, and weaklings. Of course, you accept that your imperfection causes you to have limits; one of your most glaring weaknesses, which you constantly—and humbly—acknowledge, is your lack of patience for those individuals who are too stupid to realize that you're never wrong. It makes sense that they would hate you. With great power comes great jealousy. Oh well. You're here to lead, not make friends. Who cares if everyone perceives you as bossy? As long as they make sure to refer to you as "boss."

The Hall Monitor (a.k.a. the Beaver)

Yes, we know that *farther* refers to a concrete distance and *further* refers to a figurative one. We also know that we're not really supposed to receive $500 every time we hit Free Parking. And we thank you with all the sincerity in our hearts for pointing out our transgressions. Rules. The bedrock of any advanced civilization. Without them, society would fall into lawlessness. Lawlessness into chaos. Chaos into depravity. And depravity into a world in which people frequently mistake gerunds for participles. All of which you would wholeheartedly agree with if it wasn't for the fact that clauses are not sentences, and you should never start a sentence with *and*—at least that's what Ms. Welch taught you in the fourth grade.

The Earth S-mother-er (a.k.a. the Elephant)

You have one of the most difficult jobs on the planet. Your job is to ensure the self-realization of every human being on earth, or rather every human being whom you care about (which might be the same thing) by stripping away all detrimental influences, such as life experience and intuition, and removing any pesky distractions, like a career or the search for self-worth, so that everyone might see the undeniable truth: Our purpose as humans is to get married and have kids. You use unabashed affection, constant nagging, and tactical "unplanned" social introductions to evangelize any loved one who finds themselves in the pathetic situation of being single. And you hope that, in time, these former heathens, now reformed members of the "I Love the '50s" fan club, will take up your mantle when you're gone and continue your good work.

The Mob Enforcer (a.k.a. the Bear)

The German shepherd of personality types, not only are you loyalty incarnate, but you're also—congratulations!—the cog in a good percentage of the world's unhealthy relationships. Your defense of your loved ones is so staunch and resolute that Tammy Wynette thinks you're being too faithful. It can't be particularly fun to watch a murderer pop up on the news and realize that you're married to them, but hey, we don't really know them like you do, right? I'm sure things are different when the two of you are alone. And of course, your children are beyond reproach. What does it matter if your son insists on eating a diet entirely made up of chicken nuggets and your daughter refuses to listen to her English teacher? Sixteen-year-olds can eat all the pink slime they want, and Shakespeare was a twerp who never learned to write in SVO format.

THE SELFISH THRILL SEEKERS

These are the deviant roles of the Hunters. Their desire for excitement can be, at times, all-consuming, and their insistence on pushing the limits sometimes ventures into self-destructive territory.

The Con Artist (a.k.a. the Fox)

You always know the perfect thing to say and the perfect time to say it—and there are even those occasional times when you actually mean it. Being shameless, self-serving, and insincere is a recipe for financial success and getting laid, but it doesn't always lend itself to opportunities for self-realization, and if you're not careful, even your closest friends will never know who you truly are—and neither will you. But I guess all is copasetic, considering they're the ones fighting over who gets to ride in the passenger side of your Porsche 911 on the way to the *Bridgerton*-themed swingers party being held in your honor.

The Contract Killer (a.k.a. the Shark)

Of course, you've never ever considered killing anyone. Well, there is that douchebag at work who keeps insisting you join the rest of the office in their lunchtime jaunts to Chipotle and that mother at the checkout counter who was oblivious to the fact that her mucus-effusing toddler kept touching your apples and strawberries. I mean, now and again, you play out their murders in your head. Nothing obsessive, just the precise time, method, and location. What else would you do with your day off? The last book you tried to read was *The Art of War*, which was disappointing, to say the least, because there really wasn't much war in it, and it definitely didn't have any pictures. Kind of like how you thought your high school physics class was going to be super awesome until you realized there was nothing remotely physical about it.

The Narcissist (a.k.a. the Peacock)

We're all stars of our own movie. Close friends, parents, and significant others can play strong supporting roles, but no one shares top billing. That is, unless you're in the film. Whether you're playing the best friend, the boss, or "Flower Girl #2," you are the main attraction, no matter how far down you are on the call sheet. It's not that you want attention 24/7 (though you do); it's that you deserve it. After a while, the audience might find your act, as brilliant and compelling as it is, tiresome and overwhelming. But rest assured; they're just a bunch of jealous haters, destined to watch you accept your Academy Award while they continue to take small parts in student films.

The Tortured Artist (a.k.a. the Butterfly)

There is the self-portrait that seamlessly blends watercolor and oil. Or the seven-course meal featuring shark fin and foie gras substitutes that taste like the real thing. Fantastic projects that you could complete if you weren't so busy saying yes every time a close friend asks if you want to go get breakfast, see a movie, or steal a car. And when the situation does arise when you're not fluttering aimlessly with the wind like that feather from *Forrest Gump*, it usually just means that you've relegated yourself to the vintage couch you practically stole off a retiring hipster in Silverlake, reading the fancy art book you undoubtedly have laying on your designer coffee table or drooling over the culinary orgasms taking place on *Chef's Table*, all the while wishing you had enough time and/or talent to create such masterpieces.

THE SELF-RIGHTEOUS DO-GOODERS

These are the deviant roles of the Shamans. Their desire for self-identity, while being fundamentally egocentric, frequently clothes itself in righteousness and altruism.

The Cult Leader (a.k.a. the Dolphin)

You're good at convincing people to follow you. I mean, really good. It's a pity that you're borderline crazy. Imagine all the positive effects you could have on the world if you weren't busy brainwashing the uninitiated into believing things like the polar ice caps will turn into a Slurpee in a matter of weeks if we all stay on the grid or that the government will soon be raiding our homes to confiscate the entire inventory of guns that we haven't purchased yet. Maybe you haven't yet mastered the ability to coax your social media followers into being branded with your initials; joining your sex-flavored pyramid scheme; or, worse, attending lectures on self-improvement. That doesn't mean you haven't tried.

The Svengali (a.k.a. the Giant Panda)

What's worse than a person who prescribes advice with all the caution of Michael Jackson's doctor and all the zealousness of the BeyHive (Beyoncé superfans, for those without *Urban Dictionary*). The person who dispenses said advice and then two hours later completely changes their mind (or, rather, their mood because it's pretty clear their mind is already far gone) and counsels their poor puppet of a friend to take a course of action completely opposite to their previous advice. Let's be real, though; is it really your fault the world is a cesspool of superficialities and degradations? And plus, your mentoring is all for a good cause: so that you're ensured of having a group of like-minded friends who can attend your Sunday barbecue at the beach to commemorate the end of the world.

The Bomb Thrower (a.k.a. the Baboon)

Is it petty you're still harboring a grudge against your AP literature teacher for indoctrinating your fellow students with brag sheets and memorization-based exams? Does your quest to instill the masses with a sense of authenticity and independence become devoid of meaning if it's fueled by lucid dreams of vengeance on those who have wronged you in the past? You believe your words can uplift, inspire, and motivate the human spirit to noble action. More often than not, however, they lead to a messy overthrow of the status quo, leaving only chaos and rubble in the remains, the pros and cons of which, to avoid utter recklessness, you've thoroughly ruminated over before taking on the role of herald to the oppressed and breaker of invisible chains. Riiiiiiight. Who are we kidding? The inspiration for your latest revolution came to you this morning over a bowl of Cap'n Crunch.

The Martyr (a.k.a. the Humpback Whale)

When you're not moping around the house listening to your Nick Drake and Elliott Smith albums, you're usually out trying to convince everybody of your status as the next messiah by taking an emotional beating by those who would dare to persecute you—basically, everybody. You feel a lot of pain. You feel your pain. You feel our pain. You feel Anne Frank's pain. We know this because you rarely miss an opportunity to tell us about it. And you have every right to; society should appreciate you more. The sacrifices you've made so we can understand the depths of the human condition. It's like the film *Minority Report*; you use your preternatural, precognitive abilities to predetermine that a person's an asshole and, thus, not to be interacted with. No evidence needed. Repeat the cycle enough times, and you end up not interacting with anybody because you've predetermined we're all assholes. Brilliant.

THE HIGH-FUNCTIONING SOCIOPATHS

These are the deviant roles of the Smiths. Their desire for information comes at a cost: Sometimes, they lose connection to the very world they're gathering information on, including its people.

The Dominatrix (a.k.a. the Killer Whale)

Are you familiar with the Freudian sentiment (most often attributed to Oscar Wilde) "Everything in the world is about sex except sex—sex is about power"

(Seelig, 2002)? Of course, you are. For you, desire and power are intertwined, mainly because all that you desire you attain by beating those who stand in your way into submission with an ambition that would make Macbeth blush. You're no shrinking violet. You're no rose, either, except for maybe the thorns. If society were a garden, you would most resemble a weed. Unapologetically imperialistic, to you, the artistic sensibilities of the daintier "flowers" are unnecessary trifles (you would have razed Notre Dame during the French Revolution); and the people who promote such bourgeois values, mere speed bumps on your path to utter domination.

The Supervillain (a.k.a. the Spider)

Schemes within schemes, plots within plots, the complex nefarious machinations you devise behind closed doors (i.e., the pupils of your eyes). It's a shame you're constantly stereotyped as an antisocial force of cold malevolence. It's not like you're always trying to avoid human interaction. I mean, as long as you can control the dynamics, a conversation with another person can be quite useful. You don't suffer fools, but you understand that they serve a purpose—mainly, to follow the orders that you have assigned to them and listed down in easily comprehensible bullet-point format. And just because you readily admit that the world would be more efficient if it were run by robots, it doesn't mean that you lack warmth—though, when you think about it, with global warming, sunstroke, and irrational decisions made in the heat of passion, is warmth really something we should be striving for?

The Mad Scientist (a.k.a. the Chimpanzee)

On the good side, you can count Nikola Tesla and Madame Curie as kindred spirits. On the bad side, your extended family also includes Victor Frankenstein and Josef Mengele. However, this would only be relevant if you cared about the idea of family enough to exit the laboratory/workshop/Chuck E. Cheese ball pit you've created for yourself to explore all the puzzles life has to offer. One day, you'll learn that, just because self-experimentation led you to the discovery that mango juice is the perfect complement to smoking ganja out of an apple (pencil required), it doesn't mean that, every time that cartoonish lightbulb turns on in your head, you need to enlist yourself as guinea pig number 1. That's what other people are for.

The Forty-Year-Old Virgin (a.k.a. the Owl)

Wait a minute. Doesn't reading a book about the human need for connection count as human connection? Probably not, if you're reading it in the privacy of your log cabin nestled deep in the woods, somewhere between Ted Kaczynski's summer house and the pristine lake you refuse to enjoy. To be fair, you would pull that book out in any situation: the middle of a party, the seventh inning stretch at Dodger Stadium, midconversation with a friend you haven't seen in years. Anything to escape from the din of superfluous noise (i.e., your friends talking about the things going on in their lives). Unfortunately, this doesn't make companionship very easy, and it makes in-person socialization close to a nightmare. But if interacting face to face with other humans was absolutely vital, then you wouldn't have invented the internet for all us ingrates in the first place.

CHAPTER FOURTEEN

FINAL THOUGHTS

ELON MUSK IS AN ABERRATION

I was reading a random article on Elon Musk the other day, and it sparked a thought (it's probably more accurate to say it reminded me of one): When it comes to understanding different personalities, we have a long way to go. In fairness, this was not some heavily researched essay on human psychology published in *The Atlantic*. It was a clickbait-ish, blurb of a thing, with phrases like *business savant* and *his gift is not empathy* in the title (Sauer, 2021); however, the article does reveal, almost by accident, a certain societal blind spot.

There is an incredulity shared between the writer and her source, an author and journalist, toward the idea that Musk could lack "interpersonal empathy" but have "empathy for mankind," calling it the "weirdest kind of empathy" because "he has a completely different set of emotions than the average person does" (Sauer, 2021). After reading most of this book, you've probably already determined that the traits ascribed to Musk are clearly Smith in nature. And while Smiths make up approximately 8 percent of the population (not exactly a huge portion), the writer and her source treat their existence as an aberration that's "completely different" from the norm.

It's as if they've never met anyone like Musk before and had never considered that, while his personality traits might veer from common norms (a.k.a. Gatherer values), they might also be the reason for his success as a CEO and innovator. In fact, the article proceeds to do exactly the opposite, citing random surveys in which respondents felt more "consistently innovative at work" with "highly empathic senior leaders" versus "'less empathetic' bosses," while implying, albeit accurately, that Musk fits into the latter category—because we all know that Tesla is a company not associated with creativity and innovation. Here's a tip: If you're going to write an article pushing for empathy in the executive suite, it might behoove you to practice a little empathy yourself.

Perhaps that's the greatest danger when othering someone; aside from it being the most entitled douchebag of moves, in seeking to minimize the other, society only succeeds in minimizing its own awareness. Look, I don't want to sound like a condescending asshole; you've gotten enough of that fairy dust sprinkled throughout this book. I'm aware that personality typing is a wonkish topic that not everyone nerds out about, but it's not like theorizing about different types of people is a new concept; I mean, I did write a whole chapter on its history, with enough name-drops to rival the Game dropping verses on *The Documentary*. Perhaps personality ignorance is intentional, and just like how different personalities choose to value different things, society (i.e., the ruling majority of our fellow humans) has chosen to honor other priorities. But that doesn't mean society is right.

I'm sure if you gave the average American a choice, they'd spend the day lounging on the couch, binging the latest reality-show garbage on their Netflix feed while their Roku remote becomes stained otherworldly red from the Hot Cheetos they've been inhaling. So yeah, the life choices of the average member of society might not always be the best to emulate, which always reminds me of what George Carlin (2013) said: "Think of how stupid the average person is, and realize half of them are stupider than that." Damn it. I guess I am a condescending asshole.

Howard Gardner, a developmental psychologist best known for his 1983 book *Frames of Mind: The Theory of Multiple Intelligences*, posits that there are eight forms of intelligence. Bear in mind, the following descriptions are loose paraphrases and, most likely, not sanctioned by Howard Gardner in any sense of the word.

1. **Logical-mathematical:** enables us to know some Einstein kind of shit
2. **Linguistic-verbal:** enables us to use more elegant, pinkie-lifting, tea-sipping words than *shit*
3. **Visual-spatial:** enables us to visualize images, recognize the space between objects, and pee in the toilet with reasonable accuracy (disclaimer: when sober)
4. **Musical-rhythmic:** enables those of us who dance like Elaine from *Seinfeld* to bob our heads to the beat instead
5. **Bodily-kinesthetic:** enables us to shoot a basketball, do a handstand, and show up all those people on the dance floor who are just bobbing their heads to the beat

6. **Interpersonal:** enables us to understand other people (sound familiar?) so that we can then mansplain to them, about them
7. **Intrapersonal:** enables us to understand ourselves (also familiar?) and justify our narcissism

Note: The eighth intelligence, while not in *Frames of Mind*, was proposed by Gardner in 1995:

8. **Naturalistic:** enables us to work with animals and plants, whether it's training our pets to do stupid animal tricks or knowing how to cultivate weed in the basement

Notice how two of the eight intelligences are solely focused on understanding people? And yet, they rarely get the attention of the other six. They're not even prominent enough to warrant distinct names, at least to the point where you're not constantly forgetting which one is which. When you represent 25 percent of the intelligences on the list and are getting barely the amount of attention as, let's say, logical and linguistic intelligence (a.k.a. the stuff they test for on an IQ test), there is clearly something wrong with your branding.

I don't mean to diminish the importance of reasoning or language skills, but why should they dominate the conversation? Unless you're a hermit, I'm guessing you live in a civilization made up of people. These people include your family, your friends, and the girl at the supermarket who always asks if you want a bag even though you're only buying one bunch of bananas and a bag of lentils; they constitute the fabric of your life more than mere numbers or books ever could. It only makes sense that you should devote a good portion of your time to studying people.

Nevertheless, society seems to treat interpersonal and intrapersonal intelligences like an afterthought, an amuse-bouche for an already-satiated intellectual palate, a fun conversation to have where you get to shit-talk other people and justify that philosophy degree you earned despite your parents wanting you to major in biology. It's depressing to think how much more time is spent delving into other fields and even more depressing to realize how much progress has been made in those fields—at the expense of understanding differences in personality—because of that delving. Take baseball, for example. Ten years ago, terms like *launch angle* (the vertical angle at which the ball leaves the bat) and *spin rate* (amount of spin on a pitched ball, measured in revolutions per minute) were not even on the radar gun, but now they've revolutionized the way players are scouted and developed. And it's not just about new discoveries; sometimes it boils down to paying attention to the details. In professional poker, a player mentally processes every little factor. How did my opponent bet preflop? After the flop? On the turn? The river? What cards came out at each respective stage?

Would it kill us to put that much care into how we understand people? If we did, then we'd stop fetishizing Musk for being both a brilliant genius and all-around weirdo. We'd start realizing that people who think like him and share similar values exist all around us, close to 10 percent, in fact. I bet if we did, then we'd find an entirely new dimension we never knew existed.

THE FOURTH DIMENSION

I was talking to a friend about the show *Hawkeye*, mentioned briefly in the chapter 9 discussion on Hunters, and how I loved the chemistry between its two leads, played by Hailee Steinfeld and Jeremy Renner (Thomas, 2021). Eventually, I steered the discussion toward personality typing, as the dynamic between the two protagonists, fueled by the aforementioned chemistry, powers the show:

> Me: It's cool how Kate and Hawkeye are different and yet almost the same personality.
> Friend: What? They're not even close to the same.
> Me: Not exactly but pretty close.
> Friend: They're totally different. She's supertalkative, and he's an introvert.
> Me: That's true, but extroversion and introversion aren't really that important when it comes to personality differences.
> Friend: They're the most important!

Again, with the emphasis on extroversion and introversion. You'd think we had evolved past the beginning of the twentieth century. I don't want to belabor the point (though actually, maybe I do), but extroversion and introversion are not particularly accurate indicators of a person's personality. And the fact that most people still believe these two easily identifiable but fairly superficial traits are important distinguishing characteristics shows that we, as a society, might not fully appreciate what makes individuals truly unique. There are far deeper differences than someone being more talkative than another person, and it's these differences that cut to the heart of how we view ourselves; for the person who values family above all else, it's almost impossible to fathom an individual who doesn't without judging their heresy as aberrant. Much like how the writer of the Musk article couldn't understand how he could treat his employees like garbage but be committed to the health of the planet as a whole. It's hard to see value differences as anything but alien, and for many people, it's unlikely they see them at all.

When I was a kid, I watched Carl Sagan demonstrate—probably on one of his *Cosmos* shows—the possibility of a fourth dimension. He had these paper cut-outs laid out on a table and proposed that they were living in a two-dimensional realm called Flatland. Being of two dimensions, the shapes could perceive length and width but nothing else. Now imagine if we, a three-dimensional being, entered Flatland and called out to our two-dimensional friends. Because they would be unable to perceive height (the additional third dimension), they would be unable to see us. They could hear us, they could know we were there, but we would be beyond their visual cognition. All they would be able to see is our shadow, an imperfect two-dimensional representation of our three-dimensional form (Malone, Kennard, and McCain, 1980).

Now imagine us three-dimensional beings, living in a three-dimensional world and encountering someone from a fourth dimension. Much like the shapes in Flatland, we would be able to hear our fourth-dimensional friend and know that they were there, but we'd be unable to see them. We cannot perceive a fourth dimension or know what it looks like, but we can theorize its existence; Sagan used a model of a cube within a cube to represent it. But of course, that model is only an imperfect three-dimensional facsimile—kind of like our shadows in Flatland—of a fourth-dimensional shape. My *Hawkeye* conversation sparked the memory of this Carl Sagan demonstration and for good reason. It was a reminder that, when it comes to personality typing, we live in a two-dimensional world (Gatherers and Hunters) where the existence of the other dimensions is acknowledged but any understanding of them is as limited as looking at a shadow.

The average person, regardless of whether they know anything about personality types, has a subconscious recognition of the Gatherer and Hunter types and which one they fit into. The other types, not so much. Gatherers and Hunters make up approximately 85 percent of the population. That's a lot of people. It's understandable that most Gatherers and Hunters grow up thinking there are only two types of people. Quite possibly, most Shamans grow up thinking it, too—and that they're some flawed, second-rate version of one or the other, not structured enough to be a Gatherer and not visceral enough to be a Hunter. And this two-dimensional thinking is the root of many of our misunderstandings about people.

Back when I owned an education company, tutors were required to attend a monthly group where we would discuss their students together. There was this one time when the personality demographics of the group made for an interesting dynamic. Said group consisted of one Bear (approximately 12 percent of the population) and three Chimpanzees (approximately 2 percent); that's one Gatherer and three Smiths, but I shouldn't have to remind you of that at this point, should I? I'm going to go out on a limb and say that the Bear tutor, unless she's attended a symposium on gravitational physics or an anime convention, had never encountered that many Smiths in one time and place, let alone be dominated by them numbers-wise. And out of the Smiths, Chimpanzees are not particularly shy about expressing their opinions in rapid-fire fashion.

The group discussion flitted from topic to topic. One moment, they were analyzing a student's inability to draw conclusions; the next, the Chimpanzees were arguing on behalf of their favorite John Carpenter film (my personal favorite, because I didn't really get to jump into the debate back then, is *Big Trouble in Little China*, FYI). The look in the Bear's eyes was one of utter discombobulation. It was like someone had picked her up and dropped her off in another country, where everyone was speaking another language and the street food consisted of entirely unfamiliar proteins. Probably for the first time, she felt like an alien.

IN A BOX? WITH A FOX?

Perhaps that's why I decided to write a book on personality. As the Bear being surrounded by Chimpanzees illustrates, constituting 12 percent of the population does not exempt you from feeling alone. Of course, there's always a push and pull between wanting to be part of a group and wanting to feel special and unique. That's why I wanted to focus on typing people with context and consideration of numerous factors, both deep and broad, one that doesn't involve feeling like you're being put into a box. There's a reason some people hate this kind of stuff, and I get it. We frequently associate categorization with marginalization; even as we're being sorted into unique groups of nuts, bolts, and screws, it still feels like we're all just insignificant cogs in a massive, sterile machine.

The first thing I like to tell people skeptical of personality typing is, you're already doing it. You're just doing it, to borrow from Sagan again, two-dimensionally. Think about it. How many people readily accept simple cultural categorizations—not stereotypes—as fact? Whether it's American individualism, European collectivism, or hating Asian drivers and loving Asian students, we put people into boxes all the time, bringing forth two serious problems:

1. Some of these "facts" are not distinguishing at all. I've seen enough food shows to know that every culture loves food, and every culture seems to think that the love of food is theirs and theirs alone. But beware. Cultural pride can easily warp itself into cultural vanity or a sort of twisted nationalistic patriotism Oscar Wilde once referred to as the "virtue of the vicious" (quoted in Cooper-Prichard, 1931).

2. Just because a culture has accepted certain traits as part of their identity doesn't mean that every person from that culture adheres to that reality. Such homogeneity is crass in a way, like the old joke about how, in Heaven, all police are British, all cooks are French, all engineers are German, all lovers are Italian, and the government is run by the Swiss, while in Hell, all police are German, all cooks are British, all engineers are Italian, all lovers are Swiss, and the government is run by the French. More often than not, personality type trumps culture. Your animal type is not determined or affected by the culture in which you grew up; the effects of growing up in that culture are determined by your animal type. And trust me, those two things can clash. Imagine a Peacock, the most touchy-feely of all the types, growing up in a traditional household in Japan, where social touching is not the norm. Or an Owl, huge proponents of personal space, to say the least, growing up in Latin America, where casual physical contact is prevalent. In both situations, the respective animal types will feel almost foreign. If you ever find yourself in a similar situation, understanding personality typing can be a boon to your emotional health. There's nothing wrong with you; you're just different from the culture you were raised in—and that's okay.

We also want to avoid quick generalizations. They might be funny, but they're frequently untrue (I genuinely like meat pies, Cornish pasties, and fish and chips, and though I can't speak from experience, I'm a bit hesitant to say that all Swiss people are bad in bed). I know that stereotypes can be easy and appealing, especially positive ones. We want so much to be personally validated, which is why all Owls are geniuses, all Butterflies are virtuosos, and all Pandas have the power to read people's minds. And the list goes on. But just like being born German doesn't make you a fascist cop (I grew up in Los Angeles in the '80s and '90s; overaggressive police work is not exclusive to Germany), being born into a certain personality type doesn't automatically bequeath you with its peak capabilities. Skill isn't a birthright, and tendency doesn't always lead to talent, at least not without putting in the work.

I know, I know, nobody likes a Debbie Downer. What's the harm in positive thinking? Just because someone hasn't yet reached their potential doesn't mean that they won't, and perhaps a little fan-gushing will help the actualization process along. Doesn't everyone want a hype man? It's kind of like *Dumbo*'s Timothy the mouse (basically the Flavor Flav of Disney characters) when he gives Dumbo the feather and tells him that it'll enable him to fly (Armstrong, Ferguson, and Jackson, 1941). There's nothing wrong with believing you can fly (it's taking all my self-control not to refer explicitly to a certain Humbert Humbert–esque R&B singer with a penchant for golden showers). However, we all must be careful not to accept our personality type's "powers" as self-evident certainties. There's a danger in that sort of lazy gratification. It's stifled with an air of Calvinistic predestination, as if our strengths and weaknesses have already been predetermined and what we do doesn't matter.

This is where personality-typing skeptics and I find common ground. They would argue (not a hypothetical; trust me, my ears can vouch for it) that the whole process disregards life experience. I mean, anyone who's seen *Batman Begins* knows that (voiced in the style of Christian Bale with his strange, raspy voice) "it's not who we are underneath, but what we do that defines us," and if that's not true and who we are and what we're to become has already been predestined, then what's the point of living in the first place (Nolan, 2005)? All of which I agree with unequivocally. But believing that my actions are vital to my identity does not prevent me from also believing two fundamental tenets: (1) the actions of different individuals are likely motivated by different values, and (2) accepting the reality of those inherent differences broadens rather than limits the scope of our life experiences. Like Carl Sagan said, it's highly probable that there are more dimensions beyond what we know, and while we might not be able to see them, we can still acknowledge their existence and do our best to comprehend the shadows of reality they reveal to us.

Personality typing isn't about pigeonholing people into categories. It's about letting people know that you care about really understanding them—the true them. It makes us all feel like it's okay to be who we are while also reminding us that we're not alone.

LET'S PUT IT TO USE

One of the awesome things about learning how to personality type is that it teaches us to appreciate the differences in others. I mention this for about the thousandth time because I wholeheartedly adhere to the research that shows that a child needs to try an unfamiliar food at least twelve times to like it, which also, I guess, retroactively justifies my dad force-feeding me cilantro all those years, for which I'm thankful. And trust me, you, too, will be thankful for my nagging sanctimony on the topic of personality tolerance. Look at it this way: Even if you're the most self-centered, self-serving, transactional ass-hole on the planet, you have to admit that learning about personality typing is beneficial; at the very least, people will better understand why you're a self-centered, self-serving, transactional asshole.

I was watching an interview on *Real Time with Bill Maher* where Neil deGrasse Tyson, astrophysicist and popular "explainer of complex theories to simple people," waxed poetic about Albert Einstein. Now, a modern-day scientist emitting effusive praise for Einstein is nothing new, but what caught my attention was the specificity of his admiration, a glowing example of one personality type fully appreciating the unique and subtle differences of another. Tyson is most likely a Chimpanzee, a charismatic and articulate communicator who can turn dense and occasionally arcane theories into digestible intellectual bites for the average viewer; Einstein, of course, is the prototypical Owl. In theory, these two personality types are closer to each other than to any other type, which makes Tyson's tribute all the more telling in how it crystallizes both their similarities and differences.

As mentioned in chapter 11, Chimpanzees and Owls are both novelty-minded personality types who seek knowledge for its own sake. This can commonly cause them to butt heads with those who would prioritize solutions to present-day problems over innovations with imperceptible future prospects. Tyson spoke of these more practical types when he said, "If you were around back then, you'd say, 'Why are you wasting your time? We can't even see atoms. Do something productive, you know, like stop the First World War from unfolding.'" Taking a different path (or flight path, considering his Owl nature), Einstein chose to publish a paper in 1917 titled "On the Stimulated Emission of Radiation," according to Tyson, an "obscure paper with an odd, complex derivation." Was there any semblance of a realistic benefit in sight? Certainly not. Was stimulated emission (take a deep breath . . . Don't. Take. The. Bait.) the most pressing concern at the time? Perhaps only to Einstein. But "at the time, he is not thinking, nobody is thinking, lasers, but that [paper] is the intellectual foundation of the laser. He's not thinking bar codes or Lasik surgery. Nobody is thinking that" (Maher, 2015).

Being a Chimpanzee, Tyson appreciates and, maybe more importantly in this context, understands the general public's appreciation for tangible inventions that change the world. Their benefits can be felt and understood at a visceral level. Your breath can be taken away at the wheel of a Tesla S Plaid as it accelerates and leaves a one-thousand-horsepower McLaren in its dust. Your tweet about the horrors of capitalism and corporate exploitation can be sent from the comfort and convenience of your iPhone (that you purchased with a 15 percent off holiday code on Amazon). Theory, though, is the abstract realm of academics, an ivory tower wrapped in ivy whose walls are covered with, according to Chucky, the proverbial common man from *Good Will Hunting*, a "bunch of equations and shit" (Van Sant, 1997). Theoretical physicists like Einstein, while frequently the kings and queens of university physical science departments (think Sheldon from *The Big Bang Theory*), often receive very little popular praise when compared to cutting-edge inventors like Elon Musk and Steve Jobs, even as ingenious Chimpanzee creations frequently derive from equally ingenious Owl formulations.

However, this societal bias toward invention over theory did not go unnoticed by Tyson. He stood up for his fellow Smiths, beseeching Bill Maher's audience to not "get in the way of new research that's going to new places because you never know how that will come back" (Maher, 2015). Tyson was able to not only show reverence for the unique talents of another type but also demonstrate how the contributions of all types are intermingled with each other. An important reminder that civilization merely survives when our differences coexist, but it progresses when they learn to collaborate.

Effective collaboration consists of two things (it must seem like I'm always listing things down, but would you really prefer blocks and blocks of paragraphs?):

1. **Lose yourself.** Every personality type has a bias. Don't forget that not everyone is like you.
2. **Throw out the book.** In the immortal words of Yoda, "You must unlearn what you have learned" (Kershner, 1980).

These are not always easy things to do. The second one, especially, is easier said than done. There's a reason people stick to the tried and true method: They've usually tried it, and the results have been true. But at a certain point, life gets harder. For most of us, I'm guessing it was that moment in junior high when we realized that human beings are horrible monsters and that the moral character of boys and girls is made up of things much more ambivalent than snips, snails, and puppy dog tails or any semblance of sugar and spice. Life has a way of humbling us, taking everything we thought we knew about it, and throwing those preconceptions into a garbage can—a literal junior high experience for some of us. Or in the sagacious phrasing of Mike Tyson (2018), "Everyone has a plan till they get punched in the mouth." This epiphany makes me think of Hermione Granger of Harry Potter fame—exceedingly random, yes, but if you've read up to this point, you should know by now that I'm the Barry Bonds of left-field references. Anyway, stick with me here.

In the sixth Harry Potter book, *The Half-Blood Prince*, Hermione, inarguably the best and most clever student at Hogwarts, is academically upstaged by Harry in potions class. Unbeknownst to Hermione, Harry is using what amounts to a cheat code; someone has scribbled elaborate modifications to the potion recipes in his loaner textbook. An extra sprig of peppermint, one additional clockwise stir, crushing a bean instead of cutting it to better release its juices—these recipe tweaks enable him to surpass even Hermione, who's incredulous. Harry has always been terrible at potions, and she, precise as ever, is following the textbook to a tee. No matter. Try as she might, Hermione's lack of creative risk taking in the classroom prevents her from being able to match Harry's alchemical success (Rowling, 2005).

There is an oft-used Latin proverb, famously quoted in Virgil's *Aeneid*: "Audentes Fortuna iuvat," or "Fortune favors the bold." Generally speaking, it's not that Hermione is unwilling to take chances, as she's broken plenty of rules during the course of the group's extracurricular adventures, but when it comes to school, going by the book has always worked in her favor. Until now. It takes a certain amount of bravery to venture past the boundaries of what we know to be acceptable, but when we do, we often find ourselves being rewarded for our audacity. As Jonathan Swift said (as we travel from Hogwarts to ancient Rome to Augustan-Age Dublin), "He was a bold man that first ate an oyster" (Swift, [1738] 2019).

I once had a Butterfly student who, during the middle of a tutoring session, confided to me that she had punched a boy in the face that day at school. There were a couple ways I could respond in the moment. I could repeat the line Mr. Carroll, my elementary school principal, once reprimanded me with in his office when I was ten: "Violence does not solve the world's problems." Or I could ignore words entirely and just shake my head in disapproval. Instead, I chose an even simpler reaction: "Cool."

Now, I'm guessing my response isn't exactly the solution taught in most teaching credential programs, but it's exactly what years of personality-typing experience has taught me. My student was thirteen years old, the oldest of three sisters, a title that carried absolutely no authority because—not to sound redundant—she was a Butterfly. Butterflies are gentle and deferential by nature, especially ones in the midst of adolescence, so it makes no difference where they fall on the birth-order chart. Rest assured, if personality trumps culture, then it most assuredly trumps birth order. The idea that the oldest sibling is usually the take-charge, responsible one is only applicable when that sibling is a Gatherer (the pack most likely to adhere to sibling-age hierarchy), which is the case approximately half the time (probably why birth order is casually accepted as true). In this case, my student's two younger sisters were both Gatherers: one, a friendly, easygoing Elephant who liked being around everyone else and feeling like part of the group, and the other, a firm, strong-willed Stag, easily the one in charge despite her being the youngest of the three. These interpersonal sibling dynamics are important to understand the reason for my response.

My student's biggest problem wasn't her grades, which were middling. It was her tentativeness. Being dominated by her youngest sister daily was, for lack of a better term, emasculating, and this loss of power was evident in her schoolwork. She frequently found herself mentally drifting from one topic to the next without being fully committed to learn either, rarely taking initiative. She had been apparently picked on incessantly by this boy who, let's be honest, probably had a crush on her, as we all know that's what extremely mature boys do (another story from my own life) to girls they like. She finally had enough of the "flirting" and decided to make a physical connection: Her fist kissed his face.

Her face had a look of relief when I told her it was cool. I'm sure she expected me to admonish her at some point or perhaps lecture her with the safe answer about how fighting is wrong and how she should leave that to more mature adults who are larger, more dangerous, and have years of emotional baggage fermented into rage. Instead, I told her it was good that she stood up for herself and that, if she ever disliked a situation she was in, she should never hesitate to do something about it. Perhaps it was this moment, in addition to all those clips of Arya Stark that we analyzed together, that helped my student attain agency. Her academic performance dramatically improved—and that boy never disrespected her again.

WORK

I love that story about the Butterfly student. Not only does it elucidate how personality typing enables us to venture beyond reflexive reactions and "acceptable" behavior, but it also helps to demonstrate how different personality types should be treated in their own unique way. Simply put, she was a Butterfly. A common Butterfly weakness is indecision that leads to inaction. I encouraged her to not be afraid to fight for what she wanted—literally. If she was a Shark, my advice and method would've been drastically different; Sharks sometimes have the issue of being too aggressive, so I usually encourage my Shark students to focus their aggression, and I do so with tough, straightforward discipline. Much of this book has been about how to accurately type another person. I'd like to conclude it with a couple examples on how knowing an individual's personality type can be used to our advantage—and theirs as well!

Back when I used to own an education company, I had multiple contracts with school districts to provide free tutoring to underprivileged students. My company was not the only one. We had numerous competitors (and by numerous, I mean over a hundred other companies in some districts), all fighting to see who could best convince parents to sign up with them. For this express purpose, school districts would hold recruitment fairs where all the businesses could politely, and in the spirit of congeniality, share their programs with interested parents and students. Riiiiiiight. These were private companies. Most of them didn't see parents and students; they saw dollar signs. The fairs would inevitably devolve into a free-for-all of carnival barkers, pharmaceutical reps, and used-car salesmen, with all the loudness of a spice market in Marrakesh but none of the culture.

I knew I was at a clear disadvantage. I detest sales, and I'm borderline incompetent when it comes to marketing; when I hear the word *branding*, I think cows and NXIVM sex trafficking, not logos and social media reach. Not only that, I was twenty-seven at the time and Asian (I'm no longer twenty-seven but still Asian), so I looked like I had just stepped out of fifth period on the way to my first-floor locker. And the director of the company, who was five years my junior, looked even younger. I swear, one time a parent came up to our booth and asked my director if her parents knew she was working there. So yeah, we sucked at marketing and looked straight out of the cast of *Degrassi*; it was going to be an uphill battle. Thank God for my ability to personality type. It gave us a window into the best way to connect with the parents. In this scenario, because I had to type quickly, I resorted to broader pack designations (Gatherers, Hunters, Shamans, and Smiths) instead of individual animal types.

For starters, I knew Gatherers would make up a substantial portion of the fair's attendees. As an industry, education is heavily populated by Gatherers (Shamans, too, at least relative to their approximately 8 percent share of the general population) who, by and large, possess tremendous respect for its institutions and traditions: exactly the type of parent who would go to a district-organized fair to find tutoring for their child. Gatherers would also be the hardest to convince. Their emphasis on established credentials, experience, and authority didn't exactly compel them to visit our youngish-looking booth. For those who did stop to talk to us, we knew we had to compensate by hitting them hard with information; like an undersized defensive end, we wanted to add a little extra oomph to let the quarterback know we were there.

We would drop terms like *Bloom's taxonomy* and *kinesthetic learning*—you know, stuff that's not particularly complex, but to a parent who's unfamiliar with them, we might as well have been speaking Dothraki. For Gatherers, youth might not equal expertise, but fancy-sounding jargon sure does. On a side note: Bloom's taxonomy is, in actuality, pretty awesome, though (big surprise) I'm skeptical of a strict adherence to any pedagogy. Anyhow, it might seem crude, or even manipulative, to use academic terminology as window dressing to add credibility, but I figured there were two possible outcomes, and both were positive: Either the Gatherer parent would be familiar with the concepts and impressed with our knowledge of them, or they'd be unfamiliar with the concepts and would still be impressed with our knowledge of them. It was a win-win. Did we sometimes go a little too far? Probably. I'm pretty sure an explanation of the five major pedagogical approaches is not exactly what a parent is dying to hear after a day of work, but hey, a person can take only so many dubious looks because of their appearance, age-related or otherwise, before having to release some of the frustration.

Hunter parents were different. In the past, a lot of them probably hated school. In the present, a lot of them probably hated attending a school fair surrounded by a bunch of Gatherers, the kids at school who always made them look bad by following the rules and doing their homework and yet ended up in literally the same place as they did fifteen years later. However, despite those residual feelings of enmity, Hunters love their kids, too, and are always open to the idea that their kids' school experience will be different than their own. For Hunters, instead of going heavy with the jargon, I'd emphasize how we encourage our tutors to devise lesson plans that are both creative and fun, a claim bolstered by my performance of magic (card tricks, more precisely) at our booth. Aside from enjoying the trick itself, Hunters would come to understand that, regarding our philosophy of practical knowledge and making the lesson engaging, we put our money where our mouth is.

I guess that's what attracted them to our booth in the first place. They saw some dude wearing a vest making cards go through people's hands and thought, "That booth looks fun!" A stark contrast to Gatherers, who only were attracted to our booth the moment we started drawing a crowd. Despite looking like she just threw on her mother's suit, our director was extremely knowledgeable about educational concepts, and when one parent stopped to listen, it usually led to another and another.

Shaman parents, though, were naturally drawn to our booth. Shamans love underdogs and iconoclasts, and here we were: a small boutique company that eschewed the excessively cheerful colors and schoolroom logos normally associated with K–12 education. I mean, our logo was an acronym of our company name, in black and white. Not exactly apples, A-plusses, and school buses. For the Shamans, idiosyncrasy recognized idiosyncrasy, and we rewarded their curiosity by demonstrating to them how we use a personality-typing system—a less-evolved version of the one in this book— to work individually with our students. There's only one thing that Shamans love more than talking about a person's personality traits, and that's talking about their own personality traits or those of the people closest to them. So being able to converse about their child's personality and what teaching method would work best for them was just the cherry on top of the Shamans' dream sundae.

Smith parents were a completely different animal (four to be exact!) and had the discipline of a thousand Spartans and samurai combined. They would try to talk to every single booth (keep in mind, at some fairs this meant fifty-plus tables), not because they were particularly excited about any of them, but because they figured if they were going to go to the trouble of attending one of these garish events, they might as well make the most of it. Some Smiths had their process figured out from previous years of experience and were able to save time by going to specific booths. Sometimes we were one of them; sometimes not. But those Smiths who did visit us almost always left happy. We focused on critical thinking and how our program would help their child to use reason to solve problems. This was a passion project of our director, a Smith herself (a Spider, if you remember from previous anecdotes), and her ability to give specific examples and point to relevant materials assured parents that it was more than just lip service. And much like it was with Shaman parents, our youthful and unorthodox appearance was more boon than hindrance, as it gave us a rebellious quality that resonated with the two groups most likely to be skeptical of the system.

LOVE

You're probably thinking, "About damn time! This is what I've been waiting for!" In all my years talking about and teaching personality typing, there has been no topic more asked about than romantic matching. So yeah, I understand if you're a little frustrated it took me this long to explicitly discuss it. Of course, you'll probably be even more frustrated about the abbreviated length of the discussion, but let's kick that can a few paragraphs down the road. For now, let's just appreciate how illuminating personality typing can be when it comes to understanding different types of people and how it can reveal the motivations and desires hidden beneath their actions, especially as they become more apparent when romantically coupled with another type.

When it comes to relationships, Gatherers see other Gatherers as people who are perfectly ready to settle down: steady, responsible, conscientious—you know, the type of partner your parents got overly excited about (to your embarrassment) when you brought them home for dinner. That and the fact that Gatherers are the most plentiful type would make it safe to assume that Gatherer-Gatherer couplings are the most common, but they're not. The most popular pairing is Gatherer-Hunter.

This is where I lay down this disclaimer: Any personality type can have a healthy relationship with any other type. I say this partly because it's true but mostly so I don't have a bunch of angry people sending me death threats and yelling, "You trying to say that my wife of ten years is a bad match?!" Here's the thing: It doesn't take a personality expert to know that all pairings come with difficulties. Just like how your unique personality type bequeaths you with certain strengths and weaknesses, the strengths and weaknesses of your relationships are heavily dependent on the combination of you and your partner's types. That and your personal baggage.

Whether the relationship works has less to do with the specific personality differences and more to do with you and your partner's willingness to accept and learn from them. This is how we as individuals mature into fuller human beings. I know the concept isn't exactly original, and writing it makes me feel all sorts of derivative, not to mention cheesy, treacly, and saccharine. But regardless of the idea's sentimental nature—and my inability to come up with any more food-related adjectives to describe it—something tells me that we all, on a subconscious level, know it to be true.

The reason Gatherers are more attracted to Hunters than other Gatherers (this is relative, of course, as Gatherer-Gatherer is the second-most common coupling) is because they're afraid that being with someone too much like them would probably be boring. Any Gatherer who knows themselves well knows that their caring but cautious, play-it-safe approach isn't exactly electrifying. They might even bore themselves sometimes. So why in the world would they want to be in a relationship with someone similar? They want the spontaneous Hunters. Sure, Hunters can be flighty, and trying to get them to commit to anything can be an exercise in futility, but Gatherers, for the most part, believe that one day they'll be able to wrangle their Hunter paramours and convince them to settle down.

Hunters, on the flip side, see other Hunters and think, "Whoomp, there it is!" (Gibson and Glenn, 1993). These are their fellow party people, and they know a tag team with them would lead to instant fun—with or without the early-'90s hip-hop references. However, just like with Gatherers, Hunters tend to be wary of pairing with another Hunter for too long. They must sense instinctively the relationship's potential to burn hot and fast, like F. Scott and Zelda Fitzgerald, or actually burn, like Andre Rison and Lisa "Lefteye" Lopes. Even if they might come to this realization later than other types, Hunters do want something substantial. Their natural attraction to Gatherers, people who make sure the property is secure, the kids are safe, and the house never runs out of toilet paper, is indicative of this subconscious desire for growth.

When it comes to the abstract types, a Shaman-Smith coupling is extremely beneficial. A Shaman's penchant for empathy compensates for their Smith partner's occasional insensitivity, and a Smith's objective worldview comes in handy when their Shaman partner's hypersensitivity kicks into high-gear neurosis. Essentially, a Smith ensures that a Shaman doesn't lose sight of themselves, and a Shaman prevents a Smith from becoming a sociopath. However, Shaman-Shaman and Smith-Smith pairings frequently work just as well—a godsend considering their relatively small percentage of the population (approximately 15 percent combined). And much like the opposing nature of the previously mentioned pairings, Shaman-Shaman and Smith-Smith relationships often work best when they derive from opposite poles of their respective spectrums: the ambitious, commanding Killer Whale coupled with the big-picture-oriented, thoughtful Owl or the verbose, charismatic Baboon coupled with the guarded, empathetic Giant Panda.

"ADIEU, ADIEU, ADIEU, TO YOU AND YOU AND YOU" (WISE, 1965)

I know this information is incomplete. I know it must feel rushed. I know that, when it comes to the topic of how personality typing can help us in our lives (work, love, family, etc.), we've barely skimmed our hands across the surface of a deep, dark ocean. And that's okay. The purpose of this book is to teach you how to become the test. It is my hope that, almost eighty thousand words later, you have gained not only the ability to read people and their personality differences but also the requisite context to understand those differences and how they interplay with your own unique quirks.

If you skimmed this book desperate to discover who your perfect soulmate is, I'm sorry to disappoint. When you think about it, though, what good is that information if you've typed everyone incorrectly in the first place? Let's face it: The topic of love and personality types could easily fill an entire book on its own. A simple chapter or two allotted to it would be an injustice. So I won't go any further, except to say, if you want that book in some form or fashion, consider your purchase of this book part Kickstarter campaign, part contribution to my "finally pay off your damn college loans" fund.

I humbly thank you for both. I also, humbly, ask you to recommend this book to a few hundred friends. And remember . . .

Figure 14.1 Big Ass Reminder

REFERENCES

Apple, R. W., Jr. 1990. "After the Summit; Gorbachev Urges Major Changes in the World's System of Alliances." *New York Times*, June 5, 1990.

Armstrong, Samuel, Norman Ferguson, and Wilfred Jackson, dirs. 1941. *Dumbo*. Walt Disney Productions.

Baldwin, James. 1963. "A Talk to Teachers." *Saturday Review*, December 21, 1963.

Bazaar. 2017. "The World According to Coco Chanel." August 12, 2017.

Benton, Robert, dir. 1991. *Billy Bathgate*. Touchstone Pictures.

Besson, Luc, dir. 1994. *Léon: The Professional*. Gaumont Buena Vista International.

Black, Jack. 2006. MTV Video Music Awards. Aired August 31, 2006, on MTV.

Bodhi. 1995. *The Middle Length Discourses of the Buddha: A New Translation of Majjhima Nikaya*. Boston: Wisdom.

Boyle, Danny, dir. 2019. *Yesterday*. Universal Pictures.

Brontë, Charlotte. 1847. Letter to G. H. Lewes. November 6, 1847.

Brown, Peter Harry, and Patte B. Barnham. 1992. *Marilyn: The Last Take*. Dutton.

Buffett, Warren. 1974. "Look at All Those Beautiful, Scantily Clad Women Out There!" *Forbes*, November 1, 1974.

Burrows, James, dir. 1994. *Friends*. Season 1, episode 1, "The One Where Monica Gets a Roommate." Written by David Crane and Marta Kauffman. Aired September 22, 1994, on NBC.

Byrne, David. 2012. *How Music Works*. McSweeney's.

Byron, Lord. (1821) 1833. "Observations on an Article in *Blackwood's Magazine*." In vol. 15 of *Works of Lord Byron*, edited by John Wright. John Murray.

Caldwell, Christopher. 2005. "Daughter of the Enlightenment." *New York Times Magazine*, April 3, 2005.

Callner, Marty, dir. 2008. *Chris Rock: Kill the Messenger*. HBO.

Carlin, George (@TheGeorgeCarlin). "Think of how stupid the average person is, and realize half of them are stupider than that." Twitter, May 7, 2013, 5:59 p.m. https://twitter.com/thegeorgecarlin/status/331936277140230144?lang=en.

Carpenter, John, dir. 1986. *Big Trouble in Little China*. 20th Century Fox.

Cheney, Margaret. 2001. *Tesla: Man Out of Time*. Touchstone.

Churchill, Winston S. 1937. "The Mission of Japan." *Collier's*, February 20, 1937.

Cookie Monster (@MeCookieMonster). 2020. "Today me will live in the moment, unless it's unpleasant in which case me will eat a cookie." Twitter, May 15, 2020, 3:03 p.m. https://twitter.com/mecookiemonster/status/1239311209104642049? lang=en.

Cooper-Prichard, A. H. 1931. *Conversations with Oscar Wilde*. Phillip Allan.

Coppola, Francis Ford, dir. 1972. *The Godfather*. Paramount Pictures.

Darabont, Frank, dir. 1994. *The Shawshank Redemption*. Columbia Pictures.

Daum, Kevin. 2016. "18 Quotations from Tom Hanks on Life, Leadership, and Heroism." Inc. September 16, 2016. https://www.inc.com/kevin-daum/18-quo tations-from-tom-hanks-on-life-leadership-and-heroism.html.

De Laurentiis, Giada. 2013. *Paris!* Grosset and Dunlap.

D'Elia, Bill, dir. 2000. *Ally McBeal*. Season 4, episode 1, "Sex, Lies, and Second Thoughts." Written by David E. Kelley. Aired October 23, 2000, on Fox.

Demme, Jonathan, dir. 1991. *Silence of the Lambs*. Orion Pictures.

Dickinson, Emily. (1862) 1935. "We Grow Accustomed to the Dark." *Commonweal* 23 (November 29).

Doménech, Francisco. 2015. "Tesla vs. Edison: A Mythical Rivalry." Open Mind BBVA. May 18, 2015. https://www.bbvaopenmind.com/en/technology/vision aries/tesla-vs-edison-a-mythical-rivalry/.

Dora Dore, Giovanna Maria, Jae H. Ku, and Karl Jackson, eds. 2014. *Incomplete Democracies in the Asia-Pacific: Evidence from Indonesia, Korea, the Philippines, and Thailand*. Palgrave Macmillan.

Dostoyevsky, Fyodor. (1873) 1946. *Bobok: From Somebody's Diary*. Translated by Constance Garnett. Penguin Classics.

Dutton, Denis L. 1988. "The Cold Reading Technique." *Experientia* 44, no. 4 (April): 326–32.

Dylan, Bob. 1963. Letter to the Emergency Civil Liberties Committee. December 13, 1963.

———. 1964. *The Times They Are a-Changin'*. Track 1, "The Times They Are a-Changin.'" Columbia.

Eames, Charles, and Ray Eames, dirs. 1977. *Powers of Ten*. IBM.

Ebert, Roger. 2002. "Film Review for *Blade II*." *Chicago Sun-Times*, March 22, 2002.

Edison, Thomas. 2016. *Quotable Edison: An A–Z Glossary of Quotes from Thomas Edison*. Edited by Alex Ayres. Quotable Wisdom Books.

Einstein, Albert. 1973. *Albert Einstein: Creator and Rebel*. Compiled by Banesh Hoffman. Penguin.

———. 2013. *The Ultimate Quotable Einstein*. Edited by Alice Calaprice. Princeton University Press.

EPMD. 1987. *Strictly Business*. Track 5, "It's My Thing." Fresh/Sleeping Bag.

Faber, Nancy. 1985. "An Irreverent Best-Seller by Nobel Laureate Richard Feynman Gives Nerds a Good Name." *People*, July 22, 1985.

Favreau, Jon, dir. 2020. *The Chef Show*. Season 2, episode 2, "Roy's Italian Cuisine." Hosted by Roy Choi and Jon Favreau. Aired September 24, 2020, on Netflix.

Fey, Tina. 2012. *30 Rock*. NBC web exclusive, "Ask Tina." December 14, 2012.

Feynman, Richard. 1964. "What Is and What Should Be the Role of Scientific Culture in Modern Society." Lecture, Galileo Symposium, Italy.

France, Anatole. 1909. *The Life of Joan of Arc*. Translated by Winifred Stevens. John Lane.

Frank, Anne. (1947) 1995. *The Diary of a Young Girl: The Definitive Edition*. Edited by Otto H. Frank and Mirjam Pressler. Translated by Susan Massotty. Doubleday.

Freed, Fred, and Len Giovannitti, dirs. 1965. *NBC White Paper*. "The Decision to Drop the Bomb." Aired January 5, 1965, on NBC.

Gandhi, M. K. 1909. Introduction to *Letter to a Hindu*, by Leo Tolstoy. N.p.

Gardner, Howard. 1983. *Frames of Mind: The Theory of Multiple Intelligences*. Basic Books.

———. 1995. "Reflections on Multiple Intelligences: Myths and Messages." *Phi Delta Kappan* 77, no. 3 (November 1995): 206–9.

Gibson, Stephen, and Cecil Glenn. 1993. "Whoomp! (There It is)." Lite Records.

Gladwell, Malcolm. 2007. *Blink: The Power of Thinking without Thinking*. Back Bay Books.

Gore, Martin. 1985. *Black Celebration*. Track 1, "Stripped." Mute.

Graves, Alex, dir. 2013. *Game of Thrones*. Season 3, episode 4, "And Now His Watch Is Ended." Written by George R. R. Martin, David Benioff, and D. B. Weiss. Aired April 21, 2013, on HBO.

Habashi, Fathi. 2000. "Zoroaster and the Theory of Four Elements." *Bulletin for the History of Chemistry* 25, no. 2: 109–14.

Hanson, Curtis, dir. 2000. *Wonder Boys*. Paramount Pictures.

Hanson, Marilee. 2015. "Lord Byron and John Keats Rivalry and Dislike Summary." English History. February 6, 2015. https://englishhistory.net/keats/lord-byron-john-keats-rivalry/.

Heckerling, Amy, dir. 1995. *Clueless*. Paramount Pictures.

Hedegaard, Erik. 2002. "*Smallville*: A New Superman for a New Century." *Rolling Stone*, March 28, 2002.

Hemingway, Ernest. 2003. *Ernest Hemingway: Selected Letters 1917–1961*. Edited by Carlos Baker. Scribner Classics.

Heraclitus of Ephesus. 2001. *Fragments: The Collected Wisdom of Heraclitus*. Translated by Brooks Haxton. Penguin Classics.

Hoff, Benjamin. 1982. *The Tao of Pooh*. Dutton Books.

Isaacson, Walter. 1997. "In Search of the Real Bill Gates." *Time*, January 13, 1997.

Iverson, Allen. 2002. Press conference, May 7, 2002.

Jefferson, Thomas. 1788. Letter to Alexander Donald, February 7, 1788.

Johnson, Shawn. 2012. *Winning Balance: What I've Learned So Far about Love, Faith, and Living Your Dreams.* Tyndale Momentum.

Jordan, Killian. 1997. *Legends: The Century's Most Unforgettable Faces.* Little, Brown.

Jordan, Michael. 2009. Speech, Hall of Fame induction, September 11, 2009.

Jouanna, Jacques. 2012. "The Legacy of the Hippocratic Treatise *The Nature of Man*: The Theory of the Four Humours." In *Greek Medicine from Hippocrates to Galen: Selected Papers*, 335–59. Studies in Ancient Medicine, vol. 40. Brill.

Jung, C. G. (1921) 1971. *Psychological Types: Collected Works of C. G. Jung*, vol. 6. Translated by Gerhard Adler. Princeton University Press.

Kalachanis, Konstantinos, and Ioannis E. Michailidis. 2015. "The Hippocratic View on Humors and Human Temperament." *European Journal of Social Behavior* 2, no. 2: 1–5.

Keats, John. 1819. Letter to George Keats, September 17, 1819.

Keirsey, David. 1998. *Please Understand Me II: Temperament, Character, Intelligence.* Prometheus Nemesis.

Kelly, S. H. 1999. "Bush Tells Gulf Vets Why Hussein Left in Baghdad." *Pentagram*, March 3, 1999.

Kershner, Irvin, dir. 1980. *Star Wars: Episode V—The Empire Strikes Back.* 20th Century Fox.

Kimball, John, Bob Zamboni, and Alan Zaslove, dirs. 1989. *Chip 'n Dale: Rescue Rangers.* Season 1, episode 2, "Catteries Not Included." Written by Tad Stones and Bruce Talkington. Aired March 5, 1989, on the Disney Channel.

Landis, John, dir. 1988. *Coming to America.* Paramount Pictures.

Leary, Denis. 2008. *Why We Suck: A Feel Good Guide to Staying Fat, Loud, Lazy and Stupid.* Viking Adult.

Lehmann, Michael, dir. 1989. *Heathers.* New World Pictures.

Letterman, David, host. 2013. *Late Show with David Letterman.* Season 21, episode 56, "Jennifer Lawrence; Taraji P. Henson." Written by Doug Brady, R. J. Fried, and Matt Kirsch. Aired November 20, 2013, on CBS.

Lucas, George, dir. 1977. *Star Wars: Episode IV—A New Hope.* 20th Century Fox.

Maher, Bill, host. 2015. *Real Time with Bill Maher.* Season 13, episode 29. Aired October 2, 2015, on HBO.

Malone, Adrian, David Kennard, and Rob McCain, dirs. 1980. *Cosmos.* Season 1, episode 10, "The Edge of Forever." Hosted by Carl Sagan. Aired November 30, 1980, on PBS.

Mandela, Nelson. 1995. *Long Walk to Freedom: The Autobiography of Nelson Mandela.* Back Bay Books.

McGilligan, Patrick. 1999. *Clint: The Life and Legend.* HarperCollins.

McGuigan, Paul, dir. 2012. *Sherlock.* Season 2, episode 1, "A Scandal in Belgravia." Written by Steven Moffat, Mark Gatiss, and Arthur Conan Doyle. Aired January 1, 2012, on BBC One.

McTiernan, John, dir. 1988. *Die Hard.* 20th Century Fox.

Mead, Margaret. 2003. *Sex and Temperament in Three Primitive Societies.* HarperCollins.

Merkel, Angela. 2009. Remarks, joint session of Congress, November 4, 2009.

Mischel, Walter, Ebbe B. Ebbesen, and Antonette Raskoff Zeiss. 1972. "Cognitive and Attentional Mechanisms in Delay of Gratification." *Journal of Personality and Social Psychology* 21, no. 2 (February 21): 204–18.

Mother Teresa. 2007. *Come Be My Light: The Private Writings of the Saint of Calcutta.* Image.

Myers, Isabel Briggs, and Peter B. Myers. 1980. *Gifts Differing: Understanding Personality Type.* Davies-Black.

Myerson, Alan, dir. 1995. *Friends.* Season 1, episode 13, "The One with the Boobies." Written by David Crane, Marta Kauffman, and Alexa Junge. Aired January 19, 1995, on NBC.

New York Times. 1931. "Tesla Says Edison Was an Empiricist." October 19, 1931.

Nichols, Mike, dir. 2004. *Closer.* Columbia Pictures.

Nietzsche, Friedrich. (1883) 1961. *Thus Spoke Zarathrustra.* Translated by R. J. Hollingdale. Penguin Books.

———. (1886) 1998. *Beyond Good and Evil: Prelude to a Philosophy of the Future.* Translated by Walter Kaufmann. Vintage.

Nolan, Christopher, dir. 2005. *Batman Begins.* Warner Bros. Pictures.

Norrington, Stephen, dir. 1998. *Blade.* New Line Cinema.

Obama, Barack. 1995. *Dreams from My Father.* Times Books.

O'Connor, Sandra Day. 2005. Concurring opinion, *McCreary County v. American Civil Liberties Union*, 545 U.S. 844. June 27, 2005.

Paine, Thomas. 1775. "African Slavery in America." *Postscript to the Pennsylvania Journal and the Weekly Advertiser*, March 8, 1775.

Plato. (360 BCE) 2009. *The Republic.* Book 6. Translated by Benjamin Jowett. Wayback Machine.

Q Magazine. 2008. "Madonna: Question and Answer." May 2008.

Rand, Ayn. 1964. *The Virtue of Selfishness.* Signet.

Richet, Charles. 1910. "An Address on Ancient Humorism and Modern Humorism." International Congress of Physiology, Vienna, September 27–30, 1910.

Roosevelt, Eleanor. (1960) 1961. *The Autobiography of Eleanor Roosevelt.* Harper and Brothers.

Rose, Charlie, host. 2010. *Charlie Rose.* "Remembering John Wooden; Rene Redzepi."
    Aired June 11, 2010, on PBS.
Rose, Jalen. Postgame interview. January 22, 2006.
Rowland, Ian. 2002. *The Full Facts Book of Cold Reading.* Full Facts Books.
Rowling, J. K. 2005. *Harry Potter and the Half-Blood Prince.* Bloomsbury.
Russell, Bertrand. 1991. *History of Western Philosophy.* Routledge.
Salinger, J. D. 1961. *Franny and Zooey.* Little, Brown.
———. 1963. *Raise High the Roof Beam, Carpenters and Seymour: An Introduction.*
    Little, Brown.
Santayana, George. (1905) 2013. *The Life of Reason: The Phases of Human Progress.*
    Critical ed. MIT Press.
Sappho. 1971. "Fragment 16." Translated by Eva-Maria Voigt. Athenaeum.
Sarkis, Stephanie. 2012. "31 Quotes on Gossip." *Psychology Today*, April 11, 2012.
    https://www.psychologytoday.com/us/blog/here-there-and-everywhere/201204
    /31-quotes-gossip.
Sauer, Megan. 2021. "Elon Musk Is a Business 'Savant,' but 'His Gift Is Not
    Empathy,' According to His Brother Kimbal." CNBC. December 28, 2021.
    https://www.cnbc.com/2021/12/28/elon-musk-business-savant-with-limited
    -empathy-says-brother-kimbal.html.
Schumacher, Joel, dir. 1987. *The Lost Boys.* Warner Bros.
Scorsese, Martin, dir. 2006. *The Departed.* Warner Bros.
Seelig, Beth J. 2002. *Constructing and Deconstructing Woman's Power.* Karnac Books.
Shakespeare, William. (c. 1600) 2016. *Hamlet.* 2nd ed. Arden Shakespeare.
Shaw, George Bernard. 1932. *Our Theatres in the Nineties Vol. 1.* Constable & Co.
Sheindlin, Judith. 1996-2021. *Judge Judy.* CBS Media Ventures.
Silver, Carole B. 1999. *Strange and Secret Peoples: Fairies and Victorian Consciousness.*
    Oxford University Press.
Singer, Peter. 1979. *Practical Ethics.* Cambridge University Press.
Smith, Warren Allen. 2002. *Celebrities in Hell.* Barricade Books.
Spielberg, Steven, dir. 1998. *Saving Private Ryan.* Dreamworks.
Swift, Jonathan. (1738) 2019. *Polite Conversation.* Alpha Editions.
Tarantino, Quentin, dir. 1994. *Pulp Fiction.* Miramax.
———, dir. 2003. *Kill Bill: Volume 1.* Miramax.
Thomas, Dana Lee, and Henry Thomas. 1954. *Living Adventures in Science.* Hanover
    House.
Thomas, Rhys, dir. 2021. *Hawkeye.* Season 1, episode 2, "Hide and Seek." Written
    by Elisa Lomnitz Climent, Jonathan Igla, and Katrina Mathewson. Aired
    November 24, 2021, on Disney+.
Thoreau, Henry David. 1854. *Walden.* Ticknor and Fields.
Time. 1953. "Art: Mexican Autobiography." April 27, 1953.

Tipoe, Eileen, Abi Adams, and Ian Crawford. 2022. "Revealed Preference Analysis and Bounded Rationality." *Oxford Economic Papers* 74, no. 2 (April): 313–32.

Tyson, Mike (@MikeTyson). 2018. "Everyone has a plan till they get punched in the mouth." Twitter, October 17, 2018, 2:01 p.m. https://twitter.com/MikeTyson/status/1052665864401633299.

USA Today. 2004. "Jimmy Fallon's Pleasant Tomorrow." October 8, 2004.

Van Meter, Jonathan. 2013. "*The Hunger Games*' Jennifer Lawrence Covers the September Issue." *Vogue*, August 11, 2013.

Van Sant, Gus, dir. 1997. *Good Will Hunting.* Miramax.

Venkatesan, Satish. 2013. *Ayurvedic Remedies: An Introduction.* Vyiha.

Washington, George. 1776. Letter to the president of Congress, Heights of Harlem.

Watson, Emma. 2014. "Emma Watson: Gender Equality Is Your Issue Too." UN Women. September 20, 2014. https://www.unwomen.org/en/news/stories/2014/9/emma-watson-gender-equality-is-your-issue-too.

Watterson, Bill. 1991. *Calvin and Hobbes.* May 26, 1991.

Weir, Peter, dir. 1989. *Dead Poets Society.* Touchstone Pictures.

Whedon, Joss, dir. 2012. *The Avengers.* Walt Disney Studios.

Winfrey, Oprah, host. 2011. *Oprah's Lifeclass.* Season 1, episode 13, "When People Show You Who They Are, Believe Them." Aired October 26, 2011, on OWN.

Wise, Robert, dir. 1965. *The Sound of Music.* 20th Century Fox.

Zemeckis, Robert, dir. 1997. *Contact.* Warner Bros.

Zhao, Chloe, dir. 2021. *The Eternals.* Walt Disney Studios.

Zucker, Jerry, dir. 1995. *First Knight.* Sony Pictures.

ABOUT THE AUTHOR

Eric Gee has performed personality type–based life coaching for more than twenty years. He built a successful education company that used his personality-typing method to better the lives of more than twenty thousand students, parents, and teachers. As creator of youtopiaproject.com and the Youtopia 16 assessment, he has disseminated his method to more than a half-million users since the website's creation in 2016. *The Power of Personality* is the culmination of tens of thousands of hours of research and application, insights honed by personality typing upward of fifty thousand people throughout his career.

Eric graduated from UCLA, where he studied English literature and screenwriting. Coincidentally, he's also a classically trained pianist, backyard-trained barbecue dilettante, three-time fantasy football champion, professional mentor, amateur magician, and seasonal film nerd. He owns Youtopia Creative, a shared creative workspace in Los Angeles (projectyoutopia.com/creative), where he administers life coaching (projectyoutopia.com/university) and an arguably ample amount of profanity.